LUISA MONCADA is an editor and writer. She has contributed
to several volumes on genre fiction. She has also published
essays on popular culture, gender, literature and history.
Luisa is the editor of New Holland's
Poems and Readings for Funerals and Memorials.

SCALA QUIN is an editor. She has contributed to magazines
and books, writing about children's literature, science fiction,
crime fiction and popular culture.

Published in 2011 by New Holland Publishers (UK) Ltd
London • Cape Town • Sydney • Auckland
www.newhollandpublishers.com
Garfield House, 86–88 Edgware Road,
London W2 2EA, United Kingdom
80 McKenzie Street, Cape Town 8001, South Africa
Unit 1, 66 Gibbes Street, Chatswood, NSW 2067, Australia
218 Lake Road, Northcote, Auckland, New Zealand

10 9 8 7 6 5 4 3 2 1

A catalogue record for this book is available from the British Library.

ISBN 978 1 84773 467 9

Publisher: Aruna Vasudevan
Senior Editor: Charlotte Macey
Editors: Jolyon Goddard, Sally Maceachern
Inside Design: Vanessa Green
Cover Design: Vanessa Green
Production: Melanie Dowland

Reproduction by Pica Digital Pte. Ltd, Singapore
Printed and bound in India by Replika Press

The paper used to produce this book is sourced from sustainable forests.

READING
ON LOCATION

GREAT BOOKS SET IN TOP
TRAVEL DESTINATIONS

**LUISA MONCADA
AND SCALA QUIN**

NEW
HOLLAND

CONTENTS

FOREWORD

At some point in our lives, we have all been armchair travellers, whether it be sitting by a log fire in the depths of winter and dreaming of exotic, steamy locales, or sweating away in the maddening heat of a tropical forest and imagining a much cooler place. Some of us have gone a bit further and wiled away many an hour at home or work imagining ourselves running around Jamaica in the company of James Bond (*Dr No*), having dinner on the Orient Express, careering across Europe with Hercule Poirot (*Murder on the Orient Express*) or simply yearning to be that person (Peter Mayle) who gave up everything to live in the South of France (*A Year in Provence*). But is there an even greater pleasure in reading a book set in a particular city or region, while you're actually visiting it? For those of us who want to do this, the question is: where do we start? How do we choose from the billions of books available to us in bookshops, libraries or online? Where do we find the books that are set in the places that we either dream about or intend to or actually are in the process of visiting? *Reading on Location* aims to give you a little bit of help along the way.

This book is by no means a definitive guide to every book written about every place in the world – that would be impossible – rather it includes some of the most popular and intriguing destinations in the world and many of the best-known or most evocative books (fiction and non-fiction) set in them.

In compiling a book of this size, it would be impossible to please everyone. While we have taken advice on the books that are included in this volume, the choice is primarily our own. Please forgive any omissions, as they are not meant to cause offence. Instead we hope that when you are delving into this volume, you will find something new or intriguing to read, something that will enrich your visit to a specific location or simply bring you new insights into or a greater appreciation of the place in which you live.

Anyway, we hope you enjoy this volume and the places (familiar and new) to which these books will take you.

Luisa Moncada and Scala Quin
London and Canada

Thank you: Aruna Vasudevan, our publisher, who provided a huge amount of advice and help; Julia Shone and Melanie Dowland and the rest of the team at New Holland for all their hard work; Vanessa Green, the designer of the book; and a host of others including Nicci Walker, Sarah Elphick, Lauren Gurteen, Lesley Henderson, Philippe Barbour, Karen Midgen and Brian Young.

HOW TO USE THIS BOOK

Reading on Location is divided by continent or geographical region. Each section is separated out into countries or regions. Most begin with some general books that look at culture, society or travel. This is followed by fiction and non-fiction set in or around major cities (such as London, Paris, Rome, Mumbai or Havana) or in counties, states or regions.

The entries: these features the English title of the literature in question followed by the year of the English edition (in most cases) and the author. A concise summary of the book picks up on themes, characters and key places, real and imagined, where possible. Many entries include further information such as TV and film adaptations, references to author houses or museums and useful websites (see the key below).

Feature boxes: In addition to the main entries, there are a number of feature boxes, dotted throughout the book, that focus on authors who are associated with a particular destination – such as 'Dickens' London' (page 209) or 'An Independent People: Halldór Laxness's Beloved Iceland' (page 163) – a particular book, such as *A Raisin in the Sun* (page 76) or a particular theme, such as 'the Orient Express: murder and intrigue' (page 203), which looks at books set on the famous train.

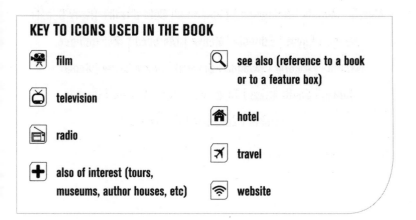

KEY TO ICONS USED IN THE BOOK

🎥 film

📺 television

📻 radio

➕ also of interest (tours, museums, author houses, etc)

🔍 see also (reference to a book or to a feature box)

🏠 hotel

✈ travel

📶 website

AFRICA

Algeria | Angola | Botswana | Cameroon | Côte d'Ivoire (Ivory Coast)
Congo | Egypt | Ethiopia | Kenya | Morocco | Mozambique
Namibia | Nigeria | Rwanda | Senegal | Sierra Leone | Somalia
Sudan | South Africa | Tanzania | Togo | Tunisia | Uganda
Zambia | Zanzibar | Zimbabwe

AFRICA

Fiction

The Sheltering Sky (1949)
Paul Bowles

Bowles's critically acclaimed book focuses on an American couple, Port and Kit Moresby, as they travel aimlessly though Africa from north to south in the post-war years. Bowles effortlessly presents the emptiness of the Moresbys' lives and the superficiality of their existence against the beauty and majesty of the African landscape.

🎬 *The Sheltering Sky* (1990)

A Good Man in Africa (1981)
William Boyd

Boyd's first novel is a satirical look at the British in Africa. Set in the fictional country of Kinjanja, Morgan Leafy is a morally suspect diplomat who bumbles through life. The comedy and writing is reminiscent of Evelyn Waugh.

🎬 *A Good Man in Africa* (1994)

Non-fiction

Dark Safari: The Life behind the Legend of Henry Morton Stanley (1990)
John Bierman

Bierman's brilliant account of the life of Welsh explorer of Africa Sir Henry Morton Stanley is a great read, with deep insight into Stanley, considered by some to be a 'Walter Mitty' character. The book describes his meeting with Livingstone and his journey into the Congo.

The Zanzibar Chest: A Memoir of Love and War (2003)
Aidan Hartley

Winner of the Samuel Johnson Prize for Non-fiction in 2004, *The Zanzibar Chest* is a mesmerizing read. A white Kenyan, with colonial ties to Africa, Hartley was a former Reuter's correspondent who had reported on several wars in the continent. He mixes accounts of his own experiences with those of Peter Davey, a young British officer and friend of his father's, who was found murdered in 1948. Hartley found Davey's diaries in his father's Zanzibar chest and in the book merges modern African history with that of the past. Through uncovering the details of Davey's life, Hartley attempts to reconnect with his own father and also with Africa.

📶 http://www.thezanzibarchest.com/
(more information about the book and author)

Green Hills of Africa (1935)
Ernest Hemingway

In December 1933 author and fan of big-game hunting Ernest Hemingway journeyed to East Africa with his wife, Pauline, to go on safari. This book, an account of the people, the lure of the hunt and the beauty of the African plains, was his second non-fiction book. In *Green Hills*, Hemingway describes the glory of the landscape and notes, even then, how man was encroaching on the wilderness.

The Shadow of the Sun: My African Life (2001)
Ryszard Kapuscinski

Kapuscinski's book, based on his own life and experiences of working and travelling in Africa over more than 40 years, provides an intimate introduction to the continent. His descriptions of the African peoples, landscape and every day life are beautifully observed. Each chapter presents a new story and aspect of life there.

🔍 Ethiopia – *The Emperor*

Dark Star Safari: Overland from Cairo to Cape Town (2003)
Paul Theroux

Theroux's entertaining book recounts his travels to a land where he worked in the 1960s. Journeying by every form of transport possible – from dugout canoe to armed convoy – Theroux experiences Africa, speaking to tourists, janitors, aid workers and missionaries to present a vivid, if critical, portrait of this extraordinary continent. By the end of his travels, Theroux seems reluctant to return to his home in Hawaii.

ALGERIA

Fiction

The Lovers of Algeria (2001)
Anouar Benmalek

Set in post-colonial Algeria, Benmalek presents the love story of Anna and Nassredine over 70 years from the late 1920s to the late 1990s. Moving between past and present, the author allows us to see the brutal reality of Algeria's history.

The Savage Night (2001)
Mohammed Dib

Viewed by many as the father of North African literature, Mohammed Dib was born in Tlemcen in western Algeria. His 1952 novel *La Grande Maison* (the first of a trilogy, followed by *L'Incendie* in 1954 and *Le Métier à Tisser* in 1957) brought him critical acclaim. This collection of 13 short stories, many of which are set in Algeria, evokes the country of the past and the modern day.

Nedjma (1956)
Kateb Yacine

Born into an old Algerian family, Yacine was raised on stories hailing Algerian heroes and Arabic achievements. *Nedjma*, his most famous book, incorporates local legends and is written in a very fragmented style, using multiple voices and a broken chronology. Yacine said his greatest influence was William Faulkner. The Nedjma of the title is a beautiful ethereal character, a woman married to a man she doesn't love. She is loved by four men, all revolutionaries and the unwitting cause of much rivalry; Nedjma becomes a symbol of Algeria.

ANGOLA

Fiction

The Return of the Water Spirit (2002)
Mayombe Pepetela

First published in Portuguese in 1995, *The Return of the Water Spirit* is a

bitter critique of the corrupt and nepotistic Marxist ruling elite of the Angola of the 1980s.

Luuanda: Short Stories of Angola (1980)
José Luandino Vieira

Born in Portugal in 1935, Vieira, a white Angolan, emigrated with his parents to Angola three years later. He joined the Angolan liberation struggle and spent 11 years in prison in Cape Verde. He is probably best known for this collection of short stories, which are set in the slums of Luuanda in the 1940s and 50s and make clear how oppressive Portuguese control was. Although it won him the Writers' Society's Grand Prize for Fiction in 1965, *Luuanda* was banned in Angola until the overthrow of the government in 1974.

Non-fiction

Angola: Promises and Lies (1996)
Karl Maier

As a correspondent for the *Washington Post* and London *Independent*, Maier wrote despatches on Angola. Drawing on his own experiences of the country and people, he offers a chronological account and explanation of the civil war that ripped Angola apart.

BOTSWANA

Fiction

A Question of Power (1972)
Bessie Head

Head's largely autobiographical novel, written while she was recovering from a psychotic breakdown, features Elizabeth as the main protagonist. Like Head she is the product of an illegal union in her native South Africa between her white mother and black father and has to deal with the repression of living under apartheid. Elizabeth leaves South Africa for the comparative liberalism of Botswana, settling in a rural part of the country where she lives largely in isolation because she is viewed as different. She is racially much lighter than the local people and, in their eyes, more like the much-hated 'bushmen'. Head also left South Africa in the early 1960s, settling in Botswana, where she lived without recognized citizenship for 15 years.

🛜 http://www.bessiehead.org/ (official Bessie Head website)

Non-fiction

Cry of the Kalahari (1984)
Mark and Delia Owens

This best-selling title by Mark and Delia Owens and winner of the 1985 John Burroughs Medal for Natural History Book of the Year is a loving portrayal of the Kalahari desert as seen by two Americans who gave up everything in 1974 to follow a dream. Travelling to Africa after auctioning off their possessions, the Owens drove into the wilderness, where they spent seven years conducting groundbreaking research into the black maned lions and brown hyenas. The Owens established a foundation for wildlife conservation and also helped promote eco-tourism in Zambia.

🛜 http://www.owens-foundation.org/index.html (Owens Foundation for Wildlife Conservation)

🔍 Zambia – *Secrets of the Savanna: Twenty-Three Years in the African Wilderness Unravelling the Mysteries of Elephants and People*

Botswana's first lady detective: Precious Ramotswe

For many people Precious Ramotswe, the heroine of *The No. 1 Ladies' Detective Agency* series, is synonymous with Botswana. Alexander McCall Smith's first novel, after which the series of currently 11 books is named, introduces Botswana's first and only lady detective to his readers. As the author himself says, Precious is a 'cheerful woman of traditional build', about whom he was inspired to write after visiting friends in Mochudi. After writing the first novel, which was lauded after its publication, McCall Smith felt it would be rude to stop writing about Precious and so began the series of books that would bring him and his protagonist so much fame. In the novels, Botswana becomes as much of a character as Precious – and the author evokes a country in which law, order and freedom are important. The Botswanans are also portrayed as a people of great dignity and hope. The series of books, which was optioned by the late director and playwright Anthony Minghella, has created new tourism for Botswana. The series was filmed on location in the country and the agency itself is set in the Kgale Shopping Centre on the outskirts of Gaborone.

🛜 http://www.alexandermccallsmith.co.uk/ (author site)

🎦 *The No. 1 Ladies Detective Agency* (7 episodes; 2008–9), starring Jill Scott as Precious Ramotse

CAMEROON

Fiction

The Story of the Madman (2001)
Mongo Beti

This novel is a humorous but critical look at corruption in a post-colonial African country, modelled on his native Cameroon. Its independence is clearly nominal and Chief Zoaételeu is a puppet dictator, who tries to hold onto old, traditional ways, even in the face of great change.

Your Madness, Not Mine: Stories of Cameroon (1999)
Makuchi

Makuchi's short stories tell of post-colonial Cameroon. Her female characters recount the daily struggle for survival and become empowered in a society in which women are often oppressed.

The Old Man and the Medal (1956)
Ferdinand Oyono

Oyono's work typically summarized the average African's experience of dealing with colonialism. This, his second novel, deals with disillusionment as seen through his protagonist, Meka, an old man who has served the French administration well. Oyono is very critical of the French regime but also of those Africans who colluded with and were controlled by colonial powers. Oyono was himself a diplomat, serving as ambassador to several African countries from 1961 and served in Paul Biya's cabinet, whose regime notably tried to oppress opponents such as Mongo Beti.

COTE D'IVOIRE (IVORY COAST)

Fiction

The Suns of Independence (1970)
Ahmadou Kourouma

Set in two fictional African republics (obvious to readers as the Ivory Coast and Guinea), Ahmadou Kourouma's classic novel has been hailed as one of the most important African novels written in French. It is remarkable (and has been criticized) for its disregard for French syntax as Kourouma manipulates the language, giving it a Malinke twist. The story of a prince reduced to beggardom in the independence era, the book is a blinding satire and was highly acclaimed following its publication.

🔍 *Monnew* (1990), Kourama's second novel

CONGO

Fiction

A Burnt-Out Case (1961)
Graham Greene

In the late 1950s, Greene travelled to the Belgian Congo with the beginnings of a novel on his mind – the result was *A Burnt-Out Case*. Greene's tale features Querry, a famous but world-weary architect, who has it all but still finds his life wanting. He travels incognito to work in a leper colony, where he begins to recover, but then real life intervenes.

The Poisonwood Bible (1998)
Barbara Kingsolver

Set in the Belgian Congo, just before independence, Kingsolver's international best-seller sees Nathan Price, a missionary, his wife and four daughters, arriving in a remote village with the aim of converting the 'natives'. They are seemingly unaware of their bad timing and the fact that the locals are fighting to rid themselves of their white oppressors. Through arrogance and misunderstandings, Price's plans flounder. Kingsolver herself lived in the Congo between the ages of 7 and 8 and set her novel there, as she told *The Times*, because she saw it as a 'perfect microcosm of the West's blindness of what is already there'.

A Bend in the River (1979)
V.S. Naipaul

Nobel-prize winning author Naipaul tells of Salim, a Muslim–Indian merchant, uprooted from his previous home, who sets up a store in a sleepy African town at a bend in the river (the Congo). Based on Naipaul's own visit to the region in 1975 and his own diaries, later published in 1980, the author successfully explores the themes of corruption in a newly independent nation.

🔍 *A Congo Diary* (1980)

Joseph Conrad and the Heart of Darkness

Probably one of the most famous books associated with the Congo is Joseph Conrad's novella *Heart of Darkness*. The Polish-born French-speaking writer travelled extensively after joining first the French merchant marines in the mid-1870s and later the British merchant navy. In 1890, he sailed up the Congo and it is this journey that provided the material for the inspirational book that he wrote in 1899 and published three years later. During the four months that he spent commanding a Congo river steamboat, Conrad heard a great deal about the behaviour of the men who had explored the region and the brutalities often committed by them. Kurtz, in *Heart of Darkness*, embodied many of the characteristics of these men and came to embody imperialism in Africa. In the book, the narrator, Marlow, who works for a company interested in ivory, travels up the Congo to find Kurtz, a man of almost mythical proportions, whom he expects to be a genius. When his party reaches the company's inner station, it is attacked and his helmsmen killed. Marlow finally reaches Kurtz, who is seriously ill and endeavours to get him back to civilization, but he dies on the way. His last words are 'The horror! The horror!' For Marlow the Congo comes to represent the evil of which man is capable. He chooses good over evil; Kurtz, however, chooses differently. *Heart of Darkness* has inspired many attempts to turn it into a film, most notably by Orson Welles, which failed, and Nicolas Roeg in 1993. Inspired by the book, Francis Ford Coppola produced the cult movie *Apocalypse Now* (1979), set in Vietnam and Cambodia. Visitors interested in travelling down the Congo can take a river trip (see below).

➕ http://www.hakunamatatatours.com/River_congo_cruise.html
(Hakuna Matata Tours)

Non-fiction

Blood River: A Journey to Africa's Broken Heart (2007)
Tim Butcher

Journalist Tim Butcher has created a modern travel classic as he follows in H. M. Stanley's footsteps, travelling with 'a penknife and a packet of baby wipes' as his only protection. Using a motorbike, a dugout canoe and other forms of transport along the way, he is helped by an intriguing assortment of characters from UN workers to a campaigning pygmy, as he gets to grips with the real Congo and the people who are fighting to make their way in a continuously shifting world.

EGYPT

Fiction

The Yacoubian Building (2002)
Alaa Al Aswany

Set in Cairo, in a building well past its prime, Al Aswany's book presents a microcosm of the city. In what was once an architectural gem of the 1930s, housing the cream of Egyptian society, a second community arose on the roof of the building. *The Yacoubian Building* follows the lives of some of these tenants, and Al Aswany's inclusions of themes such as homosexuality, exploitation and sex made the book both controversial and a best-seller.

🎬 *The Yacoubian Building* (2006)

Death on the Nile (1937)
Agatha Christie

Probably one of Christie's best-known works, apart from *Murder on the Orient Express*, *Death on the Nile* sees Hercule Poirot at his most charismatic and the author doing what she does best – killing off objectionable aristocratic characters with verve and considerable style in an exotic location. Set in the 1930s, beautiful and rich Linnet Ridgeway sets off a tragic chain of events when she steals the fiancé of her best friend, Jacqueline. She runs into Jacqueline in Europe and again after they find themselves on a luxury cruise on the Nile. Linnet is murdered and Jacqueline is, of course, the prime suspect. But *can* it really be that simple ... ? Christie fans may take in many of the sites featured in the book on a special Agatha Christie Nile trip with one of many tour companies.

📶 http://123egypttours.com/nile-cruises/dahabiya-nile-cruises/agatha-christie-dahabiya-nile-cruise (Agatha Christie Dahabiye Nile Cruise)

🎬 *Death on the Nile* (1978); the best film adaptation sees Peter Ustinov as Poirot and an array of Hollywood stars vying for first place, including Bette Davis, Mia Farrow, David Niven and Maggie Smith. They don't make them like this anymore

The Alexandria Quartet (1960)
Lawrence Durrell

Seen by many as Durrell's best work, *The Alexandria Quartet: Justine* (1957), *Balthazar* (1958), *Mountolive* (1958) and *Clea* (1960) is an epic account of the city of Alexandria in the 1930s and 40s. Focussing on four characters, Darley,

Pursewarden, Nessim and Justine, Durrell evokes a world full of passion before and after the Second World War.

📶 http://www.lawrencedurrell.org/works.htm (International Lawrence Durrell Society)

Moon Tiger (1987)
Penelope Lively

Born in Cairo, Lively set one of her most popular books *Moon Tiger* in the city. A multi-layered book, made richer by the use of flashbacks, memories and different voices and tenses, *Moon Tiger* won Lively the 1987 Booker Prize. It focuses on Claudia Hampton, a writer, who as she lies dying, plots her greatest work, the story of her life and the soldier whom she briefly loved and lost.

📶 http://www.penelopelively.net/

The Levant Trilogy (1982)
Olivia Manning

Following on from *The Balkan Trilogy*, we follow Guy and Harriet Pringle once more. Having escaped from war in Europe they find themselves tangled up in war-torn Egypt. Originally published as separate volumes, *The Danger Tree* (1977), *The Battle Lost and Won* (1978) and *The Sum of Things* (1980), the books appeared in one volume in 1982. Anthony Burgess called Manning's books the 'finest record of the war produced by a British writer'.

🎬 *Fortunes of War* (1987), starring Kenneth Branagh and Emma Thompson

The Cairo Trilogy

Naguib Mahfouz was one of a generation of writers who emerged in the 1940s and 50s calling for societal reform in Egypt and he believed that his writing could help bring about change and social enlightenment. *The Cairo Trilogy* follows al-Saiyid Ahmad Abd al-Jawad and his family from the backdrop of the 1919 Egyptian revolution (an event which Mahfouz credited with shaking the security of his childhood) to the 1950s. The three books – *Palace Walk*, *Palace of Desire*, and *Sugar Street* – are named after Cairo streets. In *The Cairo Trilogy*, the events that shape the family are those affecting Egypt on a greater scale. In the first book, *Palace Walk*, we are introduced to Al-Saiyid Ahad's oppressed wife, Amina and his two daughters and three sons, all of whom struggle against his patriarchal rule. *Palace of Desire* finds the family dealing with modernity and political change in 1920s Egypt. And finally, *Sugar Street* sees Al-Saiyid Ahad dealing with his grandchildren, including a Muslim fundamentalist and a communist. Mahfouz was himself born in 1911 in Gamaliya, the old quarter of Cairo, where he lived until he was 12, after which his family moved to a newer Cairo suburb. Although both places feature in his work, it is the more traditional world that informs the majority of his books, including the trilogy. The house in which he first grew up serves as a model for the Abd al-Jawad family home, including the roof, which is the scene of many family gatherings and illicit meetings.

Cairo Trilogy (2009), starring Omar Sharif

The Girl in the Nile (1992)
Michael Pearce

The fifth book in Michael Pearce's popular 'Mamur Zapt' series, *The Girl in the Nile* finds Captain Gareth Owen, the head of the British police force in turn-of-the-19th-century Cairo, investigating the death of a woman who fell from the boat of Prince Narouz. As Mamur Zapt (head of the secret police), Owen follows the trail of the woman, after her body disappears. Pearce's books give a great insight into 19th- and early 20th-century Egypt and are great mysteries too.

Mamur Zapt and the Return of the Carpet; the first book in the series

Woman at Point Zero (1975)
Nawal El Saadawi

A very influential book, Saadawi's *Woman at Point Zero* features a woman on death row who refuses to ask the King of Egypt for clemency. A journalist travels to see her to find out why she is behaving in this way and by interviewing her finds out the truth behind her story and how she came to this point.

The Map of Love (1999)
Adhaf Souef

Shortlisted for the Booker Prize, this wonderful and lyrical book sets a poignant love story against a vast historical and political landscape.

Anna Winterbourne, who is grief stricken at the death of her husband, decides to travel to Egypt. Keeping a diary and corresponding with friends and family, including her father-in-law, a fierce critic of British imperialism, Anna finds herself in the midst of an adventure. Abducted, while she is disguised as a man, she is taken to the home of Sharif Pasha al-Barudi, thus triggering a chain of events that eventually leads to their marriage and their ostracization by their respective societies. A century later, her daughter Isabel discovers Anna's letters in a trunk and, in turn, decides to travel to Egypt, prompting her own adventure.

📶 http://www.ahdafsoueif.com/ (author site)

ETHIOPIA

Fiction

Cutting for Stone (2009)
Abraham Verghese

An epic saga, spanning more than five decades, this novel focuses on Marion and Shiva Stone, the twin sons of a secret union between a disgraced Indian nun and a British doctor. Brought up in Addis Ababa, they come of age at the time of Ethiopia's revolution, but it is their love for the same woman rather than politics that tears them apart.

Scoop (1938)
Evelyn Waugh

One of Waugh's best novels, Scoop is based on Waugh's own experiences as a war correspondent for the Daily Mail covering the war between Abyssinia (Ethiopia) and Italy in 1935. The plot follows William, a naive reporter, who is mistakenly sent out to cover the war in Ishmaelia (almost geographically identical to Abyssinia). Through a series of accidents, William manages to get several big scoops, returning to England as a world-famous writer.

KENYA

Fiction

The Constant Gardener (2001)
John le Carré

This thriller is le Carré at his best. When a British diplomat's activist wife is found murdered in a remote part of northern Kenya, he sets out to discover what happened to her. Thwarted at every turn, he finds himself involved in a pharmaceutical cover up of monumental proportions.

🎬 The Constant Gardener (2005)

Out of Africa (1937)
Isak Dinesen

Probably most familiar through the beautiful Oscar-winning film version starring Robert Redford and Meryl Streep, Out of Africa is a memoir of Isak Dinesen, a young Danish woman's life on a 1,620-ha (4,000 acre) coffee plantation outside of Nairobi between 1914 and 1931. Isak Dinsen was the pseudonym of Karen Blixen, who married her second cousin, Baron

Bror von Blixen-Finecke, before travelling from her native Denmark to Africa. Twice nominated for the Nobel Prize for Literature, Blixen wrote other literature but *Out of Africa* details her very colourful life, including her famous affair with Denys Finch Hatton (played by Redford in the movie) and her own courageous struggle to come to terms with a strange and often hostile country. Blixen's lyrical descriptions of the land reveal her great love for Africa.

Out of Africa (1985)

The Flame Trees of Thika (1959)
Elspeth Huxley

Huxley's enchanting account of growing up in Kenya when, aged six, her parents took her from England to find the land that her father had purchased from a man wearing an Etonian tie. Her parents, both adventurers, set out to make their life there and establish a coffee plantation. Huxley's account of growing up in this magical land, of mixing with the Kikuyu people and the Masai and enduring the life of colonial settlers in Kenya in the early part of the 20th century is quite lovely.

The Flame Trees of Thika (1981), starring Hayley Mills

Red Strangers

Death in Kenya (1958)
M. M. Kaye

Reminiscent of early Agatha Christie, M. M. Kaye's delightful mystery finds

heroine Victoria travelling to take up a position at her aunt's estate in Kenya's Rift Valley, even though she knows that her former fiancé, Eden, awaits. She arrives in the aftermath of the Mau Mau rebellion and to find out that the household is reeling from a recent murder, that of Eden's wife. Kaye portrays colonial Kenya in great detail, evoking its atmosphere.

Petals of Blood (1977)
Ngugi wa Thiong'o

The murder of three directors of a foreign-owned brewery forms the frame for this book. The four suspects reveal their disappointments with modern Kenya, showing the reader how much its people have been let down. The book's publication was very controversial and led to the author's detainment by Kenyan authorities, although it was highly lauded by the world press and leading authors such as James Baldwin and Toni Morrison.

A Grain of Wheat (1967)

The In-Between World of Vikram Lall (2004)
M. G. Vassanji

Vassanji's acclaimed novel evokes colonial, post-colonial and also neo-colonial Kenya, showing the relationship between the colonists, Africans and Indians who helped shape the country. The protagonist narrates his story from Canada, where he has fled after earning the title as one of the most corrupt men in

Kenya. He looks back at his life there and shows the reader how he came to become the man he is today.

Non-fiction

Dreams in Time of War: A Childhood Memoir (2010)
Ngugi wa Thiong'o

Celebrated author Thiong'o's crisp account of growing up in 1950s' Kenya gives us insight into his upbringing as part of an extended family and what life was like under British colonial rule at a time of increasing nationalism. Many of the themes that became prevalent in his later work as a writer find their basis in his early childhood influences and experiences.

MOROCCO

Fiction

Hideous Kinky (1991)
Esther Freud

Hideous Kinky is an engaging tale of a mother taking her two children to Morocco to seek enlightenment. While she escapes the restrictions of English society for Marrakesh in the 1960s, her daughters seek something more stable.

This Blinding Absence of Light (2004)
Tahar Ben Jelloun

This remarkable book tells of Salim, a soldier who took part in an attack on King Hassan II of Morocco's palace.

With 60 others he was imprisoned in horrific conditions in a secret prison in the Moroccan desert, where they remained for 20 years. Although they can't see each other, the inmates struggle to survive and stay sane. Salim becomes the storyteller, relating the plots from the *Arabian Nights* to *A Streetcar Named Desire*.

Non-fiction

For Bread Alone (1973)
Mohamed Choukri

Choukri was one of Morocco's most famous writers but his beginnings were far from auspicious. Born into a dysfunctional family and suffering from poverty and malnutrition at times, Choukri was not able to read or write until the age of 20. In the early 1970s, he met the writer Paul Bowles, who encouraged him to write and helped translate Choukri's autobiographical *For Bread Alone* into English. Tennessee Williams described it as 'a true document of human desperation, shattering in its impact'. The book was banned in Morocco until 2000.

In Morocco (1920)
Edith Wharton

Influential writer Edith Wharton travelled through Morocco just before the end of the First World War, for the most part by military jeep. This account, which Wharton hoped would provide invaluable information for any travellers following in her footsteps, describes her journey across the country, the people she met and places she visited in glorious detail. From Rabat and Fez to Moulay Idriss and Marrakech, Wharton recounts events, celebrations, religious ceremonies and many other wondrous things that she witnessed.

The Caliph's House (2007)
Tahir Shah

In 2007, writer and film-maker Shah decided that he had had enough of London. He wanted to bring up his children somewhere vital, full of history and romance. Spurred on by this childhood memories of holidays long past, he moved his family to Casablanca into Dar Khalifa, a sprawling residence on the edges the city's shanty town, where the caliph was once rumoured to have resided. This book tells the story of what happened.

🏠 http://thecaliphshouse.com/(hotel)

MOZAMBIQUE

Fiction

Sleepwalking Land (2006)
Mia Couto

Selected as one of the 12 best books on Africa of the 20th century, Mia Couto's first novel is set in her native Mozambique. It describes the effects of war on a newly independent nation. A man and boy take refuge on a burned-out bus, where the boy finds a set of notebooks among the belongings of

one of the dead and begins to read the story to his companion.

🔍 *Under the Frangipani* (2008)

Meet Me in Mozambique (2005)
E. A. Markham

University professor Peter Markham has always been more at home in airports. One day he books a ticket to Mozambique on a mission to find a man named Colin Retford.

Non-fiction

Mozambique Mysteries (2007)
Lisa St Aubin de Teran

Writer Lisa St Aubin de Teran leads an impossibly romantic life. This book finds her newly divorced and off men – until she meets a Dutch journalist. They travel to the Mossuril Peninsula, a place seemingly of dreams with beautiful beaches and mangroves, cut off from the mainland and unaffected by civil war. The region also suffers from a lack of development and people die from diarrhoea and malaria. While St Aubin de Teran falls in love with the region and the people, she also falls for her journalist.

NAMIBIA

Fiction

The Purple Violet of Oshaantu (2004)
Neshani Andreas

Andreas's much-praised book takes place in post-independence Namibia.

Set in a fictional village in the rural north, *The Purple Violet of Oshaantu* tells of ordinary Namibians and particularly the friendship between two women and the issues that they have to deal with, including infidelity and domestic abuse.

NIGERIA

Fiction

Half of a Yellow Sun (2006)
Chimamanda Ngozi Adichie

Adichie's extraordinary second book tells of the Nigerian–Biafran War. Based on interviews with people who lived through that time and the author's own parents' experiences, *Half of a Yellow Sun* entwines the lives of 13-year-old Ugwu, a houseboy to a university professor, Olanna, the professor's lover, and Richard, a young Englishman, all caught up in the approaching war.

🔍 *Purple Hibiscus* (2003)

The Joys of Motherhood (1994)
Buchi Emecheta

Emecheta believes that fiction should have social merit and her books, which primarily deal with the lives of African women, do so. In this book, set in Laos, she presents the life of Nnu Ego, married, only to be cast off when she fails to produce a child for her husband. When Nnu marries again and has a child she gains the respect of her community.

The Famished Road (1991)
Ben Okri

A lyrically written book in which poet Ben Okri creates Azaro, a spirit child or the *abiku* of Yoruba myth, who is continually reborn. Challenging his fate, Azaro decides to change his existence of flitting between dreams and the poverty of African slum life and experience reality for himself.

The Icarus Girl (2005)
Helen Oyeyemi

Completed while the author was still at school, this book won huge acclaim. It tells the tale of Jessamy, a mixed-raced girl, who finds a soulmate when she visits her mother's family in Nigeria.

Sozaboy: A Novel in Rotten English (1985)
Ken Saro-Wiwa

Written in 'rotten English' (pidgin English), Saro-Wiwa's book follows a young teenager who joins the army without really knowing why. As a soldier in the Nigerian–Biafran War (1967–70), he finds himself caught up in the chaos and meaningless violence of the time. Saro-Wiwa was a successful writer who campaigned for the rights of the Ogoni peoples. Imprisoned in 1994 for his activities, he was hanged with eight other Ogoni activists in 1995.

📶 http://remembersarowiwa.com/ (Remember Saro-Wiwa, a coalition of organizations and individuals)

Chinua Achebe's Things Fall Apart (1958)

Regarded as the founding father of modern African literature, Chinua Achebe achieved great success with his first novel *Things Fall Apart*. The tale of Okonkwo, a proud Igbo tribal leader, and his fall from grace, the book is set in the 19th century. As Okonkwo sees his culture and society disintegrating before his eyes, following the arrival of British missionaries and colonizers, he is unable to find his place in this new world and loses all sense of himself. Achebe wrote the novel partly in response to what he viewed as inaccurate or offensive portrayals of Africans by British writers.

RWANDA

Fiction

A Sunday at the Pool in Kigali (2003)
Gil Courtemanche

Courtemanche's critically acclaimed novel is based on his own experiences as a journalist and his time in Rwanda. He wrote the book as a tribute to his friends who died and the 'unsung heroes', the survivors of the Rwandan genocide. The Hutu government stated in 1994 that those of the Hutu majority must kill the Tutsi minority. What followed was one of the most horrific slaughters in recent modern history. Courtemanche's book is a gentle love affair set against the backdrop of this genocide.

Baking Cakes in Kigali (2009)
Gaile Parkin

In this charming novel based in Kigali in the aftermath of the genocide, Parkin's protagonist Angel moves to Rwanda from Tanzania. Before long she establishes a cake-making business, baking for her neighbours and their friends. She is aware of the country's recent tragic past and how many of her friends and clients have suffered, but she also believes that life must go on and be celebrated as well as mourned.

Non-fiction

Shake Hands with the Devil (2005)
Roman Dallaire

This brutally frank account of the Rwandan genocide, the event on which the international community seemingly turned its back, is by the general who led the UN peace mission. In 1993 Dallaire arrived in Rwanda on what he thought would be a straightforward peace mission, sure of his intentions and his worth as a soldier. Thirteen months later, he flew home, broken in spirit and mind, after witnessing some of the worst atrocities of his career. A far from easy read it is essential in helping to understand the reasons why this horrific event happened in modern times.

We Wish to Inform You That Tomorrow We Will Be Killed with Our Families (1998)

Philip Gourevitch

New Yorker staff writer Gourevitch spent nine months in Rwanda in the aftermath of the genocide trying to find out how this horrifying event had come to pass. In 100 days in the spring and summer of 1994, more than 800,000 people were killed in what was state-sponsored genocide. This book is his account of what happened. It won several awards, including the 1999 *Guardian* First Book Award.

An Ordinary Man: The True Story Behind the Hotel Rwanda (2007)

Paul Rusebagina

Most people recognize Paul Rusebagina's name from the Hollywood, award-winning movie *Hotel Rwanda*. Portrayed in the film by Don Cheadle, Rusebagina was the heroic figure who put his life on the line to save the lives of more than one 1,200 Tutsis and threatened Hutus by giving them refuge in the hotel – Sabina Hôtel de Mille Collines – which he managed during the genocide that occurred in the spring and summer of 1994. This moving account, written by Rusebagina with the help of Tom Zoellner, tells the real story and is no less tragic, courageous or horrific in text than it is on film. In 1996, after receiving death threats in Rwanda, Rusebagina sought asylum in Belgium, where he still lives with his wife Tatiana and family.

🎦 *Hotel Rwanda* (2004)

Rwanda nature

Although Rwanda has suffered greatly in recent years from genocide and war, it is also a fantastically beautiful country, blessed with an abundance of magnificent wildlife. Chief among these are the gorillas, chimpanzees and golden monkeys that primatologists such as Dian Fossey made her life work. Fossey wrote about her experiences of living with four mountain gorilla families over 13 years in the remote regions of the Virunga Mountains of Rwanda in *Gorillas in the Mist* (1983). She was murdered two years later, many think by the poachers whom she exposed in her book. In 1988, Sigourney Weaver played Fossey in a hugely successful film. Visitors can go on official mountain gorilla treks (http://www.rwandatourism.com/primate.htm) and also see other kinds of wildlife such as golden monkeys in Volcanoes National Park.

🔊 http://gorillafund.org/ (Dian Fossey Gorilla Fund International)
🎦 *Gorillas in the Mist: The Story of Dian Fossey* (1989), starring Sigourney Weaver as Dian Fossey

SENEGAL

Fiction

Scarlet Song (1981)
Mariama Ba

This beautifully written tale finished just before Ba's death focuses on the interracial love between Ousmane, the oldest son of a poor Muslim family, and Mireille, the daughter of a French diplomat. Defying their families, the couple elopes and Mireille converts to Islam, but as time passes Ousmane begins to adhere to his traditional upbringing and Mireille finds it difficult to find peace in a life so very different from the one in which she grew up.

SIERRA LEONE

Fiction

The Heart of the Matter (1981)
Graham Greene

During the Second World War Greene was a secret intelligence officer in Sierra Leone and it was here that he based *The Heart of the Matter*. Essentially a tale of moral dilemma, Greene's central figure, the Catholic police officer Scobie, struggles to come to terms with his unhappy marriage to Louise. He promises to send her to South Africa after he is passed over for promotion but lacks the funds to do so and what follows is his gradual corruption as he struggles to fulfil his promise to Louise. Scobie also begins an affair with Helen, a widow, but how can he come to terms with all this and still hold on to his beliefs?

🎬 *The Heart of the Matter* (1953); Greene co-wrote the screenplay and Trevor Howard played Scobie

🔍 *Congo – A Burnt-Out Case*

Moses, Citizen and Me (2005)
Delia Jarrett-Macauley

Julia flies into Sierra Leone to see her uncle, Moses. What she finds is quite shocking when she meets her cousin, Citizen, and discovers that he is a child soldier. She struggles to understand him and takes the disturbed child into the bush, where they meet other child soldiers and a storyteller who tries to rehabilitate them, turning them back to children.

SOMALIA

Fiction

From A Crooked Rib (1970)
Nuruddin Farah

Written in 1968 when Farah was just 23, this is a sympathetic portrayal of women in Somalia. The title comes from a Somalian proverb, 'God created woman from a crooked rib and anyone who trieth to straighten it, breaketh it'. The book follows the life of Ebla, who suffers everything from female infibulations to marital abuse; it is a shocking insight into a chauvinistic society.

🔍 *Secrets* (1998)

SUDAN

Fiction

Season of Migration to the North (1966)
Tayeb Salih

Salih's classic novel follows Mustafa Sa'eed, a mysterious character, who lives in a small village in Sudan with his family. The unnamed narrator of this book arrives home after studying for a doctorate abroad and becomes fascinated by Mustafa, who disappears one day. Through the narrator we view snippets of Mustafa's life and through Salih's lyrical descriptions get an insight into the country's politics and culture.

Something Is Going to Fall Like Rain (2009)
Ros Wynne-Jones

Set in Adek, southern Sudan, Wynee-Jones's beautifully written book evokes the bleakness of the rural landscape. In the 1990s, a community is caught between the ravages of a brutal war and starvation. When a group of aid workers is stranded there they bring hope. The book pays tribute to the people of southern Sudan and also to the aid workers who have worked so hard to help them.

Non-fiction

What is the What: The Autobiography of Valentino Achak Deng (2010)
Dave Eggers

Eggers met Valentino Achak Deng through the Lost Boys Foundation in Atlanta. Over the next three years they worked together to write this book, which tells Valentino's story. As one of the countless children separated from their families by the civil war, Valentino walked across the desert, surviving the war, starvation and wild beasts to reach the refugee camps in Ethiopia and Kenya, where he lived for 13 years. He eventually reached the United States and there faced a very different set of obstacles.

📶 http://www.valentinoachakdeng.org (Valentino Achak Deng foundation helps to empower war-affected Sudanese people)

🔍 New Orleans – *Zeitoun* (2009)

The Translator: A Tribesman's Memoir of Darfur (2008)
Daoud Hari

This is a moving first-hand account of the Darfur conflict in western Sudan as witnessed by Daoud Hari. A Zaghawa tribesman, Hari sketches the history of his country and life before the conflict broke out, growing up in a tight-knit rural community, racing camels and playing with his friends and family. After Arab tribes known as the Janjaweed attacked his village and he watched loved ones die, Hari travelled across the border to the refugee camps of Chad. He chose to return to Darfur to help stop the conflict, working, at great personal risk, with journalists and genocide investigators as an English-language translator in order to help highlight the situation in his country.

SOUTH AFRICA

Fiction

A Dry White Season (1979)
Andre Brink

Brink's classic novel focuses on the awakening of a white teacher living in suburban Johannesburg to the racism and injustice prevalent in his country. Following the detainment and 'suicide' of a black friend, he investigates the truth and is led to question the very society in which he lives.

📽 *A Dry White Season* (1989)

In the Heart of the Country (1977)
J. M. Coetzee

Coetzee's second novel is set on an isolated farmstead in South Africa, where the protagonist, a fiercely intelligent woman excluded by those around her, including her father, reacts bitterly when he takes an African mistress.

🔍 *Disgrace* (1999)

Bitter Fruit (2004)
Achmat Dangor

Dangor's novel tells of a family trying to come to grips with the past. Set in post-apartheid South Africa at the time of the Truth and Reconciliation Commission hearings, Silas comes face to face with Lieutenant DuBoise. He had last met him 20 years earlier, while locked in a police van as Duboise assaulted Silas' wife as punishment for his involvement in the African National Congress.

Blood Knot (1961)
Athol Fugard

It might seem unusual to include plays in such a collection, but why not when they evoke the atmosphere and time of a certain place? Fugard's excellent collection of three plays, *Blood Knot*, *Hello and Goodbye* and *Boesman and Lena* are all set in Port Elizabeth and examine family relationships and the pressures put on them by apartheid. *Blood Knot*, which he wrote in 1960 and was first performed in 1961, established Fugard's reputation internationally. It deals with two mixed-race brothers, one who can pass for white, the other unmistakenly black.

🔍 *Tsotsi* (also made into an Oscar-winning movie)

The Conservationist (1974)
Nadine Gordimer

This Booker Prize-winning novel follows Mehring, a rich, white South African property owner during apartheid. Through a stream of consciousness and flashbacks, Gordimer shows Mehring's role in an unequal racial system in which being white is all that matters. After a body is found on his land, the police simply bury it and Mehring's life begins to disintegrate.

Living, Loving and Lying Awake At Night (1991)
Sindiwe Magona

This triumphant collection of short stories brings to life South African women in the last years of apartheid.

Triomf (1999)
Marlene Van Niekerk

Set in Triomf, a poor white township, van Nierkerk's Afrikaaner darkly comic novel follows the dysfunctional Benade family on the eve of the first democratic elections in 1993. They wait for the day when the sun will shine on everyone – but will it?

🎬 Triomf (2008)

Non-fiction

Kaffir Boy: An Autobiography (1986)
Mark Mathabane

Mathabane's best-selling book is a very personal account of growing up in the brutal apartheid system. Mathabane managed to escape through hard work. Today, he lives in the United States. Oprah Winfrey endorsed the book, even buying the film rights, after which it became a runaway success.

To My Children's Children (1990)
Sindiwe Magona

This widely acclaimed memoir of Magona's early life is a moving read. Born into a traditional Xhosa village, Magona had a very happy childhood and describes in great detail Xhosa culture. But when she grew up she came to realize the horror of apartheid.

TANZANIA

Fiction

Paradise (1994)
Abdulrazak Gurnah

This lyrical novel by Zanzibar-born Gurnah is set in rural East Africa. Following 12-year-old Yusuf, whose father 'sells' him to Aziz to settle a debt, the story moves from a remote village in what is now Tanzania to the highlands and interior as Yusuf joins a travelling caravan. On his journey,

---

Nelson Mandela and The Long Walk To Freedom (1995)

How could we have a section on South African literature and not include a work by one of greatest human rights leaders of our age, Nelson Mandela? This elegantly written book tells of Mandela's life and times and is a moving and troubling insight into one of the most oppressive regimes of modern history. Most of Mandela's autobiography was written in secret while he was imprisoned on Robben Island, where Mandela spent 27 years of his life. Visitors can visit the prison, which is now a museum and memorial. Ferries leave from the Nelson Mandela Gateway at the V&A Waterfront in Cape Town. A former inmate is the tour guide and tourists can see Mandela's cell and visit the lime quarry where inmates had to work in the blinding midday sun.

📶 http://www.robben-island.org.za/ (Robben Island)

➕ Let Freedom Reign (2010), a book published by New Holland focusing on Nelson Mandela's key speeches with an introduction by André Brink

Yusuf encounters all kinds of people – the different groups existing in Tanzania, each fighting for some kind of control or recognition in a region on the verge of war (First World War).

The Ice Cream War (1982)
William Boyd

In usual Boyd style, this novel is an extremely entertainingly look at how the Americans, Germans and British in East Africa coped with the outbreak of the First World War. Focusing on a forgotten part of history – the German and British engagements in Africa – during this period, Boyd successfully evokes the atmosphere of this time.

TOGO

Fiction

Waiting for the Wild Beasts to Vote (2003)
Ahmadou Kourouma

Kourouma's prize-winning book looks at post-independent West Africa as seen through the eyes of a dictator. Set in the fictional Republique du Golfe, Kourouma's book veers between fantasy and bitter reality as the author creates President Koyaga, based on the real-life President Eyadema of Togo. Kourouma writer lived and worked in Togo between 1983 and 1993.

TUNISIA

Fiction

The Pillar of Salt (1992)
Albert Memmi

This semi-autobiographical novel, set in Tunis in the 1950s, tells of Alexandre Benillouche, a boy of mixed Italian–Jewish and Berber descent. Memmi beautifully describes the people, sights and sounds of French-colonized Tunisia.

UGANDA

Fiction

The Last King of Scotland (1998)
Giles Fodden

Fodden's award-winning darkly funny book focuses on the horrific period of Ugandan history when Idi Amin was dictator. Narrator Nicholas Garrigan becomes Amin's personal physician. His arrival in Uganda coincides with Amin's rise to power and from his very privileged position Nicholas begins to witness the madness of Amin's plans.

📽 *The Last King of Scotland* (2006)
🔍 Zanzibar – *Zanzibar* (2002)

Abyssinian Chronicle (2001)
Moses Isegawa

This epic story is set in Uganda – not Ethiopia as the title suggests. As the narrator Mugezi explains, his father had once stated that 'Uganda was a

land of false bottoms where under every abyss there was another one waiting to snare people, and that the historians had made a mistake: Abyssinia was not the ancient land of Ethiopia, but modern Uganda.'
The plot spans about 30 years of the country's history and reveals a complex country, made up of many different ethnic and religious groups, who contribute to and suffer from the effects of the conflict that Uganda experiences through war, dictatorship and epidemics such as AIDS.

ZAMBIA

Fiction

A Cowrie of Hope (2002)
Binwell Sinyangwe

Set in 1990s Zambia, Sinyangwe's concise novel is one of courage and hope in times of poverty and extreme adversity. It focuses primarily on a mother's love for her daughter and her determination that education will provide an escape from their poor existence. It follows Nasula from her village to the big city of Lusaka, where she sells her last bag of beans to fund her daughter's schooling.

Non-fiction

Secrets of the Savanna: Twenty-Three Years in the African Wilderness Unravelling the Mysteries of Elephants and People (2007)
Mark and Delia Owens

An incredible tale of poaching, slavery and corruption, *Secrets of the Savanna* tells the true story of how Mark and Delia Owens helped to stop gangs of ivory traders working in the beautiful northern Luangwa Valley of Zambia. The Owens travelled there to study lions and instead found themselves caught up in gunfire as the poachers hunted elephants. This is a passionate account by the Owens who also lovingly evoke this beautiful part of the world, where they lived and worked from 1985 to 1997. The Owens also helped the government develop eco-tourism in the valley, establishing eco-walking safari tours in 1995.

🛜 http://www.owensfoundation.org/docs/ tourism2.htm (tourist information on the eco-walking tours)

ZANZIBAR

Fiction

Zanzibar (2002)
Giles Foden

Foden's third novel is set around the bombings of the US embassies in Africa in 1998 and was largely written before 9/11. A diverting terrorist thriller, *Zanzibar* brings several different characters together – a marine biologist on a USAID mission on the island, a disillusioned CIA agent and a young Zanzibari terrorist, recruited to al-Qaeda after the murder of his parents. In the book, the island, as much as the characters, comes to life and Foden presents its lush beauty in as much detail as he does home-made bombs and modern technology.

Death in Zanzibar (1959)
M. M. Kaye

In yet another classic murder romance from Kaye the protagonist Dany is invited to her stepfather's house Kivulimi ('the House of Shade') in exotic Zanzibar. She finds herself at a house party only to discover that one of the guests is a killer.

🔍 Kenya – *Death in Kenya* (1958)

ZIMBABWE
Fiction

Nervous Conditions (1988)
Tsitsi Dangarembga

Dangarembga's first novel is a coming of age story set in 1960s' Rhodesia. Protagonist Tambu, sent to a mission school to be educated, meets her British-educated cousin Nyasha. As Tambu struggles to make sense of her new world, her cousin also provides new challenges, leading Tambu to question many of the things she has taken for granted.

An Elegy for Easterly (2009)
Petina Gappah

Called 'the voice of Zimbabwe', award-winning writer Petina Gappah presents life under Mugabe in this beautiful collection of short stories. Her characters deal with their own disappointments, challenges and everyday life in a country beset with spiralling inflation, financial hardship and great political unrest.

The Grass is Singing (1950)
Doris Lessing

Lessing used the farm where she grew up in Southern Rhodesia as the inspiration for her novel *The Grass is Singing*. Focussing on a couple, Dick and Mary Turner, who live on an isolated farm, Lessing examines the growing rift between them and the tragic events that this leads to. As Mary becomes increasingly disgruntled with her life under the relentless sun, she becomes obsessed with Moses, a houseboy.

🎬 *The Grass is Singing* (1962)
🔍 *Going Home* (1957)

Without a Name and Under The Tongue (2002)
Yvonne Vera

Vera's two novels, *Without a Name* and *Under a Tongue*, published respectively in 1994 and 1996 and together in this one edition in 2002, were groundbreaking, dealing with subjects often treated as taboo and giving voice to Zimbabwean women. Set in the 1970s during the guerrilla war that raged in Zimbabwe, the first follows Mazvita as she moves from rural Mubaira to the country's capital of Harare in the later part of the decade. Here, she finds disappointment and is driven to commit a stupid act. In her second book, Vera deals with the problem of incest and the importance of words: after Zhizha is raped by her father, a hero of the war, she retreats into a world without words.

Non-fiction

Don't Let's Go to the Dogs Tonight: An African Childhood (2001)
Alexandra Fuller

This is a beautifully written memoir of a young girl growing up in a white family during the Rhodesian Bush War. The author presents a vivid, realistic, yet humorous portrayal of life during that time. Fuller, who moved with her parents to Rhodesia from England at the age of two, inhabited a world of breathtaking landscapes and natural beauty, side-by-side with war, unspeakable violence and racism.

When A Crocodile Eats the Sun (2007)
Peter Godwin

Godwin is a white African who dreams of returning to Zimbabwe to live one day. Telling the story of his parents who moved from England to the country 30 years ago, Godwin essentially presents the history of this battered and besieged land, laid low by bitterness, racism, Mugabe and AIDS, among other factors.

African Laughter: Four Visits to Zimbabwe (1992)
Doris Lessing

Lessing was banned from her homeland for almost 25 years for her opposition to the minority white government. This book describes four visits to Zimbabwe taken by the author in 1982, 1988, 1989 and 1992. A passionate account of the author's love for the country, *African Laughter* gives a great insight into the land, people and politics of that time.

THE AMERICAS

LATIN AMERICA

Central America and the Caribbean

Belize | El Salvador | Guatemala | Honduras | Mexico | Nicaragua

Panama | Caribbean | Antigua | Barbados | Cuba | Dominican Republic

Guadeloupe | Haiti | Jamaica | Puerto Rico | St Kitts | Trinidad

South America

Argentina | Bolivia | Brazil | Chile | Colombia | Ecuador

Guyana | Paraguay | Peru | Uruguay | Venezuela

NORTH AMERICA

Canada | United States of America

CENTRAL AMERICA AND THE CARIBBEAN

CENTRAL AMERICA

BELIZE

Beka Lamb (1982)
Zee Edgell

Edgell's award-winning book has Beka, who battles to fight her habit of lying, as its protagonist. Edgell's story portrays the politics of Belize during its last years as a British colony and the importance of the Catholic Church.

EL SALVADOR

Fiction

One Day of Life (1983)
Manilo Argueto

This brutal tale, Argueto's novel presents a day in the life of a peasant family caught up in El Salvador's civil war in Chalate (Chalatenango), a small rural town.

Bitter Grounds (1997)
Sandra Benitez

Benitez's epic tale spans 40 years of El Salvador's history from the 1930s to '70s and is set in the coffee-growing heart of the country. Following three generations of the Prieto family, this is a story played out against the changing politics of the time.

Non-fiction

Salvador (1983)
Joan Didion

This searing account based on the time that Didion spent in El Salvador in the 1980s presents the mood and politics of the country in vivid detail and sheds light on a dark period in the country's history.

GUATEMALA

Fiction

The President (1963)
Miguel Angel Asturias

Nobel prize-winning author Angel Asturias started this story of a dictator and his ruthless plans to get rid of a political adversary in an unnamed Latin American country as a short story, but it grew into this book. The country is generally believed to be Guatemala.

🔍 *Men of Maize: the Modernist Epic of Guatemalan Indians*

Comrades (1976)
Marco Antonio Flores

Hailed as a masterpiece when it was first published, *Comrades* caused a huge storm in Guatemala but is viewed as heralding in the age of the 'new Guatemalan novel'. It focuses on four friends and a lover whose lives are changed by the bloody civil war.

Non-fiction

I, Rigoberta Menchu: An Indian Woman in Guatemala (1984)
Rigoberta Menchu

This international best-seller won Menchu the Nobel Peace Prize. Menchu's memoir tells of the inequality and injustices suffered by and gritty reality of being an Indian woman in Guatemala.

HONDURAS

Fiction

Port Mungo (2004)
Patrick McGrath

Moving from England to Honduras via New York, McGrath's psychological study examines the relationship between two artists Jack Rathbone and Vera Savage.

The Mosquito Coast (1982)
Paul Theroux

Disillusioned with life in America, Allie uproots his family to the heart of the Honduran jungle with the mission of creating his own paradise. Seen through the eyes of Charlie, *The Mosquito Coast* is an entertaining look at the relationship between a father and son in a completely foreign locale and all the challenges that arise.

🎦 *The Mosquito Coast* (1986), directed by Peter Weir and starring Harrison Ford as Allie

MEXICO

Fiction

Caramelo (2003)
Sandra Cisneros

This novel is narrated by Lala, the youngest child in a Mexican–American family. Each summer the Reyes family make their way from Chicago to Mexico City to stay with their grandparents and each year they hear the family stories. *Caramelo* tells their tale, interweaving fact with fiction in a rich tapestry of love, hope and history.

Like Water for Hot Chocolate (1989)
Laura Esquivel

This global best-seller links recipes to love in a lovely magic-realism tale set in Mexico. Tita, the youngest daughter of Mama Elena, is bound by duty to look after her widowed mother. When Pedro, Tita's love, comes to ask for her hand in marriage, Mama Elena refuses but offers him her older daughter instead. Pedro accepts only to be near Tita and as Mama Elena will never allow them to be alone together, Tita expresses her love through the food she cooks for Pedro and the family.

🎦 *Like Water for Hot Chocolate* (1993)

The Years with Laura Diaz (1999)
Carlos Fuentes

One of Mexico's best-known writers, Carlos Fuentes chronicles Mexican history through the eyes of Laura Diaz in this novel. A renowned photographer, Diaz was also friends with the artists Diego Rivera and Frida Kahlo.

🔍 *The Old Gringo*

The Power and the Glory (1940)
Graham Greene

Viewed by many as Greene's finest work, *The Power and the Glory* follows a nameless drunken priest on the run following an anticlerical purge in 1930s' Mexico.

Under the Volcano (1947)
Malcolm Lowry

Lowry's classic recounts the last day in the life of Geoffrey Firmin, a former British consul, on the Day of the Dead in Quauhnahuac (Cuernavaca), Mexico. As Yvonne, his estranged wife, comes to find him and struggles to save him and their marriage, matters are complicated by the arrival of his half-brother, Hugh.

🎬 *Under the Volcano* (1984)

The Labyrinth of Solitude (1985)
Octavio Paz

Paz's work has long been seen as essential to understanding Mexico, its peoples and the quest for identity.

NICARAGUA

Fiction

Desperadoes (1993)
Joseph O'Connor

O'Connor's novel is set in 1985. When an estranged Irish couple are informed that there singer son, Johnny, is missing presumed dead in war-torn Nicaragua, they travel to the country to find him. It is based on O'Connor's own travels in Nicaragua as a 22 year old.

📶 www.josephoconnor.com

Non-fiction

The Country Under My Skin (2002)
Gioconda Belli

In this memoir by Belli, an acclaimed Nicaraguan writer and central figure of the Sandinista revolution, she covers her life from her upper-class upbringing to the 1970s, when her emerging social conscious led her to join the Sandinistas.

The Jaguar Smile: A Nicaraguan Journey (1997)
Salman Rushdie

This updated version of Rushdie's 1987 book includes a preface by the acclaimed author. Rushdie's first non-fiction work focuses on his trip to Nicaragua in 1986, the characters he met there and the politics and lyricism of the land.

PANAMA

Fiction

Two Serious Ladies (1943)
Jane Bowles

Bowles's novel, partly based on her life with the writer Paul Bowles, follows Christina and Frieda as they break away from their mundane lives. Christina leaves behind her wealthy conservative life and Frieda ditches her husband and falls in love with a prostitute in Panama.

🛜 http://www.paulbowles.org/enter.html
(information on Jane and Paul Bowles)

The Tailor of Panama (1985)
John le Carré

Reminiscent of Greene's *Our Man in Havana* (see *Cuba*) le Carré's Harry Pendel, a tailor in Panama City, is recruited by the British intelligence service. Pendel becomes increasingly seduced by this world of espionage, believing the intelligence that he has himself fabricated to pass on to his masters.

🎬 *The Tailor of Panama* (2001)

CARIBBEAN

Fiction

Flickering Shadows (1996)
Kwadwo Agymah Kamau

On an unnamed island in the Caribbean the inhabitants of a small ex-colony, the Hill, play out their

everyday lives as the pervasive threat of neocolonialism intrudes.

ANTIGUA

Fiction

Annie John (1983)
Jamaica Kincaid

This coming-of-age novel focuses on a young girl growing up on the island of Antigua. Kincaid's descriptions of the smells, food, traditions and spiritual life on the island bring Antigua to life.

🔍 *Lucy: A Novel*

BARBADOS

Fiction

In the Castle of My Skin (1953)
George Lamming

Lamming's first novel tells of G, a boy growing up in 1930s' Barbados. It is a wonderful insight into village life and an evocation of what it is like to grow up in a post-colonial and ex-slavery-dominated society.

CUBA

Fiction

Three Trapped Tigers (1975)
Guillermo Cabrera Infante

Originally published in Spanish in 1965, this book has been hailed as the 'Cuban Ulysses'. Cabrera Infante uses wordplay, puns and other literary devices to create pre-Castro Havana as seen through the eyes of a man living in exile.

🔍 *Infante's Inferno* (1979)

Explosion in a Cathedral (1962)
Alejo Carpentier

Carpentier was one of Cuba's leading writers. Setting this book in the late 18th century at the time of the French revolution, he tells of Victor Hugues, who led the battle to take back the island of Gaudeloupe from the English.

🔍 Haiti – *The Kingdom of this World*

Tango for a Torturer (2006)
Daniel Chavarria

This entertaining book sees a former Argentine revolutionary travelling to contemporary Havana only to have his holiday disrupted when he discovers that a former Uruguayan torturer is living there under a false identity.

Our Man in Havana (1958)
Graham Greene

Greene's entertaining but worrying tale of espionage and betrayal in Cuba is a classic. Offered more money than he can think of and desperate to finance his daughter's lavish lifestyle, Jim Wormold, who runs a British vacuum-cleaner business in Havana, finds himself an inept spy for the British intelligence. As he fabricates intelligence, his masters seem to

think he is doing a fantastic job, even though Wormold lurches from one crisis to another.

🎦 *Our Man in Havana* (1959)

Havana Red (2005)
Leonarda Padura

Lieutenant Mario Conde is a Havana policeman whose hero is Ernest Hemingway. After a transvestite is found murdered in Havana Park, he is forced to investigate, entering a world where nothing is as it seems.

Non-fiction

Reminiscences of the Cuban Revolutionary War (1968)
Che Guevara

Soon after the Cuban revolution, Che Guevara began to set down the 'true' history of the war, through articles that appeared in various periodicals and newspapers. In 1963, they were pulled together into one volume for which Fidel Castro wrote an introduction.

🎦 *Che* (2009)

DOMINICAN REPUBLIC

Fiction

Drown (1996)
Junot Diaz

Each of Diaz's excellent short stories in this collection features either a Dominican or Dominican–American

The Old Man and the Sea (1952)

Hemingway's love of Cuba is well documented but never more so as in this lyrical book, which documents a fisherman's struggle to catch the perfect fish. Its central character is based on Gregorio Fuentes, who captained Hemingway's boat El Pilar for almost 30 years. Visitors to Cuba can see many of Hemingway's favourite spots, including El Floridita bar where he used to hang out in Havana, his farm Finca Vigia, once a hot spot for celebrities and Hollywood stars and today a museum, and the village of Cojimar, 10 km (6⅕ miles) east of Havana, where he kept El Pilar (still on display) and where there is a huge monument to the world-famous writer.

📶 http://www.sprachcaffe-kuba.com/EN/In_Hemingways_Footsteps_Prices_And_Services.htm (one of several tours of Hemingway's Cuba)

character and move between rural Dominican Republic and suburban New Jersey.

The Feast of the Goat (2000)
Mario Vargas Llosa

Vargas Llosa covers the end of Rafael Trujillo's brutal regime and the dictator's assassination, and the return of a Dominican lawyer to the island after a long period of self-exile. In his usual style, the author characterizes a nation terrorized by one man known as 'the Goat'.

GUADELOUPE

Fiction

Windward Heights (1995)
Maryse Condé

Set in 18th- and 19th-century Caribbean, Condé cleverly transposes *Wuthering Heights* to the island of Guadeloupe.

HAITI

Fiction

The Kingdom of this World (1957)
Alejo Carpentier

Written in 1949 and translated into English eight years later, Carpentier's excellent novel tells of Haiti in the lead up to, during and after the Haitian revolution.

🔍 Cuba – *Explosion in a Cathedral*

The Comedians (1966)
Graham Greene

Set in the Haiti of Papa Doc Duvalier, Greene's novel tells of three men meeting on a boat to Haiti and how they cope with the increasing brutality of a terrorized nation.

🎬 *The Comedians* (1967), starring Richard Burton and Elizabeth Taylor

Masters of the Dew (1947)
Jacques Roumain

Considered by some to be among the island's finest works of literature, *Masters of the Dew* is set in 1930s' Haiti and follows Manuel returning home from working on a sugar plantation in Cuba, where he has become more politically aware, to his native village divided by feuds and drought. Manuel, applying the ideas to which he has been exposed, works to bring the villagers together.

JAMAICA

Fiction

Mint Tea and Other Stories (1993)
Christine Craig

A volume of stories set in Jamaica, *Mint Tea and Other Stories* tell of inequality, injustice and how women exist on the island.

A High Wind in Jamaica (1929)
Richard Hughes

This classic novel set in the late 19th century is an adventure story. The book's opening location is the ruined landscape of Jamaica, where 'earthquake, fire, rain and deadlier vegetation' has destroyed everything, and where a group of children are thrown to the mercy of pirates as they attempt to return to England.

🔍 *Lucy: A Novel*

Fruit of the Lemon (1999)
Andrea Levy

Set in the 1970s, Levy's novel, located half in England and half in Jamaica, deals with the immigrant experience. Focal character Faith Jackson's life is set up in the earlier part of the book, detailing her family's journey to the 'mother country' of England and Faith's own apparently successful career. But as Faith becomes increasingly aware of the subtle and not-so-subtle forms of racism around her, she decides to travel to Jamaica to find out where she belongs and more about her family and its past.

PUERTO RICO

Fiction

When I Was Puerto Rican (1993)
Esmeralda Santiago

Set half in Puerto Rica, where the protagonist grows up, and half in America, to where she and her family emigrate for a better life, Santiago's book beautifully evokes a young girl trying to find her identity in a dysfunctional family.

The Rum Diary (1959)
Hunter S. Thompson

Thompson began this book when he was in his early twenties. At its heart lies Paul Kemp, a disillusioned journalist who drinks and parties his way through the San Juan of the 1950s.

Mrs Rochester's Jamaica

How many writers can get away with successfully conjuring up the early life of one of the most hated characters in Victorian literature – in this case Mrs Rochester, Jane Eyre's nemesis? Jean Rhys does it with great sensitivity, style and passion in her acclaimed (and much-loved) novel *Wide Sargasso Sea*. Set in 1830s' Jamaica after the Emancipation Act, fragile Creole Antoinette Cosway lives on a beautiful estate with her beautiful mother, who is ostracized by Jamaica's elite, and her wealthy English stepfather. Rhys evocatively establishes the background for Antoinette's descent into insanity. She builds up the tension between the local, recently freed black population and the arrogant Europeans – including Mr Mason, Antoinette's often absent stepfather – who still control so much of the island's wealth and this explodes one evening into violence on the estate, when their house is set alight and her brother fatally injured. As her mother retreats into madness, Antoinette is sent to a convent school where she learns to behave like a lady and when her stepfather returns, bringing with him a group of friends, she meets her future husband, Rochester. The second part of the novel is told from Rochester's viewpoint as he finds himself dealing with his beautiful, increasingly erratic wife, whom he renames 'Bertha'. *Wide Sargasso Sea* concludes with Antoinette, completely emotionally and physically displaced in England, hidden away in an attic and guarded by servant Grace Poole. Rhys, who was herself born in Dominica and was of mixed Creole blood, imbues the book with Antoinette's increasing sense of isolation and loneliness.

France, Paris – *Quartet*

ST KITTS

Fiction

A State of Independence (1999)
Caryl Phillips

This much-acclaimed book, *A State of Independence* follows a man, returning after 20 years away, to an island very different from the one he left, becoming increasingly Americanized and increasingly independent. Phillips beautifully evokes a man lost in the place of his birth.

 A Distant Shore

TRINIDAD

Fiction

Carnival (2005)
Robert Antoni

Antoni explores racial tensions through William, Rachel and Laurence, three childhood friends who meet by accident in a New York bar and decide to return to their native Trinidad for the carnival. Retiring for some peace to the remote rainforest home of carnival king Eddoes, they discover that even in paradise there are demons.

Bond's Jamaica

Ian Fleming created one of the most famous British spies of all time – 007 James Bond. He wrote the 12 novels and 2 books of short stories featuring Bond on the island of Jamaica, where he lived in Goldeneye, the house he built in the sleepy town of Oracabessa in the north of the island. (The house is today owned by Chris Blackwell of Island Records.) Three of the 'Bond' books are located on the island – *Live and Let Die* (1954), *Doctor No* (1958) and *The Man with the Golden Gun* (1965), although we first learn that Bond has some association with the island in *Casino Royale* (1953), when he assumes the undercover identity of a wealthy Jamaican. In *Live and Let Die*, Bond visits the island and travels to the Blue Mountains along the northern coast. Of the three Jamaica-based books, *Doctor No* is probably the most famous – if only because it was the first one adapted for screen (*Dr No*, 1962) and was shot on location in Jamaica for the most part. The novel finds our 007 hero and his 'Girl Friday', Honey Rider, played so beautifully by Ursula Andress on screen, in the clutches of the villainous Dr No, after they trespass onto a secluded Caribbean island. The opening shots of the movie were filmed in Kingston, the capital of Jamaica. Bond stays initially in the Blue Hills Hotel, which is most probably the Blue Mountain Inn. Andress rises from the waves in the famous bikini shot on Laughing Waters Beach, Ochos Rios, St Ann's Bay, and Honey and Bond are later caught by the dragon tank on the beaches near Falmouth, where many of the swamp scenes were also shot. Today visitors can go to James Bond Beach and eat at the Moonraker 'Jamaican' Bar and Grill.

Salt (1996)
Earl Lovelace

Lovelace's award-winning novel looks at island politics in a post-colonial world and a teacher-turned politician involved in shaping the world around him.

A House for Mr Biswas (1961)
V. S. Naipaul

Naipaul is viewed the master of post-colonial Caribbean literature and this early work has contributed towards that reputation. A comic but poignant story set in Trinidad's Hindu community, the book has as its protagonist Mohun Biswas, the son of a contracted labourer who came to the island to work in the sugarcane fields. From the moment of his birth to his marriage into an extended Indian family who try to manipulate him, Biswas's life is full of humiliation. He rises above it, however, seeking some dignity and the only thing that he really wants, a home of his own.

A Brighter Sun (1952)
Samuel Selvon

Set primarily in a village east of Port of Spain and against the backdrop of the Second World War, *A Brighter Sun* finds central character Tiger forced to grow up to look after his child bride, Urmilla. Selvon's excellent first book reveals the multilayered, multi-ethnic Trinidadian society and the tensions between East Indians and Creoles.

SOUTH AMERICA

GENERAL
Fiction

Nostromo (1904)
Joseph Conrad

Set in the fictional country of Costaguan, a South American province between the Andes and the Pacific, *Nostromo* is considered one of Conrad's finest works (although personally we prefer *Heart of Darkness*). It is essentially a tale of corruption and greed in the mining town of Sulaco in which the Italian sailor Nostromo becomes entwined.

One Hundred Years of Solitude (1967)
Gabriel García Márquez

García Márquez wrote this novel in 18 months, locked away in his room. It is set in the fictional South American town of Macondo and follows several generations of the Buendia family over a century. Mixing fact with magic realism, the book is both comic and tragic, and a masterpiece.

Non-fiction

The Motorcycle Diaries (1997)
Che Guevara

More famous for the beautiful film adaptation of the same name, this book is based on Che Guevara's travels on a motorbike through South America in the 1950s with his friend Alberto Granado. Travelling through Argentina, Chile, Peru, Colombia and Venezuela, Guevara shows an increasing awareness of the plight of the average South American and we see his politicization as he realizes that inequality and injustice is rife everywhere.

📽 *Motorcycle Diaries* (2004)
🔍 Cuba – *Reminisces of the Cuban Revolutionary War*

ARGENTINA
Fiction

The Seven Madmen (1985)
Roberto Arlt

Set in the late 1920s, Arlt's novel follows a group of rather bizarre characters as they plot to overthrow the government.

Labyrinths (1962)
Jorge Luis Borges

This excellent collection of short pieces by this Latin American master showcases his best work. Featuring *Fictions*, short essays and other writings this is a great introduction to Borges if you haven't read him before.

The Moldavian Pimp (2006)
Edgardo Cozarinsky

This disturbing first novel follows a piece of history that many people would choose to overlook – the prostitution of Jewish women and men enticed from the Ukraine to Argentina.

Cozarinsky's journalist protagonist meets Samuel Warshauer in an old people's home while researching lost Jews. When the old man dies he finds a play called the 'Moldovian Pimp' which focuses on this subject.

The Honorary Consul (1973)
Graham Greene

Set in provincial Argentina, Greene's tragicomedy tells the tale of the bungled kidnapping of an honorary consul, the self-pitying alcoholic Charley Fortnum, by a group of revolutionaries.

🔍 Mexico – *The Power and the Glory*; Haiti – *The Comedians*

The Tango Singer (2006)
Tomás Eloy Martínez

How can one separate the tango from Argentina? In this novel by acclaimed Martínez, the protagonist is an American student who travels to Buenos Aires to find Julio Martel, an elusive tango singer, in the hope that it will help him with his thesis on Borges's essays on the tango. Martel performs for free at venues around the city that are usually associated with acts of violence against people. At the time he arrives, Argentina is gripped by hyper-inflation and civil unrest and he finds a new passion, Borges's Aleph – from Borges's story of the same name. Martínez's portrayal of Buenos Aires evokes the atmosphere of the city and also explains some recent events in Argentina's history.

BOLIVIA

Fiction

Andean Express (2009)
Juan de Recacoechea

In journalist de Recacoechea's fast-paced and often comical mystery set in 1952, a murder takes place on a train travelling from La Paz, Bolivia, to Arica, Chile.

The Fat Man From La Paz (2000)
Rosario Santos

Santos's collection introduces readers to the best of Andean short stories and is also an insight into the politics, culture and society of the region.

Non-fiction

The Bolivian Diary (1994)
Che Guevara

In October 1967, Che Guevara was executed by the Bolivian army, with the aid of the CIA, after helping support an 11-month guerilla campaign. This book is based on his actual diaries and notebooks and is a fascinating insight into the war and also one of the most important revolutionary figures in Latin American history.

🎬 *Che* (2009)

🔍 Cuba – *Reminisces of the Cuban Revolutionary War*; South America – General – *The Motorcycle Diaries*

BRAZIL

Fiction

Dona Flor and Her Two Husbands (1966)
Jorge Amado

Amado's charismatic, bawdy romp is set in Bahia. When gambler Vadinho Guimaraes dies during a carnival in Salvador, no one is particularly surprised. His widow, Dona Flor, devotes herself to her cooking school, but secretly is sexually frustrated. When she meets a pharmacist, who is everything her irresponsible first husband was not, she marries him only to find out that he is rather dull in bed. She begins to dream of Vadinho and finds his ghost visiting her one day, ready to perform.

🎬 *Dona Flor and Her Two Husbands* (1976), starring Sonia Braga

The Silence of the Rain (2002)
Luis Alfredo Garcia-Roza

Acclaimed writer Garcia-Roza's novels featuring world-weary Inspector Espinosa have garnered much attention in the crime-reading world. In this book, Espinosa is called in to investigate the death of a corporate executive in Rio de Janeiro. As Espinosa delves into the crime, his list of suspects grows and when another two people die, the inspector's interest begins to escalate. Garcia-Roza's Rio is a dark and moody place, capturing the exotic and sensual nature of the city.

The Boys from Brazil (1976)
Ira Levin

Based on real-life characters, Levin mixes fact with fiction in his usual gripping style. It's the 1970s and the horrors of the Nazi regime and the final solution are a thing of the past. But is it really? Nazi hunter Yakov Liebermann thinks otherwise when he discovers a plot developed by the 'Angel of Death' Dr Josef Mengele to kill 94 men of about the same age and background who all have sons, aged about 13, to help restore the supremacy of the Aryan race. But how?

🎬 *The Boys from Brazil* (1978), starring a very scary Gregory Peck

City of God (1997)
Paulo Lins

Lins grew up in the Cidade de Deus, a favela, or shanty town, to the west of Rio de Janeiro. Originally intended as a temporary project for people displaced by floods, it grew into a dumping ground for the poor and displaced, and a place of great violence. Lins's novel is a great insight into this slum area in one of the most beautiful locations on earth. It follows the favela's characters who want to escape to something better and the people trapped by the drugs, poverty and horrors that are everyday life. After the success of the movie of the book, visitors can now go on organized tours of Rio's various favelas.

🎬 *City of God* (2001)

The Posthumous Memoirs of Bras Cubas (1997)
Joaquim Maria Machado de Assis

Written in 1880, Machado de Assis's book is a 19th-century classic of Brazilian literature. Written as a memoir of his life as dictated by a wealthy Brazilian from the grave, the book is divided up into 160 very short chapters. It is said to have influenced many 20th-century Latin American writers, including Garcia Marquez.

Brazil Red (2004)
Jean-Christophe Rufin

Rufin's award-winning book is a work of evocatively imagined history. A great adventure story, it follows Just and Columbe, two orphans, forced to go on a French expedition to help colonize Brazil in the mid-16th century.

Brazil (1994)
John Updike

Updike's love story finds Tristao Raposa, a poor black from a Rio favela, and Isabel Leme, a wealthy white girl, meeting on Copacabana beach and triggering a chain of events that will affect both of their lives. Betrayed by their families who want to keep them apart, the couple flee to the west of Brazil.

The War of the End of the World (1981)
Mario Vargas Llosa

Vargas Llosa sets his extraordinary novel in 19th-century Brazil in the *sertao*, the desert backlands of the state of Bahia. Brazil is a nation on the verge of great change and into this comes Antonio Conselheiro, a spiritual leader who attracts the poor and disenfranchized. After the Church condemns him, Conselheiro and his followers retreat into the abandoned area of Canudos, while the government plans military action against them.

🔍 Peru – *The Green House*

CHILE

Fiction

The House of Spirits (1985)
Isabel Allende

Set in an unnamed South American country, which is really Allende's native Chile, *The House of Spirits* is a gorgeously written tale. Allende creates the Trueba family and through the three generations of its story also tells the history of Chile. Mixing magic realism with fact, Allende's book was a best-seller on publication.

🔍 *Eva Luna*

Curfew (1988)
José Donoso

A political thriller, *Curfew* is set in the days after the death of Pablo Neruda's wife and captures the oppressive mood of a country under the military dictatorship of Pinochet. Donoso was one of the many writers who lived in exile for most of the dictator's rule.

The Mermaid and the Drunks (1985)
Ben Richards

Richards's engrossing novel tells of Fresia Castillo, a young woman returning from Britain to Chile about 10 years after the end of Pinochet's dictatorship. She is drawn to two men, Joe, a university lecturer, and Roberto, a mysterious, charismatic figure, whose nephew has disappeared.

Burning Patience (1987)
Antonio Skarmeta

Some people probably know this book better under the name *The Postman*, the retitled reissue after the release of the extremely popular and award-winning film adaptation *Il Postino*. Skarmeta's poignant and engaging book is set in pre-Pinochet Chile and describes a love affair between Mario, a postman in Isla Negra, who, after falling for the local beauty, has his love helped along by his most famous client, the great poet Pablo Neruda. Visitors to Isla Negra, which is about an hour and a half from Valparaiso, can go to Neruda's seashore house (now a museum) and grave. The great poet's remains were moved there in 1992, after the restoration of democracy.

🎬 *Il Postino* (1991)

The Chilean Treasure – Pablo Neruda

Chile has produced some extremely fine poets but none more famous than the Nobel Prize-winning writer and political figure Pablo Neruda, one of the most translated poets of our time. Neruda was born Neftalí Ricardo Reyes Basoalto in 1904 in Parral, Chile. He grew up in Temuco, where he became friends with the poet Gabriela Mistral. As a teenager he began to contribute to local papers, publishing under the name Pablo Neruda from 1920. Three years later he published what was to be one of his beautiful and critically acclaimed collections *Twenty Love Poems and a Song of Despair* (*Veinte poemas de amor y una cancion desesperada*). From 1927 to 1935, he was consul to such places as Burma, Singapore, and Madrid and Barcelona in Spain, where he became friends with Garcia Lorca. The Spanish Civil War and his friend's murder affected Neruda greatly and he became increasingly politicized. When he returned to Chile, his poetry reflected this change. In 1945, Neruda was elected senator of the republic. Just two years later he was forced to go into hiding after criticizing Videla's repressive rule. He left Chile in 1949, returning in 1952. During that time he published *Canto General*, an epic work of 340 poems, which examined Latin American history from a Marxist perspective. He set up home in Isla Negra (today a museum and the site of his grave). After the election of Salvador Allende as president, Neruda served as his ambassador to France. Neruda died of leukemia in Santiago in September 1973; many think his death was accelerated by the murder of Allende and Pinochet's military coup.

📶 http://www.tourismchile.com/guide/temuco/articles/968 (Neruda's Chile)

Non-fiction

Memoirs (1977)
Pablo Neruda

Neruda's extraordinary book is essentially a history of pre-Pinochet Chile. This lyrical book tells not only of Neruda's exciting life but also provides a great insight into the politics of the time and the complex situation in Chile.

COLOMBIA

Fiction

Rosario Tijeras (1999)
Jorge Franco

This best-selling psychological thriller is set in Medellin, the drug centre of Colombia, in the 1980s. It begins with Rosario Tijeras being shot and the narrator Antonio recounting her story in a series of flashbacks.

 Paradise Travel

Love in the Time of Cholera (1985)
Gabriel García Márquez

Nobel prize-winning author Garcia Marquez is Colombia's leading novelist and short-story writer. This book is essentially a love triangle that extends over more than 50 years of Colombia's history between Florentina, Fermina and Dr Urbino. A remarkable book.

Love in the Time of Cholera (2007)
Chronicle of a Death Foretold

The Dark Bride (1999)
Laura Restrepo

Restrepo's lyrical book is a love story. It is set in Tora in the Colombian forest, where workers from the Tropical Oil Company come once a month to engage with the local prostitutes. When Sayonara, the most adored prostitute of all, breaks her rule and falls in love with a man she cannot have, it has long-reaching consequences not just for herself but also for others.

The Informers (2008)
Juan Gabriel Vasquez

The Informers is set in post-world war Bogota. When Gabriel Santoro publishes a slim volume about a family friend and Jewish immigrant Sara Guteman, he invokes the wrath of his intellectual father but cannot understand why. Years later after his father's death, helped by Sara and his father's ex-girlfriend, he gradually discovers the reasons why his father was so angry and the secrets buried in his father's past.

ECUADOR

Fiction

The Old Man Who Read Love Stories (1997)
Luis Sepulveda

This extraordinarily beautiful book tells of a man recalling his life and reading romance novels on the edge of the Amazonian jungle in Ecuador.

GUYANA

Fiction

The Counting House (1996)
David Dabydeen

Set in 19th-century Guyana, Dabydeen's novel explores the tension between indentured Indian workers and the Guyanese black population through a young Indian couple who move to colonial Guyana, seeking a better life.

The Palace of the Peacock (1960)
Wilson Harris

Harris's book follows a group of men journeying upriver in the jungle of Guyana. The crew represents every race of people that have come to Guyana. It is the first of *The Guyana Quartet*, which also incorporates *The Far Journey of Oudin* (1961), *The Whole Armour* (1962) and *The Secret Ladder* (1963).

The Ventriloquist's Tale (1997)
Pauline Melville

Set in Georgetown and moving between the 1920s and present-day Guyana, Melville's novel focuses on two affairs, one of which is adulterous.

PARAGUAY

Fiction

The Pleasure of Eliza Lynch (2002)
Anne Enright

Enright's fascinating novel is set in 19th-century Paraguay and follows the life of a beautiful Irish woman who became the mistress of Francisco Salono Lopez and was known as 'Paraguay's Eva Peron'.

PERU

Fiction

War by Candlelight (2005)
Daniel Alarcón

This exciting collection of short stories moves between New York and Peru and poetically explores internal and external conflict. Alarcón has been compared to a young Vargas Llosa.

The Green House (1968)
Mario Vargas Llosa

This novel is based on Vargas Llosa's experiences of growing up in Piura and its brothel. the story moves between that location, Santa Maria de Nieva and the Upper Maranon rain forest, and covers three generations and 34 characters. Don Anselmo builds the Green House, a brothel on the outskirts of a Peruvian town, situated between the desert and jungle, a world caught between civilization and savagery.

🔍 *Death in Andes* (1993)

The Dancers Upstairs (1985)
Nicholas Shakespeare

Shakespeare's gripping thriller was inspired by the real-life manhunt for the Peruvian Shining Path guerrilla commander Abimael Guzman. A military policeman becomes obsessed with tracking down a terrorist leader in an unnamed country in South America.

 The Dancers Upstairs (2002), directed by John Malkovitch

The Bridge of San Luis Rey (1927)
Thornton Wilder

Wilder's moral fable tells of Brother Juniper, whose life changes when a bridge that he is about to step onto collapses, killing the five people on it. Wondering if his continued life is part of a bigger plan, he begins to investigate the lives of the people who died.

URUGUAY

Fiction

The City of Your Final Destination (1985)
Peter Cameron

This extremely funny comedy of manners finds Omar Razaghi travelling to Uruguay to petition the family of a dead Latin American author to let him to write his biography.

 The City of Your Final Destination (2009)

The Shipyard (1997)
Juan Carlos Onetti

Sometimes referred to as the 'Graham Greene of Uruguay', Onetti sets his grim tale in the fictitious town of Santa Maria, where a man returns after five years in exile.

VENEZUELA

Fiction

Eva Luna (1987)
Isabel Allende

Set in a country resembling Venezuela, Allende's moving book tells the story of Eva, an orphan, who retreats into fantasy and storytelling to escape from the oppression of the world around her. Allende interweaves magic realism with reality to relate Eva's life with that of the politics of the region.

🔍 Chile – *House of Spirits*

Keepers of the House (1982)
Lisa St Aubin de Teran

Based on Englishwoman St Aubin de Teran's own experiences, her acclaimed novel follows the newly married Lydia to her husband's decaying ancestral mansion in the Venezuelan Andes.

Non-fiction

The Hacienda (1997)
Lisa St Aubin de Teran

When St Aubin de Teran was 17 she fell in love with Don Jaime Teran, a Venezuelan aristocrat (and would-be bank robber apparently) living in exile in London. In 1972 the couple returned to Venezuela to the fabled hacienda that she has heard so much about. In her husband's increasing absence, alone in a strange land, the author set out to find out as much as she could about her husband's family, whose ancestors came over on Columbus's second voyage.

NORTH AMERICA

CANADA

Fiction

Black Robe (1985)
Brian Moore

Moore's classic tale of 17th-century French Canada follows a young Jesuit priest, Father Laforgue, as he travels to convert the Huron tribe in the far North of New France to Christianity. Known as the 'Black Robe' by his Algonquin guides, both the father and his companions find their ideas and faiths challenged.

🎬 *Black Robe* (1991)

🔍 United Kingdom – *The Lonely Passion of Judith Hearne*

Selected Stories (1997)
Alice Munro

Munro is one of Canada's best-known short-story writers and *Selected Stories* includes more than 20 stories cherry-picked from her other works. A master of detail, Munroj describes everyday life and people, whether it's on the farmlands of Ontario or in the small towns of British Columbia.

WESTERN PROVINCES

BRITISH COLUMBIA

Fiction

The Cure for Death by Lightning (2002)
Gail Anderson-Dargatz

A coming-of-age novel, Anderston-Dargatz's story has as its protagonist, Beth Weeks, a 15-year-old girl living on a remote farm in British Columbia with her dysfunctional parents and brother in 1940s' Canada. Beth's home life is tough – her family are poor, her father sexually assaults her and her mother talks to her own dead mother – but despite her home life Beth struggles to find beauty and love in her landscape.

Girlfriend in a Coma (1998)
Douglas Coupland

Set in Vancouver initially in the late 1970s, a group of friends' lives change after Karen falls into a coma after losing her virginity to Richard. Years later she wakes up to find everything has changed, not least that she is a mother and the end of the world is nigh.

Swamp Angel (1954)
Ethel Wilson

Wilson's novel moves from Vancouver to the striking interior of British Columbia as a housewife walks out of her failing marriage to work at a fish lodge and strive for her personal freedom.

MANITOBA

Fiction

The Stone Angel (1964)
Margaret Laurence

Written by one of Canada's most revered writers, *The Stone Angel* is the second of five books set in the fictional town of Manawaka in Mantitoba. Laurence's main character Hagar Shipley is almost at the end of her life. Difficult, witty and awkward, Hagar looks back on her own life and her own striving for independence. Laurence was born in Neepawa, Manitoba, and visitors can tour the house where she lived, seeing where the author wrote some of her works.

🛜 http://www.mts.net/~mlhome/ (Margaret Laurence's home)

The Republic of Love (1992)
Carol Shields

Set in a tight-knit community in Winnipeg, Shields's engaging book deals with love – as seen through the eyes and experiences of Fay McLeod and Tom Avery. Shields sets up her protagonists well before they actually meet, about half way through the book; extreme opposites in the game of love, they somehow find common ground.

🎦 *The Republic of Love* (2003)

SASKATCHEWAN

Fiction

Who Has Seen the Wind (1947)
W. O. Mitchell

Mitchell's classic set in the Canadian prairies follows Brian O'Connal from the age of 4 to 12 and is viewed by many Canadians to be the nation's most important book on boyhood. Mitchell, who also grew up in small-town Saskatchewan, used his own memories to inform Brian's world. The prairie as seen through Brian's eyes is majestic and vast.

As For Me and My House (1941)
Sinclair Ross

Set in the isolated farming community of Horizon in Saskatchewan, this is a brilliant depiction of life in Depression-era Canada. Told in journal form, it describes the life of Philip Bentley, his wife and the people around them.

CENTRAL PROVINCES

ONTARIO

Fiction

The Blind Assassin (2000)
Margaret Atwood

There are so many books that one could choose from Margaret Atwood's stable, but this award-winning tome is one of her best. Covering more than

100 years of Canadian history, it is set in Ontario – in the fictional town of Port Ticonderoga and also in Toronto. Essentially a family saga, it deals with two sisters, Iris Chase Griffen, who looks back on her long life, and her late sister, Laura, who died in 1945 when her car went off a bridge, after which Iris published Laura's novel *The Blind Assassin* posthumously.

🔍 *The Handmaid's Tale; The Edible Woman*

Fugitive Pieces (1996)
Ann Michaels

This lyrically written novel moves between Greece and Canada. It is the story of Jakob Beer, a young Polish boy, coming to terms with what happened to his family during the Holocaust; Athos, the scientist who pulls him from the mud, rescuing and loving him; and Jakob's life in Toronto. Movingly told, this is a modern classic and cannot be recommended enough.

In the Skin of a Lion (1987)
Michael Ondaatje

Ondaatje's beautifully realized novel finds Patrick Lewis arriving in Toronto from the wilderness. He immerses himself in the people around him – the immigrants who have come from so many places to create new life and help shape the city itself – and we get a clear picture of Toronto in the 1920s.

Jalna (1926)
Mazo de la Roche

De la Roche's 16 'Jalna' books based in Ontario have been translated into many languages. This first novel won the author an *Atlantic Monthly* prize. It introduces the Whiteoak family and its estate in rural Ontario. It became a best-selling romance of its time. Based loosely on de la Roche's own life, the 'Whiteoak' series spanned 1854 to 1954.

🎬 *Jalna* (1935)

A Map of Glass (1987)
Jane Urquhart

When artist Jerome, spending the winter on Timber Island in the mouth of the St Lawrence River, discovers a body in a forest, he becomes embroiled in the dead man's affairs. A year later in Toronto, Jerome is visited by a woman claiming to be the dead man's lover; she tells him about Andrew and the timber empire that he and his ancestors had helped build.

QUEBEC

Fiction

Next Episode (2001)
Hubert Aquin

Aquin's book was first published in Canada in French in 1965 and is largely autobiographical. It finds a Quebec nationalist in the psychiatric ward of a Montreal prison, writing a spy story based in Switzerland. Aquin wrote this book while he was similarly incarcerated for carrying a firearm and driving a stolen car.

Two Solitudes (1945)
Hugh MacLennan

MacLennan's novel deals with the relationships between English and French Canadians between the First and Second World Wars.

🎬 *Two Solitudes* (1978)

The Apprenticeship of Duddy Kravitz (1964)
Mordecai Richler

Richler's comic classic tells of Duddy Kravitz's coming of age on the mean streets of Montreal in the 1950s.

EASTERN PROVINCES

NEWFOUNDLAND AND LABRADOR

Fiction

River Thieves (2002)
Michael Crummey

Crummey explores the last days of the Beothuks, the 'Red Indians' of Newfoundland and their interaction with a group of European settlers, including the Peytons, who live and work the island's shores in the 19th century.

🛜 http://www.exploretheonlyplace.com/ PlacesToGo/ScenicTouringRoutes/ AllAroundCentral.aspx?route=13 (Beothuk trail)

The Bird Artist (1994)
Howard Norman

Set in Witless Bay, a remote part of Newfoundland, in 1911, Fabian Vas is the bird artist of the title. But Fabian is more than he appears: he is the murderer of the local lighthouse keeper. Through contained prose, Howard Norman reveals why Fabian was driven to commit his crime. Norman paints a picture of the harsh and relentless landscape of the area, which in turn toughens the inhabitants. Witless bay is situated on the Avalon Peninsula, about a 30-minute drive from the capital, St Johns. Captain Whittle, a Dorset man, was one of its first inhabitants and the original European settlers came from the West Country and Ireland.

🛜 http://www.explorenewfoundlandand labrador.com/communities/witless-bay.htm (about Witless Bay)

The Shipping News (1993)
Annie Proulx

Proulx's engaging book evokes Newfoundland as no other book set on the island. At once beautiful and bleak, the sea and the long, often harsh winters define the place and its inhabitants. Central character Quoyle is rescued by Agnis, his aunt, after his estranged and unpleasant wife dies in a car crash. An unsuccessful journalist and a misfit, Quoyle is glad to leave New York with his two daughters for somewhere new, especially when he finds in his new job – writing the shipping news on the island – a new life, a measure of respect, friendship with the odd assortment of characters he meets and love. The movie, starring Kevin Spacey, was filmed largely at Bonavista Bay on the island. Tourists can visit that area of the island in one of the many tours on offer.

🎬 *The Shipping News* (2001)

📶 http://www.crazyaboutnewfoundland.ca/tours/tour.php?t=23 (tour of island, taking in the beautiful Bonavista Bay)

NOVA SCOTIA

Fiction

Island: The Complete Stories (2002)
Alistair Macleod

Macleod grew up in Cape Breton. These stories, set on Canada's eastern shore, focus on community and family.

🔍 *No Greater Mischief*

PRINCE EDWARD ISLAND

Fiction

Anne of Green Gables (1908)
Lucy Maud Montgomery

The first in a series featuring the enchanting character Anne Shirley, Montgomery's book captured the imagination of many children and adults around the world. Set on Prince Edward Island, it follows the life and adventures of an orphaned girl who comes to live by mistake with siblings Marilla and Matthew Cuthbert. Her charm and spirit win over the Cuthberts, their neighbours and bring her love and friendship. Sequels in the series include *Anne of Avonlea* (1909) and *Anne of the Island* (1915).

📶 http://www.tourismpei.com/pei-anne-itinerary (Anne of Green Gables Prince Edward Island tour)

Lucy Maud Montgomery's Prince Edward Island

Better known as the creator of Anne of Green Gables, Lucy Maud Montgomery was born in Clifton (now New London) on Prince Edward Island in 1874. After her mother's death, Montgomery's father left the 21-month-old Lucy Maud to be brought up by her elderly maternal grandparents in Cavendish, while he moved to Saskatchewan and remarried. Montgomery's world became that of her imagination and she began to write, first in journals. She was also close to her aunt and uncle, Annie and John Campbell, and her paternal grandfather, Senator Donald Montgomery. After leaving school, she trained to be a teacher, and also studied for a year at Dalhousie University in Halifax, Nova Scotia. Returning to Cavendish she continued to write, eventually finishing her first novel, *Anne of Green Gables* in 1905. It was finally accepted for publication in 1908 and became an immediate best-seller. She married in 1911, after which she moved from Prince Edward Island, never to live there again. For many, Montgomery is synonymous with the island through her accounts of life, people, nature and community in her works. All but one of her books are set there.

🔍 Prince Edward Island – *Anne of Green Gables*

UNITED STATES OF AMERICA

GENERAL

Fiction

What We Talk About When We Talk About Love (1981)
Raymond Carver

The best American short-story teller of the 20th century (in our opinion), Carver was a master of understatement. This beautiful collection – one of his best known – is about love and American life and culture as presented in Carver's unique style of prose.

Short Cuts (1993), Robert Altman's gorgeously shot film based on Carver's short stories

Underworld (1997)
Don DeLillo

An epic work, this is DeLillo's attempt at the great American novel. Moving back and forth between time, this book opens with a baseball game between the New York Giants and Brooklyn Dodgers, attended by Frank Sinatra, J. Edgar Hoover and Jackie Gleason, in 1951, and moves through the Cold War and on to how the nuclear age has affected post-war America.

Invisible Man (1947)
Ralph Ellison

This incredible book caused a sensation when it was first published. Following an African American's travels through the Southern states to New York, it is essentially his journey to find meaning and identity in a country in which he is largely invisible because of his race.

On the Road (1958)
Jack Kerouac

The great American road adventure novel, Kerouac's semi-autobiographical *On the Road* follows writer Sal Paradise and crazy Dean Moriarty as they race around America, through sleepy towns, cities, deserts and the wilderness, testing the American Dream to its limit. Kerouac allegedly wrote the book in three weeks in 1951, basing it on a trip he took with Neal Cassady.

The Last Empire (2001)
Gore Vidal

Vidal's fictionalized histories of America are among the best around. In this book, he recreates America's emergence as a global power, from the end of the 19th century onwards, as seen by central character of Caroline Sanford.

Non-fiction

A Walk in the Woods (2000)
Bill Bryson

After 20 years away from his native America, travel writer Bill Bryson returns home with his English wife and children. To reacquaint himself with his country, he decides to walk the 3,380 km (2,100 mile) Appalachian

Trail, which stretches from Georgia to Maine and is the longest continuous footpath in the world. Travelling through some of the most spectacularly, remote and wild scenery in the States, Bryson and his old friend Stephen Katz encounter a whole range of characters, animals and insects.

God Bless America: Diaries of an Englishman in the Land of the Free (2009)
Piers Morgan

Journalist Piers Morgan achieved 'fame' in the United States as the nasty Brit on the television series *America's Got Talent*. In this book, Morgan travels the States, meeting such celebrities as Arnold Schwarzenegger and Paris Hilton. Morgan gives a detailed account of a relatively unknown Barack Obama during his campaign in the race for the US presidency. This book gives a good insight into an America on the verge of great historic change.

United States: Essays 1952–92 (1993)
Gore Vidal

This National Book Award-winning volume of 114 essays showcases Vidal at his best as a master of letters and historical chronicler and cultural observer of the United States for more than 40 years. The book is divided into three sections: 'State of the Art', which covers literature, including essays about novelists and critics; 'State of the Nation', which examines American politics; and 'State of Being', which includes personal essays.

EAST COAST

NEW YORK AND ENVIRONS

Fiction

The New York Trilogy (1985–6)
Paul Auster

Essentially three novellas, *City of Glass* (1985), *Ghosts* (1986) and *The Locked Room* (1986), the *New York Trilogy* is one of Auster's most popular works. Combining his usual sense of dark humour, suspense and elements of noir, Auster's books explore the pursuer and the pursued and the nature of identity.

Another Country (1962)
James Baldwin

Set primarily in Greenwich Village in the 1960s, Baldwin's much-acclaimed book tells of the bohemian lifestyle of a group of musicians and artists. Dealing with themes such as racism and homophobia, Baldwin's book became a classic.

Sex and the City (1997)
Candace Bushnell

This book contains the columns, based on Bushnell and her friends' dating experiences, that were written for the *New York Observer*. They inspired the television series *Sex and the City*. The series struck such a chord with young, single women that they flock to New York to visit some of the places featured in the book and series, including The Plaza Hotel, where Carrie says goodbye to Mr Big and Buddakan, the restaurant where Big and Carrie host their rehearsal dinner in the first film.

📺🎬 *Sex and the City* (1998–2004), HBO series starring Sarah Jessica Parker as Carrie Bradshaw; two movies in 2008 and 2010

📶 http://www.screentours.com/tour.php/satc/(Sex and the City tour)

Ragtime (1975)
E. L. Doctorow

Doctorow's book captures the spirit of turn-of-the-20th-century New York through the eyes and experiences of three families. Mixing real-life characters such as Harry Houdini, Henry Ford and J. P. Morgan with fictional ones, Doctorow creates a textured story of the city's multicultural life.

🎬 *Ragtime* (1981)
🔍 *Billy Bathgate*

Manhattan Transfer (1925)
John Dos Passos

Although probably better known for the trilogy *USA*, Dos Passos evokes a Manhattan of the past – one with gas lamps and horse-drawn milk carts – in this novel. He describes lovingly the different scenes of the city from the deserted harbourside at dawn to the party scene of downtown New York.

🔍 *USA*

American Psycho (1991)
Bret Easton Ellis

Easton Ellis's savage satire on the New York 'me culture' centres on protagonist Patrick Bateman who seemingly has it all. A Wall Street stock trader, living on Upper East Side, obsessed with restaurants, bars and sex, Patrick also likes to spend his time torturing and murdering women.

🎬 *American Psycho* (2000)

The Catcher in the Rye (1951)

J. D. Salinger's classic coming-of-age novel sees Holden Caulfield, holed up in a psychiatric institution, recovering from a breakdown. In a series of flashbacks we see the events that led up to his current state. Mostly set in New York, where Holden spends three days wandering around the city a week before the Christmas break, *Catcher in the Rye* has a protagonist at odds with the society in which he lives. He is someone who views everyone he meets as 'phony' and the only person he can relate to is his younger sister, Phoebe. Many of the places that Holden visits during his wanderings of the city are real and still popular destinations. These include the Rockefeller Center skating rink, where Holden takes a date; Radio City, where he sees the Rockettes; the American Museum of Natural History, which he loves; the zoo and carousel in Central Park, where he takes Phoebe; Grand Central train station; and the Metropolitan Museum of Art, with the Egyptian wing that Holden finds spooky.

The Great Gatsby (1922)
F. Scott Fitzgerald

Set predominantly on the Gold Coast of Long Island, New York, Fitzgerald's celebrated novel is a study of the jazz age and the prosperity that America experienced in the Roaring Twenties. After renting a cottage between two large estates in West Egg (really Great Neck), Long Island, Nick Carraway gets involved with Jay Gatsby, a fabulously wealthy man of mystery. Carraway discovers that Gatsby was once in love with Nick's cousin, Daisy. The relationship is rekindled but ends in Gatsby's death.

 Great Gatsby (1974)

A Rage in Harlem (1957)
Chester Himes

In this classic work of crime fiction, Chester Himes did for Harlem what Raymond Chandler did for Los Angeles. Fast paced, it follows hapless Jackson, who enlists his savvy twin brother's help to rescue his wily girlfriend Imabelle.

 A Rage in Harlem (1991)

Bright Lights, Big City (1984)
Jay McInerney

Set in mid-1980s' New York and written in the second person, this book follows the frenetic week in a Manhattan man's life. By day a writer, he loses himself at night in the hedonism of coke and the city's nightlife.

 Bright Lights, Big City (1988)

The Interpretation of Murder (2006)
Jed Rubenfeld

In 1909, Sigmund Freud arrives in New York, accompanied by Carl Jung. His visit coincides with the vicious attack on a young heiress, Nora Acton, who is unable to speak or talk about her ordeal. Aristocrat and analyst Stratham Younger, a follower of Freud, enlists his help to find out what happened to Nora and in doing so unlocks the door to New York's more depraved society.

Last Exit to Brooklyn (1964)
Hubert Selby, Jr

Selby's controversial book deals with the underclass in Brooklyn. His stories focus on those people normally ignored – prostitutes, drug dealers, hoodlums, and transsexuals.

 Last Exit to Brooklyn (1989)

The Age of Innocence (1920)
Edith Wharton

Wharton's novel – set in the rarefied atmosphere of old New York in the 1870s – is much revered for its detail of time and place and also for its representation of the customs and etiquette of the upper echelons of the city's society. Wharton sets up her characters to represent the old and new. May Welland and her fiancé Newland Archer come from old established families. When May's cousin, the intriguing but controversial Ellen Olenska returns from Europe having reportedly left her brutal husband, Newland is attracted to her as she is a free spirit, unbound by New York's high-society conventions.

🎬 *The Age of Innocence* (1993)

Non-fiction

Tower Stories: An Oral History of 9/11 (2007)
Damon DiMarco

Recent history is really divided into that of the pre-9/11 and that of the post-9/11 world. It's hard to go to New York and not be aware of the effects of the horrific terrorist attack on the city. DiMarco wandered around the city, in the weeks after the collapse of the World Trade Center, collecting stories from survivors, rescuers and witnesses. This is an updated edition of the original 2004 publication.

MARYLAND

Fiction

Chesapeake Bay Saga (1998–2002)
Nora Roberts

A romance writer who branched off into suspense, best-selling author Roberts sets many of her books in Maryland. These four books, *Sea Swept* (1998), *Rising Tides* (1998), *Inner Harbour* (1999) and *Chesapeake Blue* (2002) tell of the Quinn brothers, Cam, the playboy, Phil, the successful advertising man, Ethan, the quiet waterman, and Seth, the acclaimed artist, all rescued by extraordinary people, who took them out of abusive

backgrounds and introduced them to the beauty of Chesapeake Bay.

📶 http://www.baydreaming.com/ (Chesapeake Bay)

Dinner at the Homesick Restaurant (1982)
Anne Tyler

Tyler's book, set in 1960s' Baltimore, finds Pearl Tull looking back on her life. After her husband left her, Pearl had to bring up her three children by herself.

NEW ENGLAND

Fiction

Little Women (1868–9)
Louisa May Alcott

Set in Concord, Massachusetts, this much-loved book has been adapted to radio, television and cinema time and time again. Following the lives of the March sisters, Meg, Jo, Beth and Amy, Alcott used her own family experiences as a basis for the plot. Visitors can go to Orchard House, the Alcott home in Concord, where Louisa May Alcott lived and wrote *Little Women*.

🎬 *Little Women* (1933 and 1994)
📶 http://www.louisamayalcott.org/

The Scarlet Letter (1850)
Nathaniel Hawthorne

Hawthorne's broody book is set in 17th-century New England and focuses on Hester Prynne, a young woman accused of adultery and forced to wear a scarlet letter 'A' pinned to her breast. Her husband, who had sent Hester ahead of him from England to Boston, arrives to discover his wife now also has a baby. He becomes obsessed with finding out the identify of the man with whom Hester has had an affair and a child.

🎬 *The Scarlet Letter* (1979)

The Friends of Eddie Coyle (1972)
George V. Higgins

Higgins's debut novel, which Dennis Lehane has called the 'quintessential Boston novel', has a small-time crook and informant as its protagonist. It covers a range of Boston locales, including a suburban railway station in Sharon and Memorial Drive in Cambridge, where gunrunners conduct their business.

🎬 *The Friends of Eddie Doyle* (1973)

🔍 *Following the Detectives,* Maxim Jakubowski (editor)

Practical Magic (1997)
Alice Hoffman

The Owen sisters are rumoured to be local witches and they are blamed for everything that goes wrong in their Massachusetts town. When their two orphaned nieces come to live with them, they are tarred with the same brush. But even as they are ostracized, the girls watch lonely women sneak into their aunts' house for love potions.

🎬 *Practical Magic* (2000)

The Cider House Rules (1985)
John Irving

Irving's popular novel, set in Maine between 1930 and 1950, follows Homer Wells, an orphan, and Dr Wilbur Larch, founder and director of the orphanage where Homer lives.

🎬 *The Cider House Rules* (1999)

The Bostonians (1886)
Henry James

James focuses on a love triangle involving suffragist Olive Chancellor, Verena Tarrant and Basil Ransom in this classic tale set in 19th-century Boston.

🎬 *The Bostonians* (1984)

Mystic River (2001)
Dennis Lehane

Set in the fictional town of East Buckingham, Lehane's novel concerns events that happened in the childhood of a group of characters coming back to haunt them in adulthood. The locations are based on Charlestown, the actual area just across the Mystic River from Boston, Boston's South End ('Southie'), across the Fort Point Channel, and Dorchester, where Lehane himself grew up. The 2003 film was shot on location, mostly in Southie but also in Charleston. Miller's Market at 366K Street in Southie is where Sean Penn works in the movie.

🎬 *Mystic River* (2003), directed by Clint Eastwood, starring Sean Pean, Kevin Bacon and Tim Robbins

Peyton Place (1956)
Grace Metalious

This best-seller, which shocked the nation when it was published, follows the lives of three women – Constance MacKenzie, her illegitimate daughter Allison and Selena Cross – in a small town in New England where secrets run deep.

 Peyton Place (1957), starring Lana Turner and Hope Lange; ABC series ran between 1964 and 1969

The Weight of Water (1997)
Anita Shreve

Photographer Jean researches a century-old crime involving two women on Smuttynose Island off the coast of Maine.

The Weight of Water (2000)

The Secret History (1992)
Donna Tartt

Tartt's epic novel is set in New England and tells of a group of students caught up in murder at an elite school in Vermont. Tartt's detail is extraordinary.

Revolutionary Road (1961)
Richard Yates

Yates's cult book received a second lease of life and an outing to wider audiences after the film of the same name starring Leonardo DiCaprio and Kate Winslett. Set in Connecticut, where Frank and April Wheeler seemingly have the American Dream,

Revolutionary Road depicts their wish to escape the mundaneness of their lives for something more. The problem is if you don't know what that 'something' is how do you find it? And is there actually anything more?

Revolutionary Road (2008)

NEW JERSEY

Fiction

The Stephanie Plum series (1994–2010)
Janet Evanovich

Evanovich's much-loved wisecracking heroine Stephanie Plum has now appeared in more than 16 books. A New Jersey girl, Stephanie lives in Trenton, has an eccentric but close-knit family and a love life that is extremely complicated. A bounty hunter by trade, Stephanie lurches from one crisis to another, usually solving her crime and getting her bounty through accident rather than design.

One for the Money – the first in the series, introducing Stephanie

The Sportswriter (1986)
Richard Ford

A tale of middle-age angst in the suburbs, Richard Ford's classic *The Sportswriter* follows the protagonist Frank Bascombe over an Easter weekend in the early 1980s.

PENNSYLVANIA

Fiction

Wonder Boys (1995)
Michael Chabon

Pittsburgh professor Grady Tripp has been writing the follow-up to his great novel for seven years. Over one weekend, his life falls apart: his wife leaves him, he learns that his mistress is pregnant and his brilliant student involves him a rather bizarre crime.

Wonder Boys (2000), starring Michael Douglas and Katie Holmes

WASHINGTON DC

Fiction

Through One Administration (1881)
Francis Hodgson Burnett

Most children have read Burnett's *The Secret Garden* or *A Little Princess* but this book is one of Burnett's lesser-known works. Set in the drawing rooms and parties of the capital, *Through One Administration* gives some insight into the politics of the time. It is based on her observations while living in the capital with her husband.

The Night Gardener (2006)
George Pelecanos

Probably a name familiar to audiences through the series *The Wire*, Pelecanos writes about Washington DC and his novels are a love letter to the city. In *The Night Gardener* he captures the essence of 1985, when the city was plagued by a crack-cocaine boom. The world he describes is not that of the moneyed classes but of the city's underbelly – his characters are more likely to be cops or drug dealers than politicians or high-society dames. The city features prominently in his work, whether it's the Washington Monument, commemorating the first US president, George Washington, or Capitol Hill.

All The President's Men (1974)

Set in Washington DC, this is a story you probably couldn't make up and it's based on one of the greatest political scandals in US history. In 1972, journalists Robert Woodward and Carl Bernstein of the *Washington Post* covered the story of the arrest of several Democrats who broke into and burglarized the Watergate Hotel and Office Building. As the journalists delved deeper, what emerged were details of a shocking scandal involving then-president Richard Nixon and some of his staff. An award-winning film of the book was made in 1976 and shot on location in such places as the Watergate Hotel, which features prominently in the book.

All the President's Men (1976), starring Robert Redford and Dustin Hoffman

http://www.movie-locations.com/movies/a/allthepresidents.html#watergate

THE AMERICAN SOUTH

FLORIDA

To Have and Have Not (1937)
Ernest Hemingway

Hemingway's novel set against the background of the Great Depression sees Harry Morgan, a fishing boat captain, forced to run contraband between Cuba and Key West.

📽 *To Have and Have Not* (1944), starring Lauren Bacall and Humphrey Bogart

Tourist Season (1986)
Carl Hiaasen

This entertaining caper finds Brian Keyes, a reporter turned private investigator, trying to solve a string of odd murders that involve a group of fanatics and some reptiles.

🔍 *Following the Detectives*, Maxim Jakubowski (editor)

The Deep Blue Goodbye (1964)
John D. Macdonald

Introducing private investigator Travis McGee, *The Deep Goodbye* finds the protagonist living on a boat called The Busted Flush, anchored at Bahia Mar Marina in Fort Lauderdale (where there is now a plaque). Compared to today, Fort Lauderdale was quite a sleepy town in the 1960s.

NORTH AND SOUTH CAROLINA

Fiction

The Hornet's Nest (2003)
Jimmy Carter

Former president of the United States Jimmy Carter's first novel is set during the American Revolution in the southern states. Following Ethan Pratt and his family, Ethan moves to North Carolina in search of a better life.

The Prince of Tides (1986)
Pat Conroy

Spanning over 40 years this book is the story of Tom Wingo and his troubled twin sister Savannah as they fight to overcome the tragic legacy of their background.

Hornet's Nest (1996)
Patricia Cornwell

Police chief Judy Hammer battles to find a brutal serial killer in Charlotte, North Carolina, after some tourists are found brutally murdered.

The Empty Chair (2000)
Jeffery Deaver

Lincoln Rhyme, a quadriplegic forensic investigator, is in North Carolina to undergo an experimental treatment. When he is asked to help find a murderer, his plans change.

Cold Mountain (1997)
Charles Frazier

Frazier's popular book is set during the last year of the American Civil War and follows Inman, a deserter from the Confederate Army, on his long journey home to his sweetheart Ada, near Cold Mountain in North Carolina.

🎬 *Cold Mountain* (2003), starring Jude Law and Nicole Kidman

Look Homeward, Angel (1929)
Thomas Wolfe

Wolfe's novel, considered to be largely autobiographical, about young and brilliant Eugene Gant is set in a fictional town believed to be Asheville, North Carolina. Visitors to Asheville can go to the Thomas Wolfe Memorial, which was the author's childhood home (1906–16) and contains artifacts from his family, his father's stone-cutting shop and his New York home.

📶 http://www.wolfememorial.com/ (Thomas Wolfe Memorial)

VIRGINIA
Fiction

Cutting Lisa (1986)
Percival L. Everett

A retired Virginian obstetrician begins to question what is important to him after the end of his affair with a younger woman and after learning of a doctor who carried out an unnecessary Caesarean section on his wife.

The Confessions of Nat Turner (1967)
William Styron

Possibly one of the best-known books set in Southampton, Virginia, Styron's Pulitzer-winning novel centres on the slave revolt of 1831. It details Styron's imagined confessions by the slave leader to a white lawyer.

THE DEEP SOUTH

ALABAMA
Fiction

Other Voices, Other Rooms (1948)
Truman Capote

Capote wrote this coming-of-age slightly gothic novel when he was 23. His focal character, 13-year-old Joel, is sent to live with the father who abandoned him after his mother's death. When he moves from New Orleans to a rural mansion in the Deep South, his father is nowhere to be found.

To Kill a Mockingbird (1960)
Harper Lee

Lee's masterpiece about race and prejudice in 1930s' small-town Alabama as seen through the eyes of a child is utterly compelling. Through Jem ('Scout'), the small daughter of attorney Atticus Finch, Lee illustrates the different types of prejudice people feel towards the outsider, whether it's Boo Radley,

The Colour Purple (1982)

Alice Walker's epic story is primarily about empowerment and triumph over extreme adversity. Celie is the central character of the novel, which is set in the Deep South. Her life is one of abuse, misery and violence. She was raped by her father at 14, with the pattern of violence continuing into her marriage to 'Mister'. Through the help of Shug, her close friend, and her own personal strength, Celie finds the power to rise above her life and take a new path. The novel won the 1983 Pulitzer Prize for Walker and was turned into an award-winning film by Steven Spielberg in 1985.

the man who supposedly stabbed his father, or African–American Tom Robinson, wrongly accused of the rape of a young, abused white girl. The novel won Lee 1961's Pulitzer Prize for fiction.

To Kill a Mockingbird (1962), starring Gregory Peck as Atticus

GEORGIA

Fiction

The Ballad of the Sad Café (1951)

Carson McCullers

Set in a small town in Georgia, McCullers story is one of loneliness and the effects of unrequited love. Most of the story is told in flashback and describes the love and power struggle between a cafe owner, her estranged husband and a hunchback.

The Heart Is A Lonely Hunter

Gone with the Wind (1936)

Margaret Mitchell

Mitchell's epic book is set in Georgia and Atlanta, but as the plantation Tara is in the former we have decided to put it in this section. Probably one of the best-known novels of the Old South and featuring two of fiction's most celebrated characters, Rhett Butler and Scarlett O'Hara, most of the story takes place during the American Civil War (1861–65) and subsequent years. *Gone with the Wind* won Mitchell the Pulitzer Prize for fiction in 1937.

Gone With The Wind (1939), starring Vivien Leigh and Clark Gable

http://www.margaretmitchell house.com/ (the apartment where Mitchell wrote the book)

Wise Blood (1952)

Flannery O'Connor

Georgia-born O'Connor wrote this novel about isolated characters in their search for spiritual truth. A tragicomedy, it follows Hazel Motes, a disillusioned man returning from war to find his family in chaos. Motes then travels to the town of Taulkinham and founds the humanistic Church Without Christ.

Wise Blood (1979), directed by John Houston

The Short Stories

LOUISIANA

NEW ORLEANS AND ENVIRONS

Fiction

Zeitoun (2010)
Dave Eggers

Eggars book is based on real-life character Abdulrahman Zeitoun, a New Orleans resident, who, in the aftermath of Hurricane Katrina, rowed around the deeply flooded streets of the city by canoe, helping rescue people, only to be later suspected of being a terrorist. The book primarily tells of the city of New Orleans in crisis.

🛜 http://www.zeitounfoundation.org/

Coming Through the Slaughter (1979)
Michael Ondaatje

This fictionalized life of Buddy Bolden, one of the great jazz musicians, brings to life the colour and excitement of the brothels and slums of jazz-era New Orleans. The city that Ondaatje evokes is often brutal, violent and raw, but never dull or calm.

A Confederacy of Dunces (1980)
John Kennedy Toole

Published after the author's suicide in 1969, this novel quickly became a cult hit. The central figure, Ignatius J. Reilly, is a slothful character, living at home with his mother in the Uptown neighbourhood of New Orleans. The book follows Ignatius as he is forced to find a living and in doing so he meets an array of colourful characters and has many adventures.

James Lee Burke's Louisiana

Burke's 'Dave Robicheaux' crime-fiction series has garnered many fans, not least because of its loving portrayal of New Orleans and Louisiana. Through Dave Robicheaux, Burke evokes the spirit of the state. *Neon Rain* (1987) first introduced Robicheaux, a recovering alcoholic and former detective in the New Orleans Police Homicide Department, living on a houseboat on Lake Pontchartrain. Robicheaux constantly pops in and out of local cafes, bars and restaurants in New Orleans and elsewhere, such as The Pearl just off Canal Street, where he has a beer and oysters on the half shell, and the nearby Acme Oyster Bar. He loves the French Quarter at the break of day. Similarly Burke buys beignets at the French Market and the Café du Monde on Jackson Square. Robicheaux also lives and works in New Iberia in the nearby bayou country, where Burke himself is based for part of the year. New Iberia is about two hours from Orleans and it's here that Robicheaux has his (fictional) bait shop and eats Cajun food, such as gumbo, dirty rice and étouffée, hanging out at Victor's Cafeteria on Main Street. Burke also eats at places like The Patio, Clementine's and the Little River Inn. The haunting beauty of the countryside is lovingly evoked in Burke's work – the flooded cypress trees, sugarcane fields in autumn, blue herons and pelicans – and the smells of 'smouldering hickory' and pork from the smokehouse, all making readers want to experience these places for themselves.

OTHER REGIONS

Fiction

The Awakening (1899)
Kate Chopin

Written at the end of the 19th century, Chopin's novel was viewed as scandalous after its publication. Chopin deals with Edna Pontillier, a young woman trying to find her own sexual identity. It is set on Grand Isle, off the coast of Louisiana, and in New Orleans. Edna is seduced by the island, the ocean and the people and that enables her to see herself in a different light. Chopin evokes the beauty and peace of Grand Isle, where she herself spent time, as did many of New Orleans's Creole families too.

A Gathering of Old Men (1983)
Ernest J. Gaines

Gaines's compelling and moving examination of racism in the Deep South is set on a sugarcane plantation in Bayonne, Louisiana. After the murder of a Cajun farmer a group of old African–American men gather to confess to the crime.

Property (2003)
Valerie Martin

Award-winning novel *Property* is set in Louisiana against the background of slave unrest in the 19th century. Manon Gaudet is given, as a wedding present, a slave girl who becomes the mistress of her husband, a sugar-plantation owner.

Divine Secrets of the Ya-Ya Sisterhood (1996)
Rebecca Wells

A joyous but also bittersweet tale set in Louisiana of a group of lifelong female friends who help a playwright work out the truth about her difficult, complicated mother.

📽 *Divine Secrets of the Ya-Ya Sisterhood* (2002)

Modern Baptists (1987)
James Wilcox

Set in a fictional town in Louisiana, Wilcox's comedy follows Bobby Pickens who experiences a new lease of life.

MISSISSIPPI

Fiction

Absalom! Absalom! (1936)
William Faulkner

Considered to be among Faulkner's greatest works, *Absalom! Absalom!* is the story of Thomas Sutpen, the son of a poor white Virginian. Thomas has a great plan, to rise above his lot and make a mark on the world. After a stint in Haiti, where he marries only to find his wife has black blood in her, he eventually turns up alone in Jefferson, Mississippi. There he builds a grand house on land in Yoknapatawpha County (based on Lafayette County) and starts a new family only to have untold tragedy strike as the Civil War breaks out and the sins of his past come back to haunt him.

Delta Wedding (1941)
Eudora Welty

Welty's charming portrait of a large Southern family, the Fairchilds, who live on a plantation in the Mississippi Delta, focuses on their preparations for a wedding.

Cat on a Hot Tin Roof (1955)
Tennessee Williams

This is a play not a novel but it is an utterly fantastic piece of work. *Cat on a Hot Tin Roof* is set in a plantation house in the Mississippi Delta, where a highly dysfunctional family has gathered.

🎬 *Cat on a Hot Tin Roof* (1958), starring Paul Newman and Elizabeth Taylor

Non-fiction

Faulkner's Mississippi (1990)
Willie Norris

Norris's beautifully illustrated book examines the author's Mississippi, in particular Yoknapatawpha, the location where Faulkner set so many of his books.

TENNESSEE

Fiction

The Violent Bear It Away (1960)
Flannery O'Connor

Set in Tennessee in the 1950s, O'Connor's second novel is a darkly comic look at religion and follows young Francis Marion Tarwater, whose life takes a prophetic turn.

THE WESTERN STATES

GENERAL
Fiction

A Boy's Own Story (1982)
Edmund White

White's semi-autobiographical examination of a boy growing up gay in the 1950s' Midwest is hauntingly beautiful.

ARIZONA
Fiction

Animal Dreams (1990)
Barbara Kingsolver

Animal Dreams is set in Grace, Arizona. The lead female character, Cosima 'Codi' Noline returns to her home town on the Arizona border in search of herself, her roots, and her place in the universe. She discovers that Grace has a lot to offer her. You will delight in the descriptions of cool tiled patios, lush, fragrant gardens, and peacocks that play an important role in the story.

The Law at Randado (1954)
Elmore Leonard

Leonard's classic is set in Randado, where a young man, Kirby Frye, 25, takes up the post of deputy sheriff. While he's away tracking suspects, the men of the local wealthy cattle baron hang two drifters for stealing cattle.

They seriously underestimate Kirby, who has sworn to carry out the job he's been sworn in to do.

Naked Pueblo (2001)
Mark Poirier

Poirier's acclaimed 12 short stories, some of which first appeared in literary journals and magazines, deal with the underbelly of the society of the author's hometown, Tucson, Arizona.

CALIFORNIA
Non-fiction

My California: Journeys by Great Writers (2004)

This book shows California through the eyes of more than 25 leading writers, including Michael Chabron, T. Jefferson Parker and Ruben Martinez. All the contributors donated their pieces so that the proceeds of the anthology could help the beleaguered California Arts Council.

LOS ANGELES
Fiction

Ham on Rye: A Novel (1982)
Charles Bukowski

Bukowski's semi-autobiographical cult novel follows Henry Chinaski in a coming-of-age book set in Los Angeles.

Less than Zero (1985)
Bret Easton Ellis

Easton Ellis's novel has Clay, a student on his winter break, returning to Los Angeles where he meets up with old friends, parties and takes drugs. The author charts Clay's emotional detachment, boredom and spiritual disintegration in this tale of a lost generation.

LA Quartet (1987–92)
James Ellroy

Ellroy's *LA Quartet* is made up of *The Black Dahlia* (1987), *The Big Nowhere* (1988), *LA Confidential* (1990) and *White Jazz* (1992). Set in noir Los Angeles, Ellroy creates a city of light

Raymond Chandler's Los Angeles

Philip Marlowe is one of the best-known creations in detective fiction and it is hard to separate him – or Raymond Chandler – from the city of Los Angeles. Marlowe lives at the Hobart Arms on Franklin Avenue near North Kenmore Avenue. He works 3.2 km (2 miles) away in an office on the sixth floor of the Cahuenga Building, near Hollywood Boulevard. All of Chandler's novels take place in Los Angeles or the nearby suburbs of Santa Monica or Pasadena (apart from the *Lady in the Lake*; 1943). Visitors can take local tours that stop at places like Scoops, where they can have a Chandler-flavoured gelato and visit the Sternwood residence on Franklin Avenue and the Geiger bookshop in Los Angeles, featured in *The Big Sleep* (1939).

Dashiell Hammett's San Francisco

Hammett's character Sam Spade helped immortalize San Francisco in text and on screen through such books as *The Maltese Falcon* (1930) and the movie it spawned starring Humphrey Bogart. Focusing on the pursuit of a gold and jewel-encrusted statue, the book captured the imagination of readers immediately after its publication. Sam Spade was based on Hammett himself and the author even gave Spade the address at which he wrote the book – 891 Post Street – where he lived between 1926 and 1929. Today, visitors can take a four-hour tour of San Francisco stopping at places important to Hammett and Spade, such as John's Grill, where customers can eat the meal that Spade has in the book – a lamp chop, a baked potato and a sliced tomato!

and shadows, where the police are hard and brutal and violence lurks around every corner.

 LA Confidential (1997), starring Russell Crowe and Kim Basinger

Ask the Dust (1998)
John Fante

Fante's classic is set in 1930s' Los Angeles. It tells of Arturo Bandini, an Italian American, who moves to Los Angeles to become a writer. When he gets involved with an unstable Mexican waitress he is forced to face up to many issues.

 Ask the Dust (2006)

White Oleander (1999)
Janet Fitch

After her poet mother is sent to prison for poisoning her lover, teenager Astrid finds herself living in a series of foster homes in Los Angeles.

 White Oleander (2002)

Devil in a Blue Dress (1990)
Walter Mosley

Mosley's charismatic Easy Rawlins is introduced in this novel. Set in South Central Los Angeles, black war veteran Easy tries to track down a missing woman on the lawless city streets.

 Devil in a Blue Dress (1995), starring Denzel Washington

SAN FRANCISCO

Fiction

Carter Beats the Devil (2001)
Glen David Gold

Gold's tale of a magician and his involvement in the death of the president also covers the history of Los Angeles from the early 20th century to the Roaring Twenties.

Tales of the City (1978)
Armistead Maupin

Maupin's iconic books featuring Michael 'Mouse' Tolliver, Mary Ann

Singleton and the unforgettable Anna Madrigal, all living at 28 Barbary Lane in San Francisco, enthralled a nation. This book, the first in the series, introduces the eccentric and charming range of characters, who first saw the light of day in the *San Francisco Chronicle*. The characters became like friends but Maupin's books were also important for discussing issues previously overlooked or ignored in literature, including HIV and AIDS.

🛜 http://www.armisteadmaupin.com/TalesMap.html (author's website, including a map of key locations in the books)

The Bonesetter's Daughter (1998)
Amy Tan

Ruth, a San Francisco-based ghost writer, finds out about her ill mother's past when a packet of letters falls into her hands. Her mother, LuLing, suffering from Alzheimer's disease, has documented her own life from her birth in China.

OTHER REGIONS

Fiction

The Mistress of Spices (1998)
Chitra Banerjee Divakaruni

Banejee Divakaruni's lyrical novel follows Indian Tilo, who runs an Indian spice shop in Oakland, California. While she sells her customers spices, she has a more important role as the 'Mistress of Spices', a priestess of the secret, magical powers of spices that can bring those who seek her out all they desire. When a lonely American comes into the store, he forces Tilo to make a difficult decision. Should she follow her own desires or will her magical powers be damaged forever?

🎬 *The Mistress of Spices* (2005)

The Tortilla Curtain (1995)
T. C. Boyle

Boyle's tragicomedy sees two couples from opposing sides of Southern Californian life collide in Topango Canyon. Boyle highlights the pervasive racism inherent in American society.

The Postman Always Rings Twice (1934)
James M. Cain

Cain's taut noir tells of a man and his lover's plans to kill her husband. This novel paved the way for many other noir books.

🎬 *The Postman Always Rings Twice* (1946), starring Lana Turner and John Garfield

Run River (1962)
Joan Didion

A fifth-generation Californian descended from a Donner Party survivor, Didion's debut novel opens with a murder on the banks of the Sacramento River and charts the disintegration of a marriage.

🔍 *Play It As It Lays*

Fup (1997)
Jim Dodge

In this engaging tale, set in northern California, Tiny and Grandaddy Jake's lives change when a duck called Fup enters their lives.

House of Sand and Fog (1999)
Andre Dubus III

Set in the California hills, Dubus's engrossing novel tells of an Iranian former colonel, now a struggling immigrant in the United States, and a troubled young woman fighting for their right to a house.

🎬 *House of Sand and Fog* (2003), starring Jennifer Connelly and Ben Kingsley

Big Sur (1962)
Jack Kerouac

Kerouac spent some time in poet Lawrence Ferlinghetti's cabin in Bixby Canyon in the gorgeous Big Sur on the Pacific Coast Highway. This is the Kerouac of later years – alcoholic, depressed and slightly paranoid – escaping his fame and his fans. The novel's deteriorating protagonist, Jack Duluoz, is a thinly disguised Kerouac. The Big Sur was a popular place in the 1960s – Joan Baez and Crosby, Stills and Nash, along with other musicians gathered there in 1969. Henry Miller and Richard Brautigan also wrote about it.

🔍 America: General – *On the Road*
🔍 http://www.bigsurcalifornia.org/ (about the Big Sur area)

Angle of Repose (1971)
Wallace Stegner

A retired historian, Lyan Ward, returns to his ancestral home in the Sierra Nevada to edit the papers of his grandmother, Susan Burling Ward. He discovers the arduous journey that she made with her husband to a land that was unforgiving to most settlers but achingly beautiful.

Of Mice and Men (1932)
John Steinbeck

Steinbeck wrote several novels set in California, all masterpieces in their own right. *To A God Unknown* (1933), which is set in Southern California, *Tortilla Flat* (1935) set in Monterey, *The Grapes of Wrath* (1938), dealing with tenant farmers forced from their homes to seek work in California, *East of Eden* (1952), based in the Salinas Valley and this book are arguably his best. *Of Mice and Men* is the moving and relentless story of George and friend Lennie who find work on a ranch in Salinas Valley. They dream of having their own land but fate has other plans for them.

🎬 *Of Mice and Men* (1992)

COLORADO

Fiction

Plainsong (1999)
Kent Haruf

Plainsong tells the stories of the inhabitants of Holt, Colorado – from a pregnant high-school girl to a pair of crusty old farmers. In this small, isolated community on the Colorado plains, everyone knows everyone else's business.

IDAHO

Fiction

Housekeeping (1980)
Marilynne Robinson

Robinson sets her novel in the fictional lakeside town of Fingerbone, which is partly based on the Pulitzer Prize-winning author's hometown of Sandpoint, Idaho. In this carefully written tale, focusing on the lives of narrator Ruth and her sister Lucille, Robinson meticulously recreates the harsh Idahoan landscape.

CHICAGO

Fiction

The Man with the Golden Arm (1949)
Nelson Algren

Algren's masterpiece deals with tragic hero and war veteran Frankie Machine as he self-destructs in the Polish ghetto of Chicago. It was turned into an award-winning film of the same name.

🎬 The Man with the Golden Arm (1955), starring Frank Sinatra

Herzog (1964)
Saul Bellow

Herzog is the story of a man whose life is disintegrating around him but who still views himself as a survivor. Moving between the Berkshires, New York and finally Chicago, to where Moses Herzog travels to try to see his daughter, he looks back at his past in

A Raisin in the Sun (1959)

American playwright and painter Lorraine Hansberry's work A Raisin in the Sun was the first play by an African–American woman to be produced on Broadway. Still a classic, this award-winning work is set in the South Side of Chicago. A 'living-room drama' that takes place in a tenement apartment, it tells of the members of a black family who dream of a better life. Walter Lee is a chauffeur, who wants to open a liquor store using his deceased father's life-insurance money. His sister, meanwhile, wants to go to medical school. Their mother, Mama Lena, wants to spend the insurance money partly on funding her daughter's college education and also on getting the family a proper home in a new white neighbourhood. Walter ends up squandering the whole settlement and the white-neighbourhood resident committee tries to dissuade Mama Lena from moving in. Hansberry partly based her play on a three-year anti-segregation Illinois Supreme Court case that her real-estate broker father was involved in to allow his family to live at 6140 S. Rhodes Avenue in Woodlawn. The case concluded in 1940 and brought an end to racially discriminatory housing covenants in Chicago.

the city to figure out how he has ended up in his situation.

Sister Carrie (1900)
Theodore Dreiser

Dreiser's classic follows a young girl moving to Chicago and making her way in the big city at the turn of the 20th century.

Studs Lonigan (1932)
James T. Farrell

The book that Norman Mailer said changed his life, *Studs Lonigan* follows a young Irish–American boy growing up in the tough environs of South Side Chicago against the background of Depression-era America.

Loving Frank (2007)
Nancy Horan

Frank Lloyd Wright is one of America's most influential architects. Horan's novel focuses on his affair with Mamah Borthwick Cheney, which scandalized early 20th-century Chicago society. Visitors can go on one of many tours to see Frank Lloyd Wright's city, including his home and studio, where he lived and worked between 1889 and 1909.

📶 http://gowright.org/visit/calendar.html (Frank Lloyd Wright's Preservation Trust)

Indemnity Only (1981)
Sara Paretsky

Pretty much every city has a detective and Chicago is no different – the windy city's is V. I. Warshawski, first introduced in this book. Now more than 13 books later, V. I. has firmly established herself in Chicago's literature. Paretsky's protagonist is firmly ensconced in the city from the 92nd Street home in which she lived with her policeman father and opera-loving mother to her home in Racine Street in South Side Chicago. Visitors can take a Warshawski tour of the city.

🎥 *V. I. Warshawski* (1991), starring Kathleen Turner in the title role

Non-fiction

Dreams from My Father (1995)
Barack Obama

President Obama's much-acclaimed memoir about his heritage, family and life moves from his childhood in Hawaii and other places to Chicago, where he lived and worked as a community organizer and then political activist. It is an extraordinary account of this influential man's life but also gives a very candid insight into many of the issues that have held Chicago's black community back. Visitors to Chicago can now take one of the many tours focusing on the president and his wife Michelle's favourite haunts in Chicago, such as R. J. Grunts in Lincoln Park.

📶 http://www.choosechicago.com/ Barack_Obama/Pages/default.aspx (Presidential Chicago Tour)

OTHER REGIONS
Fiction

So Long, See You Tomorrow (1980)
William Maxwell

Maxwell's celebrated short novel focuses on the murder of Lloyd Wilson on a rural farm in Illinois. Fifty years later, a man looks back at that time and his lost friendship with Cletus, his best friend, trying to work out what led to the killing, apparently by Cletus's father.

IOWA
Fiction

A Thousand Acres (1991)
Jane Smiley

This book can be described as *King Lear* relocated to Iowa. Smiley's award-winning book deals with a patriarchal man who gives up his farm to his three daughters. Tensions rise and loyalties are stretched to breaking point in Smiley's beautifully evocative book.

KANSAS
Fiction

Prairie Widow (1992)
Harold Bakst

Set on the 1870s' frontier, Harold Bakst's moving book follows protagonist Jenny Vandermeer. Forced by her husband to leave her Ohio home to live on a Kansas homestead, Jenny is left alone there with two young children after he dies. Through the help of the local community, she learns to appreciate the beauty of the land and its people.

Frank Baum's The Wizard of Oz (1900)

Baum's classic story is probably better known to most audiences through the Hollywood movie starring Judy Garland and by countless pantomime productions performed since then, but it is a classic none the less. The author creates the enchanting but also dark world of Oz in which Dorothy and her faithful dog, Toto, find themselves after a tornado hits Kansas. Desperate to go home, Dorothy, Toto and the companions they meet along the way travel to the Emerald City to see the Wizard of Oz, who can help her and Toto return to Kansas. Essentially a tale of a good against evil and that home is where the heart is, *The Wizard of Oz* has spawned a tourist trail to Kansas for those wanting to do all things Oz. Visitors can go to two Oz Museums in Kansas: one in Liberal and the other in downtown Wamego, which has its own Oztoberfest, complete with munchkins!

🎥 The Wizard of Oz (1939)

📶 http://www.sewardcountymuseum.com/sections/dorothy/index.html
   (Dorothy's house)

MICHIGAN

Fiction

The Virgin Suicides (1993)
Jeffrey Eugenides

Eugenides's compelling and haunting tale set in a suburb of Detroit tells of the five Lisbon sisters who all commit suicide over the course of one year. The neighbourhood boys who watch them try to piece together what happened.

🎬 *The Virgin Suicides* (1999), directed by Sofia Coppola

Non-fiction

To Be Loved: Music, the Magic, the Memories of Motown (1994)
Berry Gordy

More than any other American town Detroit is synonymous with modern black music through Berry Gordy's hugely successful company Motown. Here, Gordy tells all about his life, his work and the making of some of the best music to come out of the United States. Visitors can learn more at the Motown Historical Museum.

📶 http://www.motownmuseum.com/

MINNESOTA

Fiction

Lake Wobegon Days (1985)
Garrison Keillor

Keillor's affectionate look at a small Minnesotan town shows the minutiae of life in a place made notable for a statue of the Unknown Norwegian, among other things. It is the first book in a series featuring Lake Wobegon.

Main Street (1920)
Sinclair Lewis

Main Street provides the definitive depiction of small-town America for many critics. Lewis's engaging tale follows a young woman who moves to Gopher Prairie, Minnesota, with her doctor husband only to be met with suspicion and prejudice. Gradually, she begins to challenge the hypocrisy she finds there.

Want to Play (2005)
P. J. Tracy

The first in a series of books by a mother-and-daughter team, *Want to Play* was critically well received. The novel is set in Minneapolis primarily, where a grizzly killer is carrying out murders as featured in a serial-killer computer game, devised by the Monkeewrench team. Detective Magozzi and his partner work hard to find out the identity of the real killer. But is it a member of Monkeewrench?

MONTANA

Fiction

Perma Red (2002)
Debra Magpie Earling

Earling's story focuses on a young woman, Louise White Elk, as she struggles to escape from her life on the Flathead Indian Reservation, Montana, in the 1940s.

The Horse Whisperer (1995)
Nicholas Evans

Evans's moving tale tells of Annie, a high-powered New York woman, dealing with her daughter's tragic accident and subsequent emotional displacement. In a bid to help Grace and to assuage her own guilt, she persuades a Montanan horse whisperer to help mend Grace's spiritually and physically tortured horse.

The Horse Whisperer (1999)

These Thousand Hills (1956)
A. B. Guthrie

Guthrie's enjoyable book is set in 1880s' American West and follows an ambitious cowboy who wants more from his life. Lat Evans leaves Oregon to go on a cattle drive to Montana and it is here that he decides to stay and establish a ranch and a new life. Guthrie effortlessly sets the scene, giving much detail on frontier life.

These Thousand Hills (1959)

NEBRASKA

Fiction

My Antonia (1918)
Willa Cather

My Antonia, Willa Cather's classic, is set on the prairies of the American Midwest during the period of European settlement. Through the experiences of Antonia Shimerda, the daughter of Czech immigrants, Cather presents in fine detail the relentlessness and awe-inspiring beauty of the landscape, the mix of different cultures seeking a new life alongside the Native Americans and the joys and sorrows that come as part of pioneering life.

A Lost Lady

Dalva (1988)
Jim Harrison

Harrison's elegant book tells of Dalva, who begins the long journey back to her native Nebraska to find the son she gave up for adoption years earlier. There she finds her family and discovers through the journals of her great-grandfather the story behind the extermination of the Plains Indians.

The Road Home, which continues the story of the Northridge family on the plains of Nebraska

NEW MEXICO

Fiction

Death Comes Before the Archbishop (1927)
Willa Cather

Cather's engaging novel, set in the 1840s, tells of Father Jean Marie Latour, who is sent to the wilds of New Mexico to establish a mission. The Catholic Church wants the natives to be converted and Latour does this by working with them, calmly spreading his faith. Cather's description of the landscape, different ethnic groups and customs is, as ever, superb.

St Agnes's Stand (1994)
Thomas Eideson

This compelling western finds Nat Swanson on the run from a gang of Texan cowboys who think he murdered their friend, only to find himself fighting off Apaches as they besiege two wagons that hold Sister Agnes and a group of orphans.

The Blessing Way (1970)
Tony Hillerman

Set on a Navajo reservation in New Mexico, detective Joe Leaphorn of the Navajo Tribal Police struggles to solve a string of murders that seem to be tainted by witchcraft. Hillerman's books featuring Leaphorn give insight into Navajo life, customs and society.

NORTH DAKOTA

Fiction

The Bingo Palace (1994)
Louise Erdrich

Lipsha Morrissey has reached a crossroads. He showed such promise when he was growing up but it all sees to have come to nothing. Then his grandmother summons him back to the reservation in North Dakota and he finds himself coming to

terms with his heritage and meets Shawnee Ray.

🔍 *Love Medicine*

OHIO

Fiction

Winesburg, Ohio (1919)
Sherwood Anderson

Set in the fictional town of Winesburg, which is based on the town of Clyde in south-east Ohio, Anderson's collection is made up of interrelated short stories depicting life in a small Midwestern town through the eyes of ordinary people. *Winesburg, Ohio* is credited with having influenced Faulkner, among other great American writers.

OKLAHOMA

Fiction

Paradise (1999)
Toni Morrison

Morrison's celebrated book tells the story of Ruby, an all-black town in rural Oklahoma founded on high ideals by the patriarchs of nine families (descended from freed slaves) in the 1940s, but now full of fissures and fractures. By the 1970s, four women living at the convent nearby are attacked...

🔍 *Jazz*

TEXAS

Fiction

Giant (1952)
Edna Ferber

Ferber's sweeping tale tells the history of Texas as seen through cattleman 'Bick' Benedict, his society wife, Leslie, and their family. A sweeping saga of love, hate, racism and revenge in the magnificent Texan landscape.

🎬 *Giant* (1956), starring Rock Hudson, Elizabeth Taylor and James Dean

Blood Meridian: Or the Evening Redness in the West (1985)
Cormac McCarthy

Set in the late 1840s, McCarthy's strangely lyrical work focuses on a character called 'the kid' who runs away from home and ends up on the Texas–Mexico border. Working as part of the Glanton Gang led by the unforgettable Judge Holden, the kid helps to clear the borderlands. McCarthy's descriptions of the haunting beauty of the landscape are stunning.

🔍 *All The Pretty Horses*

Horseman, Pass By (1961)
Larry McMurtry

Pulitzer Prize-winning author Larry McMurtry wrote this novel when he was just 25. Set in 1950s' Texas, it pitches the Old West against the new.

The Killer Inside Me (1952)
Jim Thompson

Thompson's mesmerizing novel is set in a small town in Texas, where Sheriff Lou Ford leads a fairly mundane life. But people don't know what really goes on inside Lou. Beneath his façade is the mind of a depraved sociopath.

🎬 *The Killer Inside Me* (2010)

UTAH

Fiction

Riders of the Purple Sage (1999)
Zane Grey

A classic Grey western in which a lone gunman rides in to help a rancher hounded by the Mormon Church, who want to secure her land.

WASHINGTON STATE

Fiction

Ten Little Indians (2003)
Sherman Alexie

Alexie's acclaimed collection features 11 stories focusing on the intricacies of Native American life.

Snow Falling on Cedars (1994)
David Guterson

Guterson's lyrical book is set on the fictional island of San Pedro, off the coast of Washington State, just after the Second World War. Focusing on the racism and hostility still felt to outsiders, particularly Japanese Americans, Guterson tells of Kabuo Miyamoto, on trial for the alleged murder of a local fisherman. A local reporter, who secretly loves Kabuo's wife, has the information that might clear his name.

🎬 *Snow Falling on Cedars* (1999)

Surveillance (2006)
Jonathan Raban

This is the second of Raban's trilogy set in Seattle and deals with technology and modern paranoia, focusing on a reclusive writer tracked down by a journalist.

ALASKA

Fiction

The Seal Wife (2002)
Kathryn Harrison

Harrison's gorgeous tale set in the haunting beauty of Alaska follows Bigelow, a scientist, sent to the region to establish a weather observatory.

📶 http://kathrynharrison.com/ sealwife.htm

The Call of the Wild (1903)
Jack London

London's classic tale of Buck, a domesticated dog in California, forced to work as a sled dog in the harsh northern conditions of Alaska is a much-loved story. Buck finds love again at the hands of John Thornton, who rescues him from his life of slavery, only for it to end in tragedy.

HAWAII

Fiction

Paradise News (1991)
David Lodge

Lodge's beautifully observed book finds theology teacher Bernard travelling to Hawaii with his father to see his aunt, who is dying of cancer. Waikiki, part of Honolulu, is the area most focused on in this book.

Hotel Honolulu (2001)
Paul Theroux

A semi-autobiographical story, Theroux's *Hotel Honolulu* focuses on a once-successful writer recounting tales of the eccentric guests who stay at his hotel in insular Hawaii.

ASIA

Bangladesh | Bhutan | Cambodia | China | Hong Kong
India | Indonesia | Japan | Korea | Laos | Malaysia
Singapore | Myanmar (Burma) | Pakistan | Sri Lanka | Taiwan
Tibet | Thailand | Vietnam

ASIA

GENERAL

Non-fiction

Empires of the Indus (2008)
Alice Albinia

In this beautifully written book, journalist Alice Albinia charts the history and course of this famous, mystical river. Albinia travels upstream through Pakistan, Afghanistan and India to Chinese-occupied Tibet, covering more than 3,220 km (2,000 miles) and more than 5,000 years of history. By the time, we reach the end of the book, the reader will have followed Albinia's many adventures and have met many different peoples, heard their stories and been introduced to different cultures and landscapes. Michael Holroyd has described this book as a 'masterpiece in the making'.

🛜 http://www.empiresoftheindus.co.uk/index.html (book website)

BANGLADESH

Fiction

A Golden Age (2002)
Tahmina Anam

Set during the Bangladesh War of Independence in 1971, Anam's moving *A Golden Age* is the story of Rehana, a mother battling to keep her family together first after the death of her husband and then as the war starts.

Non-fiction

Songs at the River's Edge: Stories from a Bangladeshi Village (1997)
Katy Gardner

A lecturer in anthropology, Katy Gardner spent 15 months in a tiny village called Talukpur. This book, a series of carefully crafted narratives, brings the people she interacted with and their lives to vivid life.

BHUTAN

Non-fiction

Buttertea at Sunrise: A Year in the Bhutan Himalaya (1997)
Britta Das

This is an intimate account of German-born Das's time in Bhutan while working for the VSO. Part travelogue, part love story and part voyage of self-discovery, the book describes Bhutan, a remote, gloriously beautiful kingdom that is inaccessible to most outsiders. Through Das's prose we are invited into the romance – and reality – of a foreign land.

🛜 http://www.brittadas.com/ (author site)

CAMBODIA

Fiction

The King's Last Song (2006)
Geoff Ryman

Ryman's seventh novel *The King's Last Song* mixes two narrative strands together, interweaving the past with the present. The life of Cambodia's first Buddhist king, Jayavarman VII of the Angkor dynasty, and the discovery of the King's final testimony centuries later make up the plot for this story. A former Khmer Rouge cadre steals the tablets and abducts its custodians, Luc Andrade, and a Cambodian general. As his friends try to find him, Luc agrees to translate the King's words so all Cambodians can understand them.

Non-fiction

Swimming to Cambodia (1985)
Spalding Gray

Spurred on by Gray's small role in the 1984 movie *The Killing Fields*, he turned his experiences into a one-man show. Some people may find this book somewhat rambling in tone, but what emerges is Gray's thoughts on Pol Pot, the Khmer Rouge regime and genocide.

Swimming to Cambodia (1987)

A Dragon Apparent: Travels in Cambodia, Laos and Vietnam (1951)
Norman Lewis

Lewis's account of his travels through 1950s' Indochina as the Viet Minh and French make war is quite extraordinary. Mixing with ex-pats, French soldiers and locals, he visited the tribes of the central highlands who were to be so devastated by the war less than a decade later. Lewis's writing preserves them and

their way of live for us and provides a gripping travelogue of this region and times gone by.

http://www.lonelyplanet.com/china/travel-tips-and-articles/42/59689

CHINA

Fiction

Empire of the Sun (1984)
J. G. Ballard

Ballard's haunting book, based on his own childhood in Shanghai and in the civilian camp at Lunghua, where he was interned with his parents, is one of the best examples of the literature of war of this period. We see the history of this era first hand, through the eyes of the young boy, Jim.

Empire of the Sun (1987), Stephen Spielberg's epic and award-winning adaptation starring the young Christian Bale as Jim

When We Were Orphans (2000)
Kazuo Ishiguro

Ishiguro's compelling novel moves between the London and Shanghai of the 1930s. His protagonist, Christopher Banks, is a detective solving famous crimes in England. He is driven to return to Shanghai, where he lived as a child, to solve the disappearance of his own parents. As the Second Sino–Japanese War wages, Banks finds himself exploring the ruined city as he tries to find his missing parents.

Classic ancient Chinese literature

For those who want some grounding in ancient China, there are several classic novels to read on location that give some insight into the country's wealth of culture, history, folklore and philosophy. Here is a selection of what we feel are the best:

Journey to the West (Monkey)
Wu Ch'eng-en

Again known to generations of people through the cult TV series *Monkey*, Wu Ch'eng-en's entertaining *Journey to the West* mixes folklore, satire, history and philosophy with humour and compassion. Following the travels of a monk, it is based on the real-life figure Xuan Zang, who travelled to India on foot in the 7th century to bring the Buddhist scriptures back to China. Wu Ch'eng-en's monk, Tripitaka, is accompanied by the Monkey King, who emerged from an egg. He journeys with the monk to redeem himself. Along the way, they meet a host of colourful characters. The book also inspired an opera (*Monkey: Journey to the West*) and an album on which Damon Albarn of Blur fame collaborated.

Romance of the Three Kingdoms
Lo Kuan-Chung

Sometimes referred to as the '*Iliad* of China', Lo Kuan-Chung's epic novel, written in the 14th century, tells of the final years of the Han dynasty during the 2nd and 3rd centuries and the struggle of three kingdoms to control China.

Outlaws of the Marsh (The Water Margin)
Shi Nai'An

This 14th-century classic is better known by the name under which it appeared in the cult TV series, *The Water Margin*. Filmed in Japanese it was dubbed in English and has fascinated audiences since it was first aired in the late 1970s. Shi Nai'An's book is set during the Song dynasty and tells the stories of the more than 100 people who lived on the outside of society and banded together to resist the corrupt and harsh government.

The Story of the Stone (The Dream of the Red Chamber)
Cao Xueqin

Written in about 1760, *The Story of the Stone* is viewed by many as one of the greatest pieces of Chinese literature. Evoking a world that would otherwise be lost to us, Cao Xueqin's epic tale is set in a Buddhist context and follows the gradual decline of the Jia dynasty in 18th-century China. It follows Jia Bao-yu, the reincarnation of a supernatural entity known as the Stone, and his cousin, Lin Dia-yu, the incarnation of the Crimson Pearl Flower, with whose fate the stone is entwined. Xue Bao-Chai, another cousin fascinated by Bao-yu, adds another dimension to their relationship. Reality merges with illusion in this vast tome and the book is filled with the main theme of the tragic love story of Dia-yu and Bao-yu, as well as a series of subplots concerning the vast and complicated family households. Once described as a 'Chinese *Upstairs Downstairs*', *The Story of the Stone* is steeped in Chinese culture, history and philosophy.

The Vagrants (2009)
Yiyun Li

Yiyun Li's much-awaited first novel is based on a real-life event. Set in the time of the Democratic Wall Movement, in the late 1970s, the book opens in a small town called Muddy River on the day of the execution of a young woman for criticizing the Communist Party. After the girl is killed, it emerges that her execution was rushed through so that a party official could receive her kidneys. The villagers organize a demonstration to protest, with tragic consequences.

🔍 *A Thousand Years of Good Prayers* (2005), Yiyun Li's award-winning collection of short stories set in China

Balzac and the Little Chinese Seamstress (2001)
Dai Sijie

This tiny volume is a lyrical piece of work. Dai Sijie's story of two young men who are sent to a part of Szechuan for re-education and who meet the daughter of a local tailor with a secret pile of Western books, is beautiful. Illustrating the power of reading, the men are transformed through words, taken away to more lyrical places far away from the harsh reality of Mao's China.

The Joy Luck Club (1991)
Amy Tan

Tan's best-selling book is set between San Francisco and China. Dealing essentially with the relationships between Chinese mothers and their Chinese–American daughters, Tan also gives us an entertaining and poignant insight into the immigrant experience. Jing-Mei joins The Joy Luck Club to take her late mother Suyuan's place alongside three women with whom she met and played mah-jong each week, first in China and then in the United States. The other women inform Jing-Mei that her mother managed to locate her 'lost sisters', the daughters that Suyuan was forced to leave behind during the Japanese invasion of Kweilin and Jing-Mei journeys to China to meet her half-sisters and tell them about the mother they never knew.

🎬 *The Joy Luck Club* (1991)

The Boat to Redemption (2009)
Su Tong

Probably best-known for his novella *Wives and Concubines* on which the film *Raise the Red Lantern* is based, Su Tong's *The Boat to Redemption* is set during the Cultural Revolution. Banished from the Party, a previously high-level official takes to the river with his son, Dongliang, joining a group of boat people who are treated with great suspicion by those on the shore. Dongliang finds himself isolated, belonging to neither group, and when an orphan, Huixian, arrives he becomes obsessed with her. Su Tong's descriptions of rural China and the divide between the river people and the shore people are extremely evocative. The author considers this to be his most important book to date.

Soul Mountain (2001)
Gao Xingjain

Nobel prize-winning author and painter Gao Xingjain embarked on a 15,000 km- (9,320 mile) journey from Beijing into the mountains and forests of Sichuan in 1983 following a period of personal crisis. The author had been told that he had terminal lung cancer, only to find out weeks later that he did not. His work had been accused of being 'spiritual pollution' and rumours began to circulate that he was about to be arrested. *Soul Mountain* is the result of that ten-month journey. It is a lyrical piece of literature, using different forms and voices and combining among other things folklore, history and a travelogue to tell its story.

Non-fiction

Wild Swans: Three Daughters of China (1991)
Jung Chang

Chang's award-winning book about three generations of Chinese women is shocking, compelling, tragic and brutal. It is a very honest account of China's 20th-century history.

Red Dust: A Path Through China (2001)
Ma Jian

On his 30th birthday poet, painter and writer Ma Jian, facing arrest for 'spiritual pollution', faked illness and escaped from Beijing to the hinterlands of China. A book of true adventure, Jian lovingly describes the vastness of the land and the characters that he meets on his three-year trip.

HONG KONG

Fiction

Noble House (1981)
James Clavell

The fifth book in Clavell's 'Asian Saga', *Noble House* is a riveting tale of bitter rivalry set in 1960s' corporate Hong Kong. Clavell vividly paints the city in which Ian Dunross heads Struan's, the 'Noble House' of the title and the largest business in Hong Kong. Others covet Dunross's position and he also becomes embroiled with the KGB, CIA and the People's Republic of China.

The Noble House (1988), starring Pierce Brosnan

Fragrant Harbour (2002)
John Lanchester

Lanchester's novel follows four people – a journalist, a hotelier, a nun and a young Chinese entrepreneur – from the 1930s to the end of 20th century in Hong Kong. Lanchester carefully describes the changing city during this time and we follow it through war and Hong Kong's growth in the post-war years to events such as the massacre at Tiananman Square, Beijing, in 1989.

The Painted Veil (1925)
W. Somerset Maugham

Moving between England and Hong Kong in the 1920s, Somerset Maughan's tale of betrayal and forgiveness finds beautiful, shallow Kitty Vane's husband discovering his wife's infidelity. He forces her to accompany him from Hong Kong to the cholera-ridden Mei-tan-fu.

🎬 *The Painted Veil* (2006), starring Naomi Watts and Edward Norton

The Monkey King (1978)
Timothy Mo

Mo's first novel, set in 1950s' Hong Kong, features Wallace Nolasco, a Macanese man, who marries May Ling, moving into the Poon family home in the old part of the island. Relegated to the bottom of the heap by his new wife's relatives, Wallace struggles to assert his independence.

Kowloon Tong: A Novel of Hong Kong (1998)
Paul Theroux

Better known for his travel writing, author Paul Theroux sets this novel in Hong Kong in the late 1990s. Neville Mullard and his mother have a textile company in Hong Kong. They live a sheltered life apart from the Chinese but when the year arrives for the British to cede the island to China, their world is challenged. Suddenly, mainland China is closer than they thought and, with the arrival of the mysterious Mr Hung, matters become even worse.

INDIA

Fiction

The Siege of Krishnapur (1973)
J. G. Farrell

This much acclaimed and award-winning masterpiece charts an important part of British–Indian history, that of the Indian Rebellion of 1857. Set in a remote outpost, Farrell sets the scene of the British daily life in the Raj. Rumours of violent clashes reach the residency but when the siege finally occurs it is a shock. As the food and water run out and disease breaks out, the very proper British residents are reduced to scrabbling around to eat insects and the siege brings out the very best and very worst of those involved.

A Passage to India (1924)
E. M. Forster

Forster's elegant and poignant novel essentially asks if the British and Indians can really be friends. The answer is 'not really' in pre-partition India. When Aziz, a Muslim Indian doctor, who has asked himself this question already, is wrongly accused of attempting to rape Adela, an Englishwoman, his trial has tragic and long-lasting effects on British–Indian relations.

🎬 *A Passage to India* (1984), directed by David Lean

🔍 Italy – *A Room with a View*

The Epics

The *Ramayana* and *Mahabharata* are the two great Indian epic poems. Originally written in Sanskrit, both influential tales are lyrical, beautiful and full of wisdom and teachings on philosophy and morality. The *Ramayana* is the shorter of the two at around 24,000 couplets and was most probably composed after 300 BC by the poet Vaimiki. It follows the life and adventures of Rama, the prince of Ayodhya, an incarnation of Lord Vishnu. Rama's adventures have fascinated adults and children alike for centuries and have informed Indian culture and society for about the same amount of time. The *Mahabharata*, written in its current form in about AD 400, is seen by many as a vital Hindu text, instructing on *dharma*, essentially a moral code on the right way for a person to live his or her life – which is a very simplistic summing up of such an extraordinary book. Telling of two sets of warring cousins, the book features epic and bloody battles. Very good translations of the *Ramayana* and *Mahabharata* have been published by Penguin.

Heat and Dust (1975)
Ruth Prawer Jhabvala

Known to many through her association with the Merchant Ivory team who produced so many lush film adaptations of classic novels, including the movie of this book, Ruth Prawer Jhabvala was an award-winning screenwriter and novelist. This book, which moves between the India of the 1920s and the 1970s, won her the 1975 Booker Prize. The narrator travels to India to find out more about Olivia, the step-grandmother who was embroiled in a scandal 50 years earlier. She discovers that Olivia, bored with her colonial life in a small Indian town, had an affair with an Indian prince and became pregnant. Prawer Jhabvala's beautiful prose gives us insight into the world of English women in British India.

📽 *Heat and Dust* (1983)

The Far Pavilions (1978)
M. M. Kaye

Kaye's historical romance set against the beautiful backdrop of 19th-century India is an exploration of identity as well as a very enjoyable love story. Ashton is English but has been brought up as an Indian after his father is killed by cholera. He never truly fits into English society. While serving at an Indian court, he meets and falls in love with Anjuli, a princess of mixed race, who also never truly belongs to her community. Their relationship takes place against the backdrop of the Second Afghan War.

Kim (1901)
Rudyard Kipling

How could you possibly have a section on literature based in India and not include Kipling? Love or hate him, Kipling's work is important in evoking a certain age. *Kim*, possibly one of his best-known books, is named after its young protagonist, Kimball O'Hara, an orphan of Irish extraction who has run free on the streets of Lahore. The book is essentially a quest to find out where he belongs. When a Tibetan lama enters the city, Kim becomes his disciple, guiding and learning from him as they journey through India to the Himalayas in search of a secret river. Set against the background of the Great Game played out by Britain and Russia in the North-West Frontier Province, and in which Kim becomes embroiled, this is a rollicking good adventure with India playing as much of a character in the story as the boy himself.

The Life of Pi (2001)
Yann Martel

This magical book won Martel international recognition. Pi Patel, the precocious son of a zookeeper, grows up in Pondicherry. Planning to move to Canada, his father packs up the family and its animals to go there by ship. After a shipwreck, however, Pi finds himself floating in the Pacific Ocean with a wounded Bengal tiger, a spotted hyena and an orangutan. As Pi battles against the animals, the shark-infested waters, hunger and the elements, his hallucinations begin to become reality.

Midnight's Children (1981)
Salman Rushdie

Rushdie's acclaimed novel, which won the Booker Prize in 1989 and went on to be named 'The Booker of Bookers', the best book to win the prize in its 25-year history in 1993, is a magic-realist tale. Saleem Sinai is a mirror of India, born at the very moment when India achieves independence from Britain at the strike of midnight on 15 August 1947. All of the babies born at that time have special powers and Saleem's is the ability to see events through the eyes of other people. This is a diverse, multilayered book, which documents key events in India's history.

The Raj Quartet (1965–75)
Paul Scott

Scott's renowned series charting the end of British rule in India as seen from different points of view, is held by many as a classic. Starting with the *Jewel in the Crown* and followed by *The Day of the Scorpion*, *The Towers of Silence*, and *A Division of the Spoils*, the books cover a five-year period between 1942 and 1947.

📺 *The Jewel in the Crown* (1984)

A Suitable Boy (1993)
Vikram Seth

This epic tome, set in the newly independent India, tracks a woman's search for a suitable husband for her youngest daughter. While Mrs Mehra plots to marry Lata to a businessman, Lata has other plans. She is in love with a Muslim student, who is unsuitable in the eyes of her family. Sent to Calcutta (Kolkata), she meets Amit and her world becomes even more confusing. With a fine sense of detail and historical accuracy, Seth provides an intricate insight into India's politics at the time.

Non-fiction

Chasing the Monsoon (1990)
Alexander Frater

'The first sounds I heard were those of following rain', thus begins Alexander Frater's lovely travel classic *Chasing the Monsoon*. After an illness, Frater embarks on a voyage of discovery, journeying to India to follow the path of the monsoon. Tracing it from Trivandrum (Thiruvananthapuram) in Kerala to the terminal point at Cherrapunji in Meghalaya, Frater meets a wide variety of people on his way, from the rich and famous to the poor and humble, each with their own story and opinion about the significance of the monsoon.

📺 *Chasing India's Monsoon* (1991)

An Autobiography (1925)
M. K. Gandhi

If you haven't read this book and want to learn about India, you should do. Mahatma Gandhi was one of the most brilliant of civil rights activists and his influence on many key political and social leaders of today, including Nelson Mandela, is far reaching. This book is the story of his life, his influences and his beliefs. There are many heritage sites in India, places were Gandhi visited or lived for some time, if you had to choose just one go to the Gandhi Ashram in Sabarmati.

📶 http://www.gandhiashramsabarmati. org/ (Gandhi Ashram)

🎬 *Gandhi* (1982)

Freedom at Midnight (1975)
Dominique Lapierre and Larry Collins

If you are travelling around India, the chances are you will see dog-eared copies of this book lying around on shelves in hotels or cafes or in second-hand bookshops. This isn't the best-written tome about the events leading up to India's independence in 1947 and the creation of Pakistan, but it is a very accessible and gripping read. Written more like a thriller, it is fast paced and based on the many interviews that the authors carried out with key players, including Lord Mountbatten, who largely orchestrated the partition.

THE NORTH AND THE INDIAN PLAINS

KASHMIR

Fiction

Death in Kashmir (1981)
M. M. Kaye

Another Kaye mystery romance, this time set in the exotic location of the Vale of Kashmir, where Sarah Parrish finds herself involved in murder and intrigue. Invited to stay on a houseboat on the idyllic Dal Lake, she discovers that someone wants to stop her talking at all costs. As usual, Kaye conjures up the beauty and magic of her location. Tourists can experience staying on a houseboat in Srinigar, although it is a good idea to check the safety situation before doing so.

Non-Fiction

The Tiger Ladies: A Memoir of Kashmir (1981)
Sudha Koul

This memoir tells of Koul's life growing up in a valley in Kashmir. Listening to tales of the Tiger Lady, Koul tells of a Kashmir almost forgotten and gives an insight into the history of this turbulent region.

THE PLAINS

DELHI

Fiction

Clear Light of Day (1980)
Anita Desai

Set in Old Delhi, Desai's novel tells of the Das family – Bimla, the teacher, who looks after her mentally challenged brother, Baba, in the home in which they grew up; Raja, their successful brother; and Tara, their estranged sister, who returns home, opening all kinds of wounds.

Delhi Noir (2009)
Hirsh Sawney (editor)

This collection of 14 stories about Delhi by established and new authors, brings life and vitality to the city often bypassed in literature. If you want to get to know Delhi, from the more popular spots such as Lodhi Gardens to the less-known locales such as Rohini, and like noir fiction, this

collection is a great way to start. Split into three sections, each titled with a slogan you would see tattooed across the city – 'With You, For You, Always' (Delhi Police), 'Youngistan' (Pepsi ad campaign) and 'Walled City, World City' (a *Times of India* campaign) – this book is also an excellent introduction to a selection of Indian authors with whom you may or may not be familiar.

🔍 *Following the Detectives,* **Maxim Jakubowski (editor)**

Non-fiction

City of Djinns: A Year in Delhi (1993)
William Dalrymple

Dalrymple's love of the city comes through in this travelogue. After visiting Delhi when he was 17, Dalrymple returned later to spend time there, peeling away the layers of the city's past, people and culture. This fascinating read is a must for anyone intending to go there.

OTHER REGIONS

Fiction

Difficult Daughters (1998)
Manju Kapur

A tale of a girl torn between love for her family and love for a married man and the desire for education, *Difficult Daughters* is lyrically written. Virmati lives in Amritsar in pre-partition India. When she eventually marries her loved one, the Professor, she moves with him to Lahore to pursue her studies but also to live with his first wife.

The Romantics (2001)
Pankaj Mishra

Samar, a young Brahmin, travels to the city of Benares (Varanasi) to complete his education and take his civil service exams. Lured by the West, he meets a group of Westerners and falls in love with a young Frenchwoman. Through Samar's eyes we get a sense of the city, its majesty and history.

Non-Fiction

The Heart of India (2001)
Mark Tully

Tully, the former BBC Chief of Bureau in New Delhi, tells various tales of life in Uttar Pradesh.

THE EAST

WEST BENGAL AND ENVIRONS

KOLKATA (CALCUTTA)

Fiction

The Blue Bedspread (2000)
Raj Kamal Jha

In a house on Main Circular Road, a man records the history of his family's past, while a baby, his niece, waits for a family to adopt her. Through his memories we see the truth behind his relationship with his sister.

Mrs d'Silva's Detective Instincts and the Shaitan of Calcutta (2009)
Glen Peters

This murder mystery is set in Calcutta in the 1960s among the Anglo–Indian community. Of great interest for its insight into this group, considered neither English nor Indian enough by both communities, the novel is based on the author's own experiences of growing up in an Anglo–Indian family (although he now lives in Wales) and his own memory of finding the body of a woman on the banks of the Ganges.

🛜 http://www.shaitan.org.uk/
(about the book)

Chowringhee (2009)
Sankar

Although published in the 1960s and often referred to as a classic of Bengali literature, *Chowringhee* has only recently been translated into English. Set in the 1950s, the story revolves around the Shahjahan Hotel, a lavish place where the rich, powerful and famous rub shoulders. Seen through the eyes of a hotel clerk, the hotel is a microcosm of the city.

🎬 *Chowringhee* (1968), hard-to-find cult movie

OTHER REGIONS

Fiction

The Hungry Tide (2006)
Amitav Ghosh

Ghosh's engaging novel is set in the Sunderban Islands in the Bay of Bengal. A place of natural and extraordinary beauty, crocodiles fight with man-eating tigers among the mangroves. It is here that Kanai meets Piyali, an American scientist studying a rare breed of dolphin. Kanai has been summoned to the islands by his aunt after her discovery of a packet of letters written by her dead husband to his favourite nephew.

🔍 Myanmar – *The Glass Palace*

Black Narcissus (1939)
Rumer Godden

Godden's evocative tale is set in the Himalayas near Darjeeling. The disciplined Sisters of Mary travel to the old palace, formerly the home

---

Tagore's Bengal

It is almost impossible to discuss the literature of Bengal without Nobel Prize-winning author Rabindranath Tagore's name coming up immediately. Civil rights activist, poet, novelist, playwright and educator, Tagore fought hard for India's independence from British rule and when he was awarded a knighthood by the British Empire, he returned it in 1919 in protest against the Amritsar massacre, during which several hundred unarmed Indians, many of them women and children, were killed when British troops opened fire during a peaceful demonstration. Born in Kolkata in 1861 to a wealthy family, he was brought up educated in both Indian and Western ideas. He wrote his first poetry at 8 years of age. Tagore published several volumes of poetry, short stories, plays and other literature but it is probably *Gitanjali: Song Offerings* that established his reputation as a writer internationally. W. B. Yeats wrote the foreword to the 1912 English edition, which Tagore translated from Bengali himself. Many of Tagore's books dealt with social or political issues, such as caste, equality, women's position in society and the plight of Bengal itself. His influence on both Indian and Western literature was great. One such book *The Home and the World* (1915) has a protagonist who encourages his wife to see herself as his equal. Visitors to Kolkata can see Tagore's family home where he was born and died at 6/4 Dwarakanath Tagore Lane. It is now a museum housing many of his personal effects, including paintings and manuscripts. It is also worth travelling to Santiniketan, meaning 'abode of peace', the school that Tagore founded in 1901 on his family's land. The residential school was based on the ancient system of *gurukul*. The city of Kolkata is about 180 km (110 miles) away and direct buses go from there to Santiniketan, today a university town, and the nearest train station is 2 km (1¼ miles) away in Bolpur. The main attractions can be found at the Visva-Bharati University, where the author himself lived in the Uttarayan complex.

🔍 http://www.santiniketan.com/ (Santiniketan)

of the local potentate's harem, high in the mountains to establish a school and dispensary for the locals. Dependent on the local, very masculine English agent for help, they struggle against the harsh environment, the traditions and suspicions of the native people, as well as their own demons and desires.

🎬 *Black Narcissus* (1947)

THE SOUTH

Fiction

Coromandel Sea Change (1982)
Rumer Godden

Set on the beautiful Coromandel Coast, Rumer Godden creates Patna Hall, a grand old-fashioned hotel, run by Aunt Sanni and peopled by a host of lively and intriguing characters.

Malgudi Days (1982)
R. K. Narayan

Narayan's popular and charming depiction of the fictional southern Indian town of Malgudi has riveted readers for decades. In this short story collection, the whole city comes to life through the range of characters who emerge from the pages. Narayan's work has been compared to that of P. G. Wodehouse. He had many famous fans, including Graham Greene, who helped to get his first book published and became a good friend. Greene said that Narayan was 'the novelist I most admire in the English language since the death of Evelyn Waugh.

Without him I could never have known what it is like to be Indian.'

🔍 *A Malgudi Omnibus*

Kanthapura (1963)
Raja Rao

Recognized as one of the most important books on modern India, Rao's classic recounts the Gandhian story for independence as seen in one village in South India.

KERALA

Fiction

The God of Small Things (1997)
Arundhati Roy

Probably one of the most famous books to be set in Kerala in recent years, Roy's *The God of Small Things* caused a huge stir around the world following its publication, particularly in India where she was brought up on obscenity charges for the descriptions of inter-caste lovemaking. Elsewhere, it received critical acclaim and won the author the 1997 Booker Prize. Based in Ayemenem, a small riverside town in Kerala, the plot sees twins Rahel and Estha living with their divorced mother, their grandmother, grand-aunt Baby and uncle Chacko. When uncle Chacko's English ex-wife comes to stay with their daughter, Sophie, the twins' lives change radically and tragedy strikes. Roy, whose mother is a Keralite and was also divorced, lived in the state until she was 16. She brings Kerala's lushness to life, a place bursting with natural beauty. She also portrays a community where different religions – including Catholicism, Hinduism, and Islam – rub along side by side, but where caste and tradition are still very important.

 http://www.weroy.org/arundhati.shtml (Arundhati Roy website)

Daughters of Kerala (2 004)
Various

As India's most literate state it is not surprising that Kerala has produced writers such as Arundhati Roy. This collection of 25 stories introduces the reader to some of the state's leading female talent.

THE WEST

MAHARASHTRA

MUMBAI (BOMBAY)

Love and Longing in Bombay (1977)
Vikram Chandra

Chandra's collection of interconnected short stories is set in modern Bombay.

🔍 *Red Earth and Pouring Rain: A Novel* (1995)

East of the Sun (2008)
Julie Gregson

An engaging read, Gregson's story of three young women travelling to Bombay in 1928 is a fine depiction of Raj society at the time and a generally very enjoyable read. The girls, Rose, a bride to be, Victoria, her bridesmaid, and Viva, their inexperienced chaperone, each seek something from their new land.

A Fine Balance (1995)
Rohinton Mistry

Set in mid-1970s' Mumbai, at the time of Indira Gandhi's state of emergency, the book focuses on four people – Dina Dalal, a widow, the two low-caste men who work for her, Ishvar Darji and Omprakash, and Maneck Kohlah, the boy who rents a room from her.

Shantaram (2003)
Gregory David Roberts

Based on real-life events, this best-selling novel follows an Australian convict who escapes from prison and flees to Mumbai, where he becomes a doctor in the slums of the city and falls in love with the people and the place. Leopold's Cafe and Bar in the Colaba district of the city features heavily in the book. The multi-cuisine eatery has been a popular tourist venue for many years and it also hit the headlines when it was targeted by terrorists in the November 2008 shootings. Despite, or possibly because of this notoriety, tourists still flock to the cafe.

 http://www.shantaram.com (author site)

Q&A (2000)
Vikas Swarap

Swarap's best-selling novel had a second lease of life after the release of the Oscar-winning film *Slumdog Millionaire*, which was based on the book. Opening in a prison in Mumbai where Ram Mohammad Thomas is being held after answering correctly all 12 questions in a quiz show, the book looks back at his life and how a poor Indian boy could know the right answers to those questions.

🎬 *Slumdog Millionaire* (2008)

OTHER REGIONS
Fiction

Bhowani Junction (1952)
John Masters

This novel is probably more familiar to audiences through the 1956 film adaptation starring Stewart Grainger and Ava Gardner, in which the latter played Victoria, an Anglo–Indian woman struggling to find out where she belongs in pre-partition India. As the British prepare to leave, Victoria kills a British officer who tries to rape her and is protected by a young Sikh man who hopes to marry her. An English officer and an Anglo–Indian man also fight for her attention. Set in Bhowani, based on the railway town of Bhusawal in Maharasta, the book is an excellent insight into the Anglo–Indian community.

🎬 *Bhowani Junction* (1956), directed by George Kukor

The Assassin's Song (2007)
M. G. Vassanji

Vassanji's tale, set mostly in Gujurat, follows Karsan Dargawalla, whose destiny is to follow his forefathers as the avatar of a Sufi shrine in Gujarat that is open to all religions. But Karsan wants more than that and rebelling against his heritage leaves India for the United States and Canada, only to return years later to the place where he grew up.

INDONESIA
Fiction

The Year of Living Dangerously (1978)
Christopher Koch

Set in Jakarta in 1965 during an insurrection against President Sukarno, Koch's tale of misplaced loyalties and love has at its heart a dwarf Chinese–Australian cameraman called Billy who works with and manipulates the newly arrived journalist Guy Hamilton into reporting on the real Indonesia.

🎬 *The Year of Living Dangerously* (1982), Peter Weir's popular film starring a young Mel Gibson and Sigourney Weaver

Max Havelaar: Or the Coffee Auctions of the Dutch Trading Company (1860)
Multatuli

This book caused a storm when it was first published. A bitter indictment of colonialism, Max Havelaar tells of a young civil servant who challenges the corruption and inhumanity of Dutch colonial rule in Java. Multatuli was in reality Edward Douwes Dekker, who had worked for the East Indian Civil Service in Java.

🔍 The Buru Quartet – *Children of All Nations* (1991), *Footsteps* (1990) and *House of Glass* (1992)

This Earth of Mankind (1990)
Pramoedya Ananta Toer

The first in the quartet that became known as the *Buru Quartet, This Earth of Mankind* is set in the last days of Dutch colonial rule. Minke, the narrator, is the descendent of Javanese royalty, and the only Javanese boy to attend an elite Dutch school. But when he goes to live in Nyai Ontosoroh's household, his eyes are opened and his political, emotional and cultural awakening begins — and so his life also begins. Toer 'wrote' this book while in prison. As he wasn't allowed to write anything down he told his story to fellow inmates, who in turn passed his stories on. The book was finally published in Jakarta in 1980 and the quartet appeared in English in the 1990s.

🔍 The Buru Quartet – *Children of All Nations* (1991), *Footsteps* (1990) and *House of Glass* (1992)

Non-fiction

In the Time of Madness (2005)
Richard Lloyd Parry

Lloyd Parry worked as a foreign correspondent based in Indonesia at the end of the 20th century when General Suharto's dictatorship was disintegrating. Lloyd Parry himself witnessed many atrocities as he reported on the brutal ethnic war. This book is divided into three sections dealing with events that happened in Borneo, Java and East Timor between 1997 and 1999.

🎬 *The Year of Living Dangerously* (1982)

JAPAN

Fiction

Rashoman and Seventeen Other Stories (2002)
Ryunosuke Akutagawa

One of Japan's most accomplished short story writers, Akutagawa published hundreds of stories in his lifetime. This collection features some of his most noted work, including the stories that inspired Japanese film-maker Akira Kurosawa's masterpiece of the same name.

🎬 *Rashoman* (1950)

Shogun (1975)
James Clavell

Another epic by Clavell this time focusing on Japan in the 1600s as seen through the eyes of John Blackthorne, a shipwrecked captain who learns to live and love the country and its people. Treated as an honoured guest, Blackthorne is assigned a translator, Mariko, so that the Japanese can learn as much from him as he can from them. Treated with suspicion by some, Blackthorne is given the honoured title of 'Samurai' by the feudal lord Toranaga, but the question is why?

📺 *Shogun* (1980)

Memoirs of a Geisha (1999)
Arthur Golden

A runaway best-seller, Golden's tale is a mesmerizing read. When a young girl is sold into a famous geisha house, she is transformed as she learns every art associated with the ancient tradition. Visitors wishing to learn more about geishas can go on working tours such as those run in Kyoto which take in the traditional tea houses of the city.

📶 http://www.japanvisitor.com/index.php?cID=359&pID=322 (Kyoto geisha walking tour)

🎬 *Memoirs of a Geisha* (2005)

Inspector Imanishi Investigates (1989)
Seicho Matsumoto

In the first Imanishi book, Matsumoto introduces his detective who is fond of haikus and gardening. Imanishi must hunt down a killer across Japan.

I Am a Cat (2002)
Soseki Natsume

This comic masterpiece written in the early 20th century satirizes Japanese society during the Meiji era. Told through the eyes of a world-weary kitten, who comments on whatever he sees, Soseki originally submitted this as a short story, but was encouraged to expand it into what appears collated in this book.

🔍 England, Yorkshire – *The Red Riding Quartet*

TOKYO
Fiction

The Earthquake Bird (2001)
Susanna Jones

Jones's award-winning book follows two women in Tokyo. When Lucy Fly is arrested for the murder of another Englishwoman, Lily, she begins to recall the events that brought her from Yorkshire to Japan and the people she has met since she came there.

Out (1997)
Natsuo Kirino

A gritty, but sometimes surprisingly funny thriller, Kirino's much acclaimed *Out* follows a group of ordinary women working at a factory making boxed lunches. When one of them strangles her abusive husband, she seeks the help of her co-workers to help her dispose of the body. Throw a ruthless nightclub owner into the equation, who becomes the prime suspect after the body parts are discovered, and the plot becomes much more grim and intense.

Norwegian Wood (1987)
Haruki Murakami

It is hard to choose one Murakami, but space dictates we must. This best-selling cult novel is a coming-of-age story set in Tokyo in the late 1960s. Told in Murakami's usual lyrical style, it follows student Toru, who is friends with Naoko, the girlfriend of his dead best friend. As Naoko retreats into her own world, Toru waits for her return.

🔍 *The Wind-Up Bird Chronicles*

In the Miso Soup (1997)
Ryu Murakami

Murakami's entertaining story of Kenji hired to take Frank, an overweight American tourist, on a tour of Tokyo's sleazier sights, provides a great insight into the city's underbelly. As Kenji gradually comes to the conclusion that Frank is in fact the serial killer terrorizing Tokyo, his worst nightmare seems to be coming true.

Tokyo Year Zero (2007)
David Peace

The first part of a trilogy based on true crimes committed in war-devastated Tokyo, the book begins with the discovery of the decomposed bodies of two raped and strangled young women. Pearce, with his usual eye for detail and sense of atmosphere, focuses on the chaos and horror of a nation recovering from war.

🔍 England, Yorkshire – *The Red Riding Quartet*

Some Prefer Nettles (1929)
Yunichiro Tanizaki

Written in the 1920s, Tanizaki's novel looks at the relationship of Kaname and Misako, who are unhappily married. As his wife pursues a liaison with another man, Kaname is urged by his father-in-law to look to the past, at the traditional ways that are dying as society progresses.

🔍 *The Makioka Sisters* (1943–8)

Kitchen (1988)
Banana Yoshimoto

Yoshimoto's critically well-received novel immediately made her the author to read. In *Kitchen* she weaves a offbeat tale of grief, love and family through her protagonist Mikage, whose grandmother has just died. Mikage goes to live with Yuichi and his mother (who is actually his father in a dress). Through Yoshimoto's eyes we see Japanese culture, with the East warring and blending with the West.

Non-fiction

Underground: The Tokyo Gas Attack and the Japanese Psyche (1997)
Haruki Murakami

On 20 March 1995, the unthinkable happened. Tokyo's underground system became the site of a terrorist attack when members of a cult released the nerve gas sarin. In an attempt to find out why this horrific event happened, Murakami interviewed many of the people who lived through that day.

OTHER REGIONS

Fiction

The Sailor who Fell From Grace with the Sea (1900)
Yukio Mishima

Set in Yokohama Harbour, Mishima's novel tells of Ryuji Tsukazaki, a merchant marine, Fusako Kuroda, a widow, and her son, misfit Noboru.

🎬 *The Sailor who Fell From Grace with the Sea* (1976), with Japan transposed to England

Nip the Buds, Shoot the Kids (1958)
Kenzaburo Oe

Often compared to William Golding's *Lord of the Flies*, Oe's book, written when he was just 23, follows a group of boys who are evacuated to a remote part of Japan towards the end of the Second World War. Treated with suspicion and cruelty by the locals, the boys are later blockaded by the fleeing villagers when plague breaks out in the valley, and they cannot escape. As time passes, the boys develop their own society and rules, caring for each other and an infirm girl also left behind. Then the realities of life outside begin to intervene.

Non-fiction

Hiroshima (1946; updated 1989)
John Hersey

Hersey's classic tells of the events that led up to the dropping of the atomic bomb on Hiroshima. Updated almost four decades after its original publication, Hersey returned to the city to find out what happened to many of the people he had originally interviewed. Despite its horrific recent history, Hiroshima is a beautiful place and a popular tourist destination and the city has a Peace Memorial Museum and the Atomic Bomb Dome, left in its original state to remind us of the effects of the bomb.

📶 http://www.asiarooms.com/en/travel-guide/japan/hiroshima/useful-information/when-to-go-to-hiroshima.html

KOREA

Fiction

Fox Girl (2003)
Nora Okja Keller

Okja Keller's novel deals with the abandoned children of GIs after the Korean War. Disowned by her parents, Hyun Jin, or Fox Girl, lives in a world where it's all about survival. Her best friends are teenagers Sookie, a prostitute kept by an American soldier, and Lobetto, a pimp.

The Poet (1996)
Yi Mun-yol

Set in 19th-century Korea, Yi Mun-yol's book tells of Kim, part of a family condemned as traitors through the actions of their grandfather. Wandering the country as a vagrant, Kim struggles for recognition as a poet. Yi Mun-yol's mesmerizing book gives us a good insight into Korean culture.

Three Generations (2005)
Yom Sang-seop

This English translation of Yom Sang-seop's 1931 classic allows us to see the Japanese-occupied Seoul of that decade through the experiences of the Jo family.

The Guest (2005)
Hwang Sok-yong

When Ryu Yosop returns to his native land after 40 years absence he must come to grips with his brother's actions during the Korean War.

LAOS

Fiction

The Coroner's Lunch (2004)
Colin Cotterill

The first book in the Dr Siri Paiboum series introduces the septuagenarian doctor, one of the last left in Laos after the communist takeover in the 1970s, who becomes the national coroner. When the wife of an official turns up dead, Siri is determined to find out how and why.

MALAYSIA

Fiction

The Malayan Trilogy (1972)
Anthony Burgess

Burgess introduces a host of colourful and entertaining characters in his three books set in post-war Malaysia, giving us a very good overview of society in the last days of British rule.

Inspector Singh Investigates: A Most Peculiar Malaysian Murder (2009)
Shamini Flint

The first in the series introducing the corpulent Inspector Singh of the Singapore police sees him travelling to Kuala Lumpur to investigate the murder of an abusive Malaysian man by his Singaporean model wife. Dogged by the young, fit Sergeant Shukor of the Malaysian police, Singh does his best to untangle the truth.

Inspector Singh Investigates: The Singapore School of Villany

The Rice Mother (2002)
Rani Manicka

Lakshmi spends her childhood in Ceylon and moves to Malaysia at the age of 14 to marry. *The Rice Mother* traces her development from young bride and mother to matriarch.

SINGAPORE

Fiction

The Singapore Grip (1978)
J. G. Farrell

Farrell's tragicomic classic is set in 1939, on the eve of the Second World War, as the Japanese are about to invade at any moment.

Foreign Bodies (1997)
Hwee Hwee Tan

This astonishing novel explores the clash between traditional and popular culture in Singapore. When Andy is arrested for allegedly running an international betting ring, he has, according to Singapore's ancient laws, nine days to prove himself innocent or will face life imprisonment. His girlfriend Mei, a lawyer, and Eugene, Andy's best friend, strive to uncover the truth as the clock ticks away.

MYANMAR (BURMA)

Fiction

The Glass Palace (2000)
Amitav Ghosh

Ghosh's beautifully written book is set in Burma, Malaya and India. Spanning more than a century, from the time when the King of Burma was sent into exile to the end of the 20th century, Ghosh presents a vibrant piece of Asian history.

🔍 India – *The Hungry Tide*

The Piano Tuner (2002)
Daniel Mason

Set in the 1880s, Mason's intriguing novel finds a middle-aged piano tuner sent to the remote jungles of north-east Burma to tune the instrument of an eccentric army surgeon.

Burmese Days: A Novel (1934)
George Orwell

Orwell served with the Imperial Police in Burma and knew his subject well. Set in the waning days of British colonial power, a European club with a whites-only policy is ordered to allow one native member through its hallowed doors, with dreadful results. James Flory detests the racism of his club but lacks the courage to stand up for his friend Dr Veraswami, who is the leading candidate for membership.

Non-fiction

Finding George Orwell in Burma (2004)
Emma Larkin

Larkin spent a year in Burma tracing Orwell's life and work. Travelling from Mandalay to the hill stations in the far north and on to Rangoon, she traced the places that inspired Orwell and brings a country and a people cut off from the rest of the world to life.

The River of Lost Footsteps: A Personal History of Burma (2006)
Thant Mying-U

A fascinating, vivid yet scholarly history of modern Burma interwoven with the story of the author's family.

Little Daughter: A Memoir of Survival in Burma and the West (2009)
Zoya Phan

Political activist Zoya Phan was born into the Karen tribe in the remote area of Burma. Her early years living with her animist parents and brother were quite idyllic but at 13, Zoya's life was shattered after the Burmese army attacked and her family was forced to fight or run. After hiding in the jungles with thousands of other refugees, She ended up in a Thai refugee camp with her sick mother. Zoya finally sought asylum in the United Kingdom. This moving book gives the reader an insight into Burma's recent history.

Letters from Burma (1995)
Aung San Suu Kyi

Nobel Peace Prize-winner Aung San Suu Kyi is one of the most inspirational human-rights activists of our time. At great personal cost, she left her husband and family behind to go back to her native Burma to help fight for democracy and has, for many years, been under house arrest while the military junta control her country. This collection of over 50 pieces, started just after she was placed under arrest, paints a vivid picture of Burma and its people, as seen through the eyes of a very extraordinary woman.

PAKISTAN

Fiction

Seasons of the Rainbirds (1993)
Nadeem Aslam

Aslam's award-winning story tells of a missing sack of letters that suddenly reappears 19 years later in a small rural town in Pakistan. As the inhabitants wait to see what will be revealed they wonder if the letters have anything to do with a judge's recent death.

In Other Rooms, Other Wonders (2009)
Daniyal Mueenuddin

A collection of linked short stories set in Pakistan, In *In Other Rooms, Other Wonders*, Mueenuddin's characters move across the vast landscape of the country. From landowners, servants and managers to politicians and mistresses, the characters present a vivid representation of life in Pakistan.

Shame (1983)
Salman Rushdie

Rushdie gives a potted history of Pakistan in this fable of two men and their families set against the lively culture, politics and religion of the country.

Broken Verses (2005)
Kamila Shamshie

When Pakistan's greatest poet is found murdered and his lover, an activist, disappears, her daughter just assumed she had been abandoned. Years later, Aasmani runs into an old friend of her mother's and begins to receive letters written in the code that the poet and her mother used to write. Believing her mother to be alive, Aasmani searches to find the truth.

🔍 *Kartography*

The Pakistani Bride (1996)
Bapsi Sidhwa

Sidhwa's acclaimed novel follows Qasim, who is caught up in the struggles surrounding the creation of Pakistan. He takes in an orphaned girl, Zaitoon, bringing her up as his daughter in the lively city of Lahore, where he is successful. Zaitoon has romantic visions of Qasim's homeland, a remote village in the Himalayas, but reality strikes when she is promised in marriage to a tribesman.

Train to Pakistan (1970)
Khushwant Singh

This classic novel examines the horror of partition. A previously peaceful place erupts into racial and religious hatred after the arrival of a ghost train, carrying the bodies of thousands of refugees.

Non-fiction

Pakistan: Democracy, Terror and the Building of a Nation (2010)
Iftikhar Malik

This critical examination of modern Pakistan by scholar Iftikhar Malik not only gives an insight into the complex political, religious and societal situation in the relatively new nation-state, but also gives much needed background to the geo-political situation, the history and tribal issues as well.

Three Cups of Tea (2006)
Greg Mortenson

'Here we drink three cups of tea to do business; the first you are a stranger, the second you become a friend, and the third, you join our family, and for our family we are prepared to do anything – even die', mountaineer Greg Mortenson was told. After a failed trip to climb K2, Mortenson found himself off course, freezing and desperate for help in a remote Pakistani village in the Karakoram mountains. Amazed by the generosity of the villagers, he returned later to build the first of what was to be more than 50 schools, not just in Pakistan but in Afghanistan as well, as the Taliban rose to power.

SRI LANKA

Fiction

Reef (1994)
Romesh Gunesekera

Gunesekera's lovely novel follows Triton's life. When Triton bumps into a former compatriot in London he begins to think back to his life in Sri Lanka. Aged 11, he joins the household of Ranjan Salgado, a marine biologist studying the changing coral reef, an allegory for his own household and country. Rising through the ranks, he is left in charge of the household, doing everything for the master to whom he is devoted, especially his cooking, which helps win over Nili, the lady of the house. Set against the disintegrating political situation in Sri Lanka, *Reef* also evokes the beauty of a spoiled paradise.

The Hamilton Case (2005)
Michelle de Kretser

Oxford-educated Sam Obeysekere practices law in 1930s' Ceylon. When a planter is found murdered, Sam is assigned the case. Clearing two natives of the crime, he charges an Englishman with murder instead and in doing so opens a can of worms.

Anil's Ghost (2000)
Michael Ondaatje

Award-winning novelist Michael Ondaatje sets his novel in Sri Lanka. Forensic anthropologist Anil Tessera returns to her native land after years away to find a country torn apart by civil war and littered with mass graves. With the help of an archaeologist she uncovers bodies and inadvertently becomes involved in the murder, betrayal and war waged by her government and country.

Funny Boy (1994)
Shyam Selvadurai

Sri Lankan–Canadian Selvadurai's gorgeous first novel is a coming-of-age treat about a young boy growing up gay in Sri Lanka. As Arjun deals with his sexuality, he also has to cope with his family and the growing uncertainty of a country on the brink of civil war. The novel won Selvadurai the Books in Canada First Novel Award in 1994.

Mosquito (2008)
Roma Tearne

A moving love story set in war-torn Sri Lanka and Venice, Tearne's novel sees artist Theo Samarajeeva returning to his country after the death of his wife, Anna. Here he meets and falls in love with 16-year-old Nulani. As the country's political situation explodes, Theo is betrayed and tortured.

Non-fiction

Running in the Family (1982)
Michael Ondaatje

Ondaatje's travelogue tells of his journey back to Sri Lanka in the late 1970s, where he traces the lives of his Dutch–Ceylonese family.

TAIWAN

Fiction

The Butcher's Wife (1986)
Li Ang

This gripping novel is based on the true story of a young woman who murders her brutal husband in a coastal Taiwanese town.

A Thousand Moons on a Thousand Rivers (1980)
Hsiao Li-Hung

A Taiwanese best-seller when it was first published, this book tells of love and family in a small town in the south of the country.

TIBET

Fiction

Red Poppies: A Novel of Tibet (1998)
Alai

An epic tale set in the first half of the 20th century, *Red Poppies* follows the rise and fall of a chieftain.

Tintin in Tibet (1960)
Hergé

Sometimes *Tintin* books make the best travel companions. This book finds Tintin and faithful canine companion Snowy travelling through the Himalayas in search of their Chinese friend Chang Chong-Chen, whose plane has crashed.

Stick Out Your Tongue (2006)
Ma Jian

Written shortly after Ma Jian's travels around China, this book, which provides a lot of description of the region and its people, focuses on a Chinese writer who travels to Tibet after the failure of his marriage.

🔍 China – *Red Dust*

Non-fiction

My Tibet (1990)
Dalai Lama XIV

One of the world's most renowned spiritual leaders, the 14th Dalai Lama provides essays in this book illustrated by Galen Rowell's dramatic images.

THAILAND

Fiction

Bangkok 8 (2002)
John Burdett

The first in a series featuring Buddhist Sonchai Jitpleecheep, a detective in the Royal Thai force, sees him investigating the murder of a US marine in Bangkok. Fast-paced, the book races through the underbelly of the city.

The Beach (1996)
Alex Garland

Garland's successful debut novel is narrated by Richard, a backpacker who is given a map to the perfect beach by a man who commits suicide. He sets off with a young French couple to find it. But does perfection exist?

🎬 *The Beach* (2000), starring Leonardo diCaprio

Sightseeing (2004)
Rattawut Lapcharoensap

This collection of stories, published when the author was in his mid-20s, brings the real Thailand to life.

VIETNAM

Fiction

The Lover (1984)
Marguerite Dumas

Dumas's poignant novel, which won her the Prix Goncourt, is set in the

Indochina that the author herself grew up in. It tells of a passionate affair between a young French girl and a Chinese man in 1930s' Saigon.

The Quiet American (1955)
Graham Greene

Greene's classic tale of innocence and betrayal in war tells of a foreign correspondent, a young American idealist and the woman who comes between them. Fowler has been covering the war for a couple of years, living with his young mistress, reportedly the most beautiful girl in Saigon, when Alden Pyle arrives to upset the status quo, in more ways than one.

🎥 *The Quiet American* (2002), starring Michael Caine and Brendan Fraser

Memories of a Pure Spring (2000)
Duong Thu Huong

Set during and after the Vietnam War, dissident Duong Thu Huong tells the story of Suong, a young peasant girl, who meets and marries Hung, joining his travelling troop. After the war, he loses his job and their life begins to unravel.

The Sorrow of War: A Novel of North Vietnam (1991)
Bao Ninh

This semi-autobiographical account tells of the dreadful reality of a soldier fighting in the Vietnam War. A poignant and often moving tale, it won the 1994 Independent Foreign Fiction Award.

The Things They Carried (1990)
Tim O'Brien

Mixing memoir with short stories, O'Brien's account of the soldiers involved in the Vietnam War has been highly acclaimed.

Non-fiction

Dispatches (1977)
Michael Herr

Herr's classic book is considered by many to be the best account of the Vietnam War. Herr, who was a journalist for *Esquire* magazine, was the first writer to really capture the feel of the conflict and how it differed from other wars.

AUSTRALASIA

Australia | New Zealand

Pacific Islands

AUSTRALIA

GENERAL
Fiction

Voss (1957)
Patrick White

Nobel Prize-winner Patrick White has been described as Australia's greatest writer. His books often depict the vastness of the Australian landscape and *Voss* is possibly one of his best. The book explores the relationship between the main protagonist, after whom the book is named, and Laura, whom Voss meets just before embarking on a journey across Australia and about whom he thinks as he travels across the continent from east to west. Voss's life is based on that of German explorer Ludwig Leichhardt (1813–48), who also crossed the continent.

Non-fiction

The Fatal Shore (1987)
Robert Hughes

Hughes's account of Britain's settlement of Australia as a penal colony is widely considered a scholarly masterpiece. Focusing on the period from the 1770s to the white settlement of the country by the mid-19th century, *The Fatal Shore* examines many of the historic, social and cultural issues that have helped make Australia the country it is today.

A Secret Country (1992)
John Pilger

In this fascinating book, journalist John Pilger chooses his homeland as his subject matter. Writing both with great affection and also a critical eye, Pilger exposes an Australia not often revealed to the public, in which race and class and the struggle for power are still major issues.

🛜 http://www.johnpilger.com/page.asp?partid=1 (author website)

MELBOURNE
Fiction

Monkey Grip (1977)
Helen Garner

Set in Melbourne in the 1970s, Helen Garner's lyrically written novel *Monkey Grip* follows Nora as she copes with her desperate relationship with heroin addict Javo. The harder the couple try to pull away from each other, the tighter the monkey grips.

Reunion (2009)
Andrea Goldsmith

Twenty years after leaving university, four friends are reunited in Melbourne. Beautiful Ava, the novelist, mediocre academic Jack, who loves her, Helen, a brilliant scientist and Connie, a philosopher, all come together, along with Ava's husband Harry, and in meeting raise questions about their own lives and their relationships with each other.

My Brother Jack (1964)
George Johnston

The first in a trilogy written by Johnston – *My Brother Jack* (1964), *Clean Straw for Nothing* (1969) and *A Cartload of Clay* (1971) – the book has been hailed as one of the best Australian novels of the 20th century. Set between the First and Second World Wars, the series is a good depiction of Australian society and history during that period. The first book follows brothers David and Jack Meredith as they cope with the return of their war-scarred father from the First World War (1914–18).

Three Dollars (1998)
Elliot Perlman

How does a man who seemingly has everything find himself with three dollars in his pocket, set to lose everything? Perlman's highly entertaining black comedy, set in the Melbourne of the 1990s, charts the rise and fall of Eddie Harnovey.

📽 *Three Dollars* (2005), screenplay by Perlman

The Getting of Wisdom (1910)
Henry Handel Richardson

Nom de plume of Ethel Florence Lindsay Richardson, Henry Handel Richardson is considered to be one of Australia's finest novelists. This book, published in 1910, is based on the author's experiences at boarding school in Melbourne, where Richardson's protagonist Laura is also sent to study at the age of 12. Given to romanticizing and daydreaming, Laura receives a shock as she is forced to face the reality of life in the school and later the loss of her own innocence.

📽 *The Getting of Wisdom* (1978)

On The Beach (1957)
Nevil Shute

This apocalyptic vision of the end of the world is perhaps an unusual book for Nevil Shute to have written but it is arguably one of his best. Set in Melbourne, the plot follows a group of people who are essentially waiting to die. Radioactive winds set off by a nuclear event that occurred several months before are heading for Australia. Shute focuses on Peter and Mary Holmes and their friend, Moira, whose way of coping is to drink to forget the impending doom. A US submarine captain, Dwight, arrives and invites Peter to go an exploratory mission with him to find out who or what might be still alive. The mission is a disaster and, as the radioactive winds approach, Moira and Dwight enter into a complicated relationship.

📽 *On The Beach* (1959) starring Ava Gardner (Moira) and Gregory Peck (Dwight), was nominated for several Oscars

📶 http://aso.gov.au/titles/home-movies/beach-home-movie-filming-1959/clip1/ (the Australian Screen Archive features some interesting footage of filming *On the Beach* in the waters of Canadian Bay, Mount Eliza, Victoria)

🔍 *A Town like Alice*

Non-fiction

More Please (1992)
Barry Humphries

Derived from the author's 'first coherent utterance', this memoir covers Humphries's childhood in suburban Melbourne and his often-spectacular rebellions against his very respectable upbringing, first as a follower of Dadaism and then in his adoption of the stage personas Barry McKenzie, Sir Les Patterson and Dame Edna Everage, which gained Humphries international acclaim. Frequently outrageous and always entertaining, *More Please* also contains penetrating comments on post-Second World War Australian society. The book concludes with personal reminiscences from a number of the author's friends, including Patrick White, John Betjeman and C. K. Stead.

VICTORIA

Fiction

True History of the Kelly Gang (2001)
Peter Carey

Set in the bleak settler area north of Sydney, this book is a great depiction of colonial life in 19th-century Australia. Carey tells the story of real-life outlaw and folk hero Ned Kelly, who was hanged in Melbourne in 1880, aged 25. Told in the first person, in the form of a letter written by the man to his unknown daughter, *True History of the Kelly Gang* is a detailed and evocative account of the man who became known as 'Australia's Robin Hood'. The book won the Booker Prize in 2001.

Picnic at Hanging Rock (1967)
Joan Lindsay

Probably more famous for the eerily evocative Peter Weir film of the same name (1975), *Picnic at Hanging Rock* focuses on the disappearance of four girls during a picnic at the real-life site near Mount Macedon in Victoria on St Valentine's Day in 1900. Part of a group of schoolgirls from the prestigious Appleyard College, the girls vanish without any explanation. Originally the book included a chapter providing a solution to the disappearances but this wasn't published in book form in 1967, prompting much speculation about what actually happened to the girls. Weir's film version was shot on location in Victoria and also features Martindale Hall in Mardindale, South Australia, as Appleyard College.

Picnic At Hanging Rock (1975)

The Broken Shore (2005)
Peter Temple

Fleeing the big city and his last case, homicide detective Joe Cashin returns to the coastal Victorian town where he grew up to lick his wounds. But when a local man is murdered and ugly prejudices and tensions come to the fore, Cashin is forced to take the lead again to find out who is the real murderer. A tightly written book, *The Broken Shore* has been called one of 'those watershed books that makes you rethink your ideas about reading', according to the *Sydney Morning Herald*.

CANBERRA
Fiction

The White Tower (2003)
Dorothy Johnston

Set in Canberra, the plot follows computer consultant Sandra Mahoney as she investigates the suspicious suicide of a teenage boy. Niall had been playing an online role-playing game and his virtual character had just been killed off; he had also recently been dumped by his girlfriend, so he had reasons to throw himself off the Telstra Tower, but Mahoney soon begins to suspect that all is not what it seems and that Niall's death may just have been murder.

📶 http://www.dorothyjohnston.com.au/index.html (author website)

Dead Set (2006)
Kel Robertson

Dead Set introduces the wisecracking Brad Chen. An Aussie of Chinese descent, Chen was a professional sportsman but is now an inspector in the Australian Federal Police. Battling with alcohol and drug problems, and hindered by a broken leg, Chen has to solve the murder of the unpopular federal minister for immigration.

📶 http://kelrobertson.net.au/main/page_home.html (author website)

SYDNEY
Fiction

Legacy (2009)
Larissa Behrendt

Simone has two lives: her life in Harvard where she's studying and her life back home in Sydney, where her father is a leading Aboriginal civil rights activist. When her father's secrets come to the fore, Simone is forced to question their relationship.

Oscar and Lucinda (1988)
Peter Carey

Set in mid-1800s' Australia for the most part, Carey's acclaimed novel won several awards following its publication in 1988, including the Miles Franklin Award and Booker Prize for that year. It follows the story of Oxford clergyman Oscar Hopkins and orphaned heiress Lucinda Leplastrier, who are polar opposites in every way – apart from their shared passion for gambling. When Oscar travels to Sydney by boat he meets Lucinda, who is on her way back from England, where she has been trying to buy machinery for her glass factory. Lucinda dreams of building a church made of glass and bets Oscar that he cannot transport it across the harsh and unyielding landscape of the Australian bush.

🎬 *Oscar and Lucinda* (1997) directed by Gillian Armstrong, starring Ralph Fiennes and Cate Blanchett

🔍 *Bliss*

Puberty Blues (1979)
Kathy Lette and Gabrielle Carey

A semi-autobiographical look at teenage life in Sydney in the 1970s, this book was written by Lette and Carey when they were teens themselves and it immediately became a cult hit, spawning a film of the same name. In hilarious and sometimes painful detail, Lette and Carey tell of drink, drugs and surfer sex in the southern suburbs of Sydney.

🎬 *Puberty Blues* (1981)

📶 http://www.kathylette.com/ (author website)

Looking For Alibrandi (1992)
Melina Marchetta

A coming-of-age story, *Looking for Alibrandi* became a best-seller on its publication. Seventeen-year-old Josephine has a lot on her plate: teased by her snooty classmates about her illegitimacy and her mixed Australian– Italian background, her life is further complicated by the arrival of her father and the two boys she's involved with and the problems those relationships bring.

🎬 *Looking For Alibrandi* (2000), screenplay by Marchetta

Fetish (1999)
Tara Moss

Struggling Canadian model Makedde (Mak) Vanderwall turns up in Sydney to visit her friend, Catherine, only to find that she's the most recent victim of the Stiletto Murderer, the city's latest serial killer. As Mak struggles to find out who killed her friend, she also has to outwit the murderer, who has her in his sights as his next victim. Mak also features in other Moss books, such as *Split* (2003).

The Harp in the South (1948)
Ruth Park

This novel by New Zealand-born writer Park depicts the lives of an Australian Irish–Catholic family who live in Surry Hills, Sydney, which in the 1940s was an inner city slum. Hughie and Mumma Darcy live in Plymouth Street, Surry Hills, with their two teenage daughters, Roie, a factory worker, and Dolour, who is still at school. Tenants in the Darcy home include a Protestant Irishman, Patrick Diamond, Miss Sheily and her adult, mentally disabled son, Johnny.

Riders in the Chariot (1961)
Patrick White

Set in the fictional Australian suburb of Sarsaparilla, widely believed to be Castle Hill, Sydney, *Riders in the Chariot* follows four interconnected characters – Mary Hare, an elderly spinster, Alf Dubbo, a half-Aboriginal artist, Mordecai Himmelfarb, former professor and survivor of the Holocaust, and Ruth Godbold, a poor housewife.

Non-fiction

Searching for the Secret River (2007)
Kate Grenville

The Secret River was one of the most acclaimed books of 2006 and is based on Grenville's own family history. In this 'book behind the book', Grenville tells us how she came to write her acclaimed novel; she looks back to the life and times of her great-great-great grandfather, following him between London and Sydney.

🔍 New South Wales – *A Town like Alice*

Unreliable Memoirs (1979)
Clive James

Journalist and broadcaster Clive James's memoir of growing up in suburban Sydney is still viewed by some critics as one of the funniest autobiographies of the 20th century. The book follows James's life from his school to college days.

📶 http://www.clivejames.com/ (author website)

NEW SOUTH WALES
Fiction

Eucalyptus (1998)
Murray Bail

This lyrical fable set in modern times tells the story of a man named Holland who moves with his daughter to a remote farm in New South Wales, where he collects hundreds of varieties of eucalyptus. When his daughter grows into a beauty of great repute, he decides to bestow her hand on the man who can name all the different species of tree. In true fairytale style, many suitors come to claim Ellen's hand but only a botanist is able to name them all. In the meantime, Ellen falls under the spell of a stranger who tells her stories and brings the different trees to life. Bail's beautifully

Eleanor Dark's The Timeless Land (1941)

Dark published 10 novels during her lifetime, three of which – *The Timeless Land* (1941), *Storm of Time* (1948) and *No Barrier* (1953) – dealt with the early British settlement of Australia from 1788 to 1813. Dark, perhaps unusually for her time, wrote about the white colonization of the country in *The Timeless Land*, not just from a white but also from an Aboriginal viewpoint, presenting what she believed was a true history of the people – black and white, convict and settler, and men and women. Others agreed with her as the book became an instant best-seller. Dark believed that the Australian landscape moulded people and her books are full of vivid descriptions of the land and countryside. Dark wrote many of her books at Varuna, the home she shared with her husband Eric, in the town of Katoomba in the beautiful Blue Mountains of New South Wales. It was from here that she also corresponded with many of the leading female authors of the time, including Stella Miles Franklin. Today Varuna is Australia's leading writing centre.

➕ http://www.varuna.com.au/ (Varuna is situated in Katoomba, in the World Heritage Area of the Blue Mountains, about 110 km (70 miles) from Sydney)

written book is a celebration of Australia and the Australian landscape through the device of the national tree.

The Sundowners (1951)
John Cleary

The Sundowners follows the trials and tribulations of a roaming sheep drover family, the Carmodys, in Australia in the 1920s. Whereas Paddy Carmody is someone who loves to sleep where the sun goes down, his wife and young son weary of the nomadic life they lead and want to settle down. This is an affectionate and loving account of life in Australia's open and empty countryside. The Sundowners was turned into a film by Fred Zimmermann (of High Noon and From Here to Eternity fame) in 1960 and was filmed on location largely in New South Wales. Probably Zimmermann's finest film, it was largely overlooked as the studio didn't believe that anyone would flock to see a film set in a largely unknown country – Australia in 1960 – despite the pulling power of its stars.

🎬 The Sundowners (1960), starring Robert Mitchum, Deborah Kerr and Peter Ustinov

My Brilliant Career (1901)
Miles Franklin

The first book written by Franklin, while still a teenager, My Brilliant Career was published in 1901. Protagonist Sybilla Melvyn lives on a rural farm in New South Wales with her parents. Although she loves the Australian landscape she longs for a more exciting life. Her wishes are answered when her grandmother invites Sybilla to live with her. She accepts and her life and dreams are brought into question when she meets Harry Beecham. Made into an acclaimed film by Gillian Armstrong in 1979, My Brilliant Career has become an Australian classic.

🎬 My Brilliant Career (1979), starring Judy Davis and Sam Neill

The Secret River (2006)
Kate Grenville

Grenville's award-winning book follows protagonist William when he is transported from London to New South Wales. William escapes a life of hard labour by winning emancipation. He rows up river and claims 40 ha (100 acres) of land in Hawkesbury that is already populated by Aborigines. The Secret River charts the new life of William and his family in Australia, an emerging country dealing with a clash between two very different cultures, old and new.

🔍 Sydney – Searching for the Secret River

The Chant of Jimmy Blacksmith (1972)
Thomas Keneally

Keneally is one of Australia's best-known authors, although readers will possibly know him best for Schindler's Ark, made into an Oscar-winning film by Steven Spielberg. The Chant of Jimmy Blacksmith is based on the real-life story of Jimmy Governor, a controversial figure in the turn of the

20th-century Australian society. Of mixed parentage, half-Aborigine and half-white, Governor suffered severe racism and prejudice when he married a white woman in New South Wales. After killing nine people, Governor became a renowned figure. Keneally's Jimmy is a much more sympathetic character than the real-life Governor and the book examines many key issues to do with the treatment of Aborigines in Australian society.

🎬 *The Chant of Jimmy Blacksmith* (1978)

BRISBANE
Fiction

Zigzag Street (1996)
Nick Earls

Earls is a Brisbane-based writer, whose novels are set in his city. Named after the road in the suburb of Red Hill, *Zigzag Street* focuses on six weeks in the life of 28-year-old singleton Richard Derrington.

📶 http://www.nickearls.com/
nicknews.html (author website)

Johnno (1975)
David Malouf

Semi-autobiographical, *Johnno* was David Malouf's first novel. Set in Brisbane, *Johnno* evokes with great nostalgia the subtropical city of the 1940s and 1950s. Malouf describes the Brisbane of his youth, including the verdant parklands, gardens, river and tramlines (now defunct) with great nostalgia. In 2004

Johnno shared the One Book One Brisbane award, as the book that most summed up Brisbane, with Rebecca Sparrow's *The Girl Most Likely*.

The Girl Most Likely (2003)
Rebecca Sparrow

In her extremely funny and witty first novel, Sparrow draws on many of her experiences growing up in Brisbane. *The Girl Most Likely* finds 27-year-old Rachel back where she started, in her parents' home, wondering how it came to this. The girl with the most promise – the one that everyone pinned their hopes on – Rachel has abandoned her travel-writer career to marry her Mr Right in Las Vegas, only for everything to go wrong. Brisbane is integral to Sparrow's book and she litters it with references to real-life locations such as RE (The Royal Exchange Hotel) and Indooroopilly Shopping Town.

QUEENSLAND
Fiction

Remembering Babylon (1993)
David Malouf

Remembering Babylon deals with the relationship between the white colonizers and the Aboriginal community in 1840s' Queensland. When a young boy, Gemmy Fairley, who was rescued and brought up by Aborigines for 16 years, walks out of the outback into a European settlement, he is treated with suspicion.

Barely able to speak English, Gemmy evokes fear in many of the settlers, who have to cope with the presence of the unsettling newcomer to their community. Malouf's novel conjures up not just the atmosphere of 19th-century Queensland but much of the hostility and suspicion with which the settlers viewed Aborigines – feelings that still exist to this day.

🔍 New South Wales –
The Chant of Jimmy Blacksmith

The Thorn Birds (1977)
Colleen McCullough

McCullough's hugely popular book *The Thorn Birds* is set, for the most part, in the sweeping Australian outback on a fictional sheep station called Drogheda. It follows the fated relationship between Meggie Cleary and a Roman Catholic priest. Forced to choose between Meggie and the Church, Father Ralph de Bricassart chooses the latter, eventually rising through its ranks to become a cardinal. Meggie marries a de Bricassart lookalike and moves to Queensland, before finally returning to Drogheda, where she brings up her daughter.

📺 *The Thorn Birds* (1983)

DARWIN
Fiction

Maestro (1989)
Peter Goldsworthy

Set in Darwin (described by one of the characters as 'a town populated by men who had run as far as they could flee'), Peter Goldsworthy's novel *Maestro* explores aspiring pianist Peter Crabbe's relationship with his music teacher, the maestro, a Viennese refugee.

Territory (2003)
Judy Nunn

At the heart of *Territory*, written by actor Judy Dunn and set against the backdrop of Darwin, lies a priceless locket, originally commissioned by a Dutch noblewoman in the 16th century. Through a shipwreck off the Western Australian coast, the locket ends up in the hands of one of the survivors, who is found washed up on the mainland by some Aborigines who take him in and help him to survive. *Territory* follows the course of the locket and the fortunes of the Galloway clan.

📶 http://www.judynunn.com.au
(author website)

NORTHERN TERRITORY
Fiction

Walkabout (1959)
James Vance Marshall

Marshall's classic *Walkabout* tells the story of Mary and Peter, the survivors of a plane crash, who are found and helped by a young Aborigine on his walkabout through the Sturt Plain in the Northern Territory. Through a clash of white and Aboriginal cultures, misunderstandings occur between them and tragedy strikes. *Walkabout* features long lyrical descriptions of the desert, nature and wildlife. It is a lovely evocation of the Australian outback and is a favourite childhood book of many readers. Nicolas Roeg made a movie of the book in 1971, starring Jenny Agutter as Girl (Mary) and his son, Luc, as White Boy (Peter).

🎥 *Walkabout* (1971)

PERTH

Fiction

Cloudstreet (1991)
Tim Winton

Set in the period between the end of the Second World War (1939–45) and the 1960s, *Cloudstreet* follows the lives and fortunes of two families, the Lambs and the Pickles, who escape the city to share a rundown house on the wrong side of the tracks in Perth. Winton, who is from Perth, presents his story of two very decent families with an affection for Western Australia that is almost palpable.

🔍 *Dirt Music* (2001)

WESTERN AUSTRALIA

Fiction

Red Dog (2001)
Louis de Bernières

When author Louis de Bernières came across a bronze statue of a dog in Karratha, north of Perth, little did he know that the dog had already inspired two biographies. De Bernières was so amazed by the story of the beloved and intrepid Red Dog that he wrote this fictionalized account of the Red Cloud Kelpie, who became a legend during his short life in 1970s' Western Australia.

Jasper Jones (2009)
Craig Silvey

Set in the fictional town of Corrigon, Craig Silvey's second novel is an amalgam of several country towns that he knows, including Dwellingup, the idyllic town in south-west Western Australia, where his parents owned an orchard. A coming-of-age story, the book focuses on the relationship between the older mixed-race Jasper Jones and 13-year-old Charlie Bucktin and his best friend Jeffrey Lu, all growing up in Australia in the mid-1960s. It has been compared to *To Kill A Mockingbird* and deals with many of the same issues, including racism and the small town fear of the outsider.

Breath (2008)
Tim Winton

Winner of the 2009 Miles Franklin Award for Literature, *Breath* is set in a tiny sawmilling town in Western Australia. The book follows 12-year-old Bruce Pike, 'Pikelet', who longs to be down on the beach but for some reason is forbidden from doing so by his parents. When he befriends local wild child Loonie, this all changes. The two boys fall under the spell of older surfer Sando. Initially they just watch, but gradually they are seduced by the 'primary thrill' of surfing, which takes them beyond their initial fear and leads them to take more and more chances, until they surf the huge waves farther out to sea where the sharks lie in wait.

Non-fiction

Follow the Rabbit-Proof Fence (1996)
Doris Pilkington

During the 1930s, under Western Australia's removal policy, in which children of mixed white and Aboriginal parentage were removed from their homes and transported to camps where they were educated to forget their native culture, Molly, Gracie and Daisy were taken from their Aboriginal home and transported thousands of kilometres away. This true-life account by Molly's daughter is the story of the sisters' escape and their 1,600 km- (995 mile) walk back home.

🎬 *Rabbit-Proof Fence* (2002)

TASMANIA

Fiction

The Sound of One Hand Clapping (1997)
Richard Flanagan

In 1954, when Sonja Buloh was three, her Slovenian immigrant mother Maria walked out of their home in a construction camp in the Tasmanian highlands into a blizzard never to return. Tasmanian writer Flanagan tells the poignant and powerful story of Sonja, as she returns to Tasmania, decades later, to face her drunken father and her past.

The World Beneath (2009)
Cate Kennedy

Acclaimed short-story writer Kennedy's first novel, *The World Beneath* is a lyrical and thoughtful exploration of relationships set against the remote Tasmanian landscape. Sandy and Rich met while protesting the proposed Franklin Dam in Tasmania in the 1980s, but the only thing they share now is their 15-year-old daughter, Sophie. When Rich, who has been absent from Sophie's life, suggests a bonding father-and-daughter trek to Tasmania, he sets off a chain of events that no one could have foreseen.

English Passengers (2000)
Matthew Kneale

Kneale's novel is a grim but often funny look at late 19th-century Tasmanian history. When Captain Illiam Quillian Kewley is forced to put his boat up for charter, the only takers are two Englishmen, both with their hearts set on going to Tasmania, but for very different reasons. One believes that it is the Garden of Eden and the other wants to explore his theories on race. In Tasmania, an Aborigine named Peevay recounts his people's struggle against the new settlers, little knowing that the English passengers approach.

Non-fiction

In Tasmania (2004)
Nicholas Shakespeare

Proclaiming Tasmania, the most beautiful place he had seen on earth, writer Nicholas Shakespeare moved his family to the island in 1999. There, he discovered that he was descended from Anthony Fenn Kemp, an early pioneer, and through his letters, Shakespeare discovers and recounts a period of Tasmanian history in which settler and Aborigine warred against each other with tragic results.

NEW ZEALAND

GENERAL

Fiction

Once Were Warriors (1990)
Alan Duff

Set in the fictional town of Two Lakes, but based on Rotorua, where Duff grew up, *Once Were Warriors* is a brutal examination of Maori life in contemporary New Zealand. Beth is married to Jake and lives with him and their five children in a slum. Jake is unemployed and spends most of his days drinking with his mates and nights beating his wife. When Grace, their daughter, hangs herself, Beth reads her diary and discovers the reason for it, triggering off a series of dreadful events.

 Once Were Warriors (1994)

The Plumb Trilogy (omnibus, 1995)
Maurice Gee

Possibly one of New Zealand's most loved authors, Maurice Gee's trilogy of books – *Plumb* (1978), *Meg* (1981) and *Sole Survivor* (1983) – follows three generations of the Plumb family. In *Plumb* the main character, clergyman George Plumb, is introduced. *Meg* follows George's daughter as she battles with life and the world wars. Finally, in *Sole Survivor*, we follow George's grandson's life. Gee often sets his books in Henderson, west of Auckland, where he grew up. In the trilogy, Henderson becomes Loomis. The books were enormously popular on publication.

Potiki (1986)
Patricia Grace

Grace's lyrical book about a coastal Maori community under threat is considered by many to be a modern classic. When developers move into the area, they want to resettle the Maoris living there, leading to a clash between the traditional indigenous culture and the push for development.

The Bone People (1984)
Keri Hulme

Keri Hulme's first novel almost didn't make it to publication. Hulme approached pretty much every publisher in New Zealand, most of whom rejected it out of hand; the few who did consider it wanted substantial re-edits. Finally, a small feminist press published the story and the rest – as they say – is history. Winner of the 1984 Booker Prize, *The Bone People* is a book you either love or hate. Essentially the book revolves around three people: the narrator, Keriwin Holmes, a painter who can't paint; Simon, a boy who can't speak; and Jo, the part-Maori man who finds Simon after he is shipwrecked on the South Island. Although Jo loves Simon, he is often violent towards him and the brutality of the book is sometimes very shocking. Hulme describes lyrically and lovingly her country's coast and also weaves Maori myth and legend into her complex story.

Whale Rider (1987)
Witi Ihimaera

Although Witi Ihimaera was inspired to write *Whale Rider* while living in New York, completing it in three weeks, the book is pure New Zealand. It evokes the tribal myth of the Maori of Whangara, where Ihimaera's people come from. According to legend, Paikea, one of the royal sons of Hawaiki, came to the North Island on the back of a whale. In *Whale Rider*, Maori chief Koro Apirana rules his family – his delightful wife, Nanny Flowers, and his grandsons Porourangi and Rawiri – with an iron hand. When Porourangi has a female child, who is named after the original Whale Rider, Koro deems her useless, but the rest of the family don't agree. Kahu loves her grandfather, Koro, but is hurt by his rejection of her even though she understands some of the reasons for his attitude. When a whale comes to the coast, Kahu has her opportunity to prove that she is worthy of him and her name. Ihimaera subverts the legend to have Kahu, a girl, ride the whale. Turned into an award-winning film in 2002, the movie was shot in the tiny beachside township of Whangara on the Gisborne and Eastland coast.

🎬 *Whale Rider* (2002)

The Book of Secrets (1987)
Fiona Kidman

Kidman lived in Waipu, where *The Book of Secrets* is set, as a child and bases her story on a group of Nova Scotians who settled in the area in the 1850s. Kidman's book follows three generations of women from Scotland to New Zealand via Canada. The settlers, who are dispossessed during the Highland Clearances of Scotland, follow the charismatic preacher Norman McLeod across the Atlantic to settle in Nova Scotia, where they live for 40 years. However, some of them want an easier life and petition to go to New Zealand. The community at Waipu is the result.

The New Zealand Stories (1997)
Katherine Mansfield

One of New Zealand's most celebrated writers, Mansfield wrote about her native land in many short stories. Collected together here for the first time and arranged in order of writing, the stories show Mansfield's unique talent for detail and are a window into politics and society of that time and place – particularly the stories based in Wellington, where Mansfield lived and was schooled as a child. Visitors can go to Te Puakitanga, the house where Mansfield grew up in Wellington. The gardens, of which Mansfield was particularly fond, are described in such stories as 'Prelude' and 'The Garden Party'.

➕ http://www.katherinemansfield.com/ (Te Puakitanga)

Vintage Murder (1937)
Ngaio Marsh

The *New York Times* called Dame Ngaio Marsh 'New Zealand's best-known literary figure'. Certainly her books, featuring aristocratic detective Roderick Alleyn and his artist wife, Troy, have put her on the map as a crime writer of distinction. Marsh wrote 32 books featuring Allen, which are mostly set in England. Four were set in her native New Zealand, including *Vintage Murder*. Seconded to New Zealand, Chief Inspector Allen finds himself investigating a murder in a touring theatre group. Did the beautiful leading lady kill her husband? Was it her lover? Or someone altogether different? Classic stuff! Visitors can see the house where Marsh lived from the age of 10 in Christchurch, New Zealand. Built by Samuel Hurst Seager, the house is today a showcase for Marsh's work as a crime writer, theatre producer and painter.

 http://www.ngaio-marsh.org.nz/ (author's house)

The Denniston Rose (2003)
Jenny Pattrick

Pattrick's novel is set in the coal-mining settlement of Denniston, in the 1880s. Located high on a plateau above the West Coast of the South Island, Denniston can be reached only via the empty coal wagons, which are hauled up the 610 m (2,000 ft) rail incline that takes coal from the Denniston mine down to a railway line on the coast. To the rough and bleak mining settlement come five-year-old Rose and her mother, who both struggle to find a place in the isolated community. *The Denniston Rose* was followed by a sequel, *Heart of Coal* in 2004.

The Stories of Frank Sargeson (2010)
Frank Sargeson

Sargeson was the first New Zealand fiction writer to capture the cadences of the local vernacular in his short stories. Narrated in the first person and usually featuring working-class characters, many of Sargeson's short stories have become classics, including *Conversation with My Uncle*, *A Great Day*, *The Hole that Jack Dug*, and *An Affair of the Heart*. The house where Sargeson lived and wrote for over 50 years, at 14 Esmonde Road, Takapuna, is preserved as a literary museum and can be visited by contacting the Takapuna Public Library.

http://www.bookcouncil.org.nz/ Readers/Book_Lovers_Guide_to_ New_Zealand/Literary%20Sightseeing (author's house)

Non-fiction

Under the Bridge and Over the Moon (1998)
Kevin Ireland

Distinguished New Zealand poet, novelist and short-story writer Kevin Ireland evokes the years of his childhood on the North Shore of Auckland, including his primary schooling at Vauxhall and his secondary education at Takapuna Grammar School. The writer's childhood and family life were severely disrupted by his parents' divorce, and the threat of invasion from the Japanese during the Second World War. In turns heartbreaking and hilarious, the memoir won the Montana New Zealand Book Award for Non-fiction in 1999 and was succeeded by a second volume, *Backwards to Forwards* in 2002.

South-West of Eden, A Memoir: 1932–56 (2010)
C. K. Stead

New Zealand writer, poet and academic C. K. Stead recounts his life from his birth to the time he first left New Zealand in the early 1950s. Aucklander Stead recalls such figures as Frank Sargeson and Janet Frame, and describes a life in which most things of real significance to him and his family 'had happened somewhere in sight from the summit of Mt Eden'.

PACIFIC ISLANDS

GENERAL

Fiction

South Sea Tales (1911)
Jack London

First published in serial form in 1907, Jack London's *South Sea Tales* was subsequently collated as a book in 1911. In typical London style, the eight short stories in this book highlight the beauty and dangers of life on the South Seas, and feature sharks, disease and natural hazards.

South Sea Tales (1996)
Robert Louis Stevenson

When author Robert Louis Stevenson announced at the height of his career in the late 1880s that he was going to travel around the South Seas, most people in the literary world were extremely surprised. This book brings together for the first time Stevenson's short stories about the region. Using different narrative styles, Stevenson examines imperialism and globalism in such stories as *The Beach of Falesa*. Stevenson lived at Villa Vailima near Mount Vaea on the island of Upola, Samoa's second largest

island. Visitors to the region can see his mansion, today a museum dedicated to the writer and his works. Stevenson is buried under the summit of Mount Vaea, facing his beloved house, as he requested.

➕ http://www.fromers.com/destinations/
samoa/A31357.html
(museum and grave)

Mr Fortune's Maggot (1927)
Sylvia Townsend Warner

Warner's beautifully written tale follows bank-clerk-turned-missionary Mr Fortune on his quest to convert the 'immoral children' of Fanua, a tiny island in the Pacific. But there, Mr Fortune finds his own faith tested as he falls for one of his converts, a native boy, Leuil.

PAPUA NEW GUINEA

Fiction

Mister Pip (2007)
Lloyd Jones

Set in the 1990s on the New Guinean tropical island of Bougainville during civil war, *Mister Pip* has a teenage narrator, Matilda. While most white people – including the teachers – have fled Matilda's village, one remains, Mr Watts, or Pop Eye as he is also known. Assuming the responsibility of teaching the children, Mr Watts instils in them a love of Dickens and Matilda falls in love with Pip, the protagonist of *Great Expectations*. Mr Watts also recounts his own story and that of others, transporting the children away from the miseries and brutal reality of rampaging soldiers and war.

SAMOA

Fiction

They Who Do Not Grieve (2001)
Sia Figiel

Figiel's sequel to *Where We Once Belonged* (1996) is a lyrically written tale of three generations of women from families in New Zealand and Samoa. An unfinished tattoo prompts Lalolagi and Tausi to pass on to their granddaughters, Malu and Alofa, many secrets from the past. Figiel invokes the mythic twin sisters who brought the tattoo custom to Samoa as guides for Malu and Alofa.

Stevenson Under the Palm Trees (2000)
Alberto Manguel

Manguel takes Robert Louis Stevenson's last days on Samoa and turns them into this strange but beautifully written and imaginative tale. When Stevenson meets a strange man called Mr Baker on a beach, little does he know the upheaval the stranger will bring to the writer's final days. Mr Baker is a missionary, an outsider, whereas Stevenson is an accepted and welcome part of the local community, many of whom believe his stories are real. Drawing on Stevenson's last letters, Manguel catches the language and tone of the time.

TAHITI

Fiction

Iolani – Or Tahiti As It Was (1991)
Wilkie Collins

Iolani, Collins's first novel, written in 1844, remained unpublished during the author's lifetime. The story of an evil high priest of Oro and Idia, the woman with whom he has a child, *Iolani* contains many of the traits and themes that Collins was to become so famous for – a love of the exotic, mystery and suspense, and also romance. As local custom dictates that the firstborn must be sacrificed, Idia flees from Iolani, taking refuge with another chieftain, but Iolani declares war on the chief, triggering a series of tragic consequences. Collins later declared that his youthful imagination had run riot 'among the noble savages, in scenes which caused the respectable British publishers to declare that it was impossible to put his name on the title page of such a novel,' but as the author did research the book meticulously it does feature quite detailed descriptions of local customs, including infanticide.

Q United Kingdom –*The Moonstone*

The Moon and Sixpence (1919)
W. Somerset Maugham

Based on the life of artist Paul Gauguin, this classic short novel follows Charles Strickland, a middle-aged man who abandons his conventional life to become an artist, first in Paris and Marseille and then on the island of Tahiti, where his work flourishes. Maugham visited Tahiti after the First World War, describing it as 'a lofty green island, with deep folds of darker green, in which you divine silent valleys'.

🎬 *The Moon and Sixpence* (1942)
🔍 *The Painted Veil*
🔍 *http://www.pgcruises.com/ (there are several tours relating to the artist Paul Gauguin. This is a cruise!)*

Breadfruit (2000)
Celestine Hitiura Vaite

Based on Vaite's recollections of growing up in Tahiti, *Breadfruit* is essentially a tale of love in a very exotic location. After 16 years together, Pito comes home one night and asks Materena to marry him. Little does he know that he's opened a can of worms. A warm evocation of the island, *Breadfruit* is Vaite's first novel.

Henderson's Spear (2001)
Ronald Wright

A story within a story, Wright's second novel, *Henderson's Spear*, is framed by protagonist Olivia, a filmmaker. As she waits out her time in a Tahitian prison on a trumped-up charge of murder, Olivia reviews her family's past, including ancestor Frank Henderson who came to Tahiti about 100 years before her. A British naval officer, Henderson undertook an epic three-year voyage to Polynesia with Prince Eddy and Prince George (later George V) that culminates in his time in Tahiti.

EUROPE

Albania | Austria | Belgium | Cyprus | Czech Republic and Slovakia
Denmark | Estonia | Finland | Former Yugoslavia | France
Germany | Greece and the Islands | Greenland | Hungary
Iceland | Ireland | Italy | Latvia | Netherlands | Norway
Poland | Portugal | Romania | Russia | Spain | Sweden
Switzerland | Turkey | United Kingdom

EUROPE

GENERAL

Fiction

The Good Soldier Svejk (1973)
Jaroslav Hasek

Hasek's biting satire *The Good Solder Svejk* follows the comic adventures of an incompetent but very likeable soldier during the First World War as he roams across Central Europe. Written originally in Czech, Hasek's book is a war novel that never really deals with the reality of war. A contemporary of Kafka, Hasek's four-volume work was banned in Nazi Germany and in the newly independent Czechoslovakia. Joseph Heller once said that he would never have written *Catch-22* but for Hasek's work.

Non-fiction

The Balkans, 1804–1999 (2000)
Misha Glenny

Acclaimed journalist Misha Glenny gives a brilliant insight into the history of the Balkans since the 19th century.

In Europe: Travels through the 20th Century (2004)
Geert Mak

In 1999, Dutch journalist Mak spent a year travelling across Europe, writing despatches for his newspaper *NRC Handelsblad*. His subsequent book presents the Continent's history from Verdun to Berlin, Saint Petersburg to Auschwitz, Kiev to Srebrenica. Through accounts from varied sources, such as the diaries of important historic figures and Mak's interviews with such varied people as the grandson of Kaiser Wilhelm II and a guard at the gates of Birkenau camp, and vivid descriptions of the places that he visits, Mak presents the Continent in its past and present days, a region at the end of a turbulent, vibrant century.

🛜 http://www.routeyou.com
(to see some of the author's routes)

Dark Continent: Europe's Twentieth Century (1999)
Mark Mazower

Mazower's brilliant overview of Europe since 1900 provides an account of the major events that shaped the Continent's political, social and cultural order.

Man in Seat 61 (2008)
Mark Smith

A career railway man and traveller, Smith has viewed much of the world, via its train systems from the viewpoint of seat 61. This book gives handy, easy-to-understand advice on traversing the world by train. Smith provides insider tips and advice on routes, as well as explaining why you should choose train travel over air or any other method of transport.

🛜 http://www.seat61.com (official site)

ALBANIA

Fiction

The Albanian Affairs (2003)
Susana Fortes

Spanish writer Fortes's novel tells of a family destroyed by the totalitarian regime in Albania. Victor and Ismail are the sons of a national hero and a Spanish mother who disappeared when they were young boys. Through their story, Fortes provides a good insight into a country under dictatorship and the secrets and social and political complexities that result from such a regime.

Non-fiction

High Albania: A Victorian Traveller's Balkan Odyssey (1909)
Edith Durham

Following an illness and depression, 19th-century traveller Edith Durham set off for the Balkans on the advice of her doctor. Spending most of her time in Albania, in the mountainous regions of the country's north, she cut quite an odd figure in her waterproof Burberry skirt and golf cape, but her love and respect for the region and its local inhabitants were clearly evident and she won the respect of the people. Durham came to be known as the 'Queen of the Mountain People'. *High Albania* is an extremely entertaining account of her journey. It has been reissued as a travel classic.

AUSTRIA

VIENNA

Fiction

The Man Without Qualities (1930–43)
Robert Musil

Set during the demise of the Austro–Hungarian Empire, Musil's three-volume work has been hailed as a masterpiece by such writers as Milan Kundera, even though it was unfinished. The story opens in 1913, when Ulrich, the protagonist, a man without 'qualities' searches for some greater meaning to life.

The Radetsky March (1932)
Joseph Roth

Banned by the Nazis, Roth's *The Radetsky March* examines the lives and fortunes of three generations of the Trotta family. Beginning in 1859 it ends with the demise of the Austro–Hungarian Empire and the end of the First World War. Roth creates great sweeping landscapes and detailed descriptions of location which give this epic tale a realistic geographic and historic frame.

The Fig Eater (2000)
Jody Shields

While investigating the death of Dora, Sigmund Freud's famous patient, who is found with figs in her stomach, an inspector finds his case seemingly hampered by his own wife, Erszebet.

Following The Third Man

Think Vienna, think Orson Welles and Joseph Cotton running through the city's streets, twangy music in the background, and Alida Valli pouting dangerously at the camera. Graham Greene's *The Third Man* sums up post-war Vienna at a time when the city was carved up between the Russians, Americans, British and French, with an international zone to spare. Originally written as a screenplay by Greene, turned into the brilliant 1949 film, *The Third Man* was published in 1950 in book form. The plot revolves around Rollo Martins (Holly in the film, played by Cotton), who is invited to post-war Vienna by old school friend Harry Lime (Welles in the film). Little does he expect to find his friend dead and himself embroiled in the mystery of whether it was murder or an accident. Martins quickly finds out that Vienna is a city in which everyone has a racket and that Lime was the 'worst racketeer who ever made a dirty living.' From Vienna's Central Cemetery, the reader is guided through the city as Martins gradually discovers what happened to his friend. Today, visitors to Vienna can take *The Third Man* tour and visit the places that inspired Greene, the cobbled and hidden courtyards of Old Vienna, the places where Harry Lime lived, disappeared and died and other locations associated with the film.

📺 *The Third Man* (1949), Carol Reed's classic

📶 http://www.viennawalks.com/ (tours)

🔍 United Kingdom, Brighton – *Brighton Rock*; Turkey – The Orient Express: Murder and Intrigue (feature box)

Helped by a young governess, Erszebet conducts a secret investigation into the death – with startling results. Shields, who was a design editor, evokes the Vienna of the early 20th century, lovingly reconstructing the clothes, meals, customs and even the class system of the city at that time.

BELGIUM

Fiction

The Sorrow of Belgium (1983)
Hugo Claus

Seen through the eyes of an adolescent, this book shows the Belgian experience of the Second World War. Louis, returning from school, is dismayed to find how his family deal with the Germans.

Niccolo Rising (1986)
Dorothy Dunnett

Dunnett's classic 'House of Niccolo' series helped establish her reputation internationally. In *Niccolo Rising*, the first book in the series, we meet Claes, a young apprentice, who through plotting and scheming becomes Nicholas de Fleury, the head of a mercantile empire in 15th-century Bruges during its golden age.

📶 http://www.dorothydunnett.co.uk/ (author website)

The Folding Star (1994)
Alan Hollinghurst

The Folding Star is an exploration of desire. Hollinghurst's protagonist Edward Manners moves to a small Flemish town to tutor two boys; he falls for 17-year-old Luc, a boy almost half his age. He also discovers the world of 19th-century Belgian artist Edgard Orst, a man obsessed with his dead lover. Hollinghurst meticulously details life in a small Flemish town.

Antwerp (2004)
Nicholas Royle

A thriller set in the port of Antwerp the book focuses on a film critic, in town to interview an American film director making a film about a surrealist, who is caught up in the deaths of two prostitutes connected to the film. A fast-paced but beautifully put together book, *Antwerp* shows us another side to Belgium, the underworld in which the diamond trade vies with prostitution and murder. The author also pays tribute to cinema, not least through director Harry Kümel, whose films are found near the bodies of the victims.

🎬 *Antwerp* (in production)

Non-fiction

Tall Man in a Low Land (1999)
Harry Pearson

Pearson's account of travelling in Belgium is a humorous and affectionate look at the eccentricities of the Belgians. Immersing himself in the culture, he worked his way through many of the hundreds of types of Belgian beer, ate local delicacies (including chips, of course), and attended many strange places and events, such as Oostduinkerke's Festival of Shrimps in June and the now defunct Underpant Museum in Brussels.

📶 http://www.harrypearson.co.uk/ (author website)

📶 http://www.planetware.com/ oostduinkerke/shrimp-festival-b-wv-prawn.htm (Oostduiinkerke festival website)

CYPRUS

Fiction

Death in Cyprus (1984)
M. M. Kaye

An old-fashioned thriller in the vein of an Agatha Christie novel, *Death in Cyprus* finds Amanda Derrington on a cruise with her uncle. Amanda decides to stop on the lovely island of Cyprus, but murder soon upsets her plans.

🔍 Africa, Kenya – *Death in Kenya*

The Cypriot (2006)
Andreas Koumi

Koumi's beautifully written love story is set in 1950s' Cyprus, at the beginning of the struggle for independence from British rule. To each community freedom and independence means different things. For the Muslim minority, union with Greece spells disaster, but for the Orthodox Christian majority it is the only option. The 1974 invasion by Turkey and the effect it has on the people of Cyprus also feature in the book's plot.

Eat, Drink and Be Married (2005)
Eve Makis

Ana has greater aspirations than the ones her Greek–Cypriot mother has for her. Through her close relationship with her grandmother, Yiayia, who tells her evocative stories of Cyprus, Anna discovers the events that have helped shaped her family and brought them to their current situation.

🛜 http://www.evemakis.com
(author website)

Non-fiction

Bitter Lemons of Cyprus (1957)
Lawrence Durrell

A lyrical, sometimes angry work, Durrell's classic is viewed as one of the best travelogues on Cyprus. His analysis of the island's history, culture, people and politics made while he was living there gives us a fascinating insight into Cyprus during a period of great change as the island's battle for independence really began.

🛜 http://www.lawrencedurrell.org/
(International Lawrence Durrell Society)

CZECH REPUBLIC AND SLOVAKIA

GENERAL
Fiction

I Served the King of England (1971)
Bohumil Hrabal

This comic novel follows protagonist Ditie, the picaresque waiter whose life is used as a frame for the greater political events happening in Czechoslovakia, including the Nazi occupation of the country and the normalization regime of the 1970s and 1980s. Many authors have hailed Hrabal as one of the greatest 20th-century Czech writers.

The Engineer of Human Souls (1984)
Josef Skvorecky

A beautifully written book, *The Engineer of Human Souls* is Skvorecky's comic exploration of Czechoslovakian politics and history, and explores the country during the war and the communist era from the viewpoint of a writer in exile in Canada.

PRAGUE
Fiction

Utz (1989)
Bruce Chatwin

Although perhaps better known for

his travel writing, Chatwin also wrote several novels, including the highly acclaimed *Utz*. An English art historian travels to the Prague of the 1960s and '70s, where he meets the intriguing Baron Kaspar Joachim Utz, a man who has lost most of his wealth and status and lives in a shabby apartment in central Prague along with his wonderful Meissen collection. Allowed to leave the country once a year to go to France, Utz can never take his Meissen with him and so remains a prisoner of his collection and of the state.

The Unbearable Lightness of Being (1984)
Milan Kundera

Kundera's brilliant study of the fragility of life and love is set in Prague in the spring of 1968, where Tomas and Tereza pursue their lives, one as a surgeon, the other as a photographer. Tomas is serially unfaithful but has a favourite mistress, Sabina. When Tomas criticizes the Communist Party, Tomas and Tereza are both forced to face up to the brutal reality of their lives.

🎬 *The Unbearable Lightness of Being* (1988)

The Book of Splendour (2003)
Frances Sherwood

Sherwood's *The Book of Splendour* is set in the 17th century, where Rudolph II is obsessed with obtaining the secret of eternal life. His quest causes many problems for the Jews of Prague and tales begin to stir about a golem, a supernatural being, living in their area. A vivid,

richly detailed book, *The Book of Splendour* is an engaging epic.

Life with a Star (1989)
Jiří Weil

Based on Weil's experiences during the war, this book was originally published in Czechoslovakia, but didn't appear in English until 1989, after Philip Roth championed its translation. It follows the life of Josef Roubicek, a former bank clerk, in Nazi-occupied Prague. One day Josef is forced to wear a yellow star, indicating that he is a Jew, and he realizes that the life and the order that he once enjoyed have all but disappeared.

Non-fiction

The Spirit of Prague (1994)
Ivan Klíma

This collection of essays charts five different decades in the history of Prague as witnessed through the eyes and experiences of the great writer Ivan Klíma.

DENMARK

COPENHAGEN
Fiction

Miss Smilla's Feeling for Snow (1993)
Peter Høeg
First published in Denmark in 1992,

Hans Christian Anderson

It is almost impossible to think of Denmark without conjuring up Hans Christian Anderson and the extraordinary tales that he wrote, mixing fact, fiction and folklore. Although Anderson wrote his tales for adults, it is from our childhoods that we are most familiar with his extremely moral stories such as 'Little Ugly Duckling' and 'The Emperor's New Clothes'. Anderson, who was born into poverty in Odense, on the island on Funen, in 1805, was the son of a shoemaker who believed he was descended from aristocracy, and a washerwoman. Although he had little formal education, Anderson was encouraged by his father in particular to write and put on puppet shows. After his father died, Anderson moved to Copenhagen where he worked in various jobs, finally becoming associated with the Royal Theatre, where he sang, danced and acted. After getting a grant to attend grammar school, Anderson went to university in Copenhagen where he completed his education. He began to write, drawing on folk tales for his initial inspiration, and also began to travel. Although he published several novels, it is for the collections of fairy tales, written between 1835 and 1872, that he made his name. By the third book, Anderson was creating his own stories, including 'The Little Mermaid', 'The Snow Queen' and 'The Princess and the Pea' – only about 12 of his 156 stories were based on folk tales. Anderson's work influenced other writers, including his friend Charles Dickens, the Irish writer Oscar Wilde and fellow Dane Isak Dinesen (Karin Blixen). Visitors to Copenhagen can to go Anderson's various houses at Nyhavn (nos 18, 20 and 67) and see the seated statue of him, holding a book, next to the City Hall of Copenhagen. A statue of the Little Mermaid, a present from the brewer Carl Jacobsen (Carlsberg breweries) to the city in 1913, also greets visitors to the harbour.

➕ http://www.andersen.sdu.dk/index_e.html (Hans Christian Anderson Centre)

this international best-seller was published a year later in English to much critical acclaim. Set initially in Copenhagen, it is essentially a thriller that explores, among other things, the relationship between Denmark and Greenland and the tensions and ethnic problems that that sometimes involves. When her six-year-old neighbour and friend, Isaiah, a Greenland Inuit, falls off the roof of their apartment block, the police rule it an accident, but Smilla knows better. Made into a film starring Julia Ormond in 1997, the opening sequence was filmed in Greenland, where the beauty of the glaciers is contrasted with

Copenhagen, the film's other main location.

🎬 *Smilla's Sense of Snow* (1997)

Music and Silence (1999)
Rose Tremain
Set in the late 1620s, Tremain's acclaimed novel follows English lutenist Peter Claire to the Danish court of King Christian IV, where he is to join the Royal Orchestra. The court is full of conflict, Christian is impoverished and married to a duplicitous, scheming, disloyal woman and the musicians are

treated badly and have to rehearse in dreadful conditions. Peter, himself recovering from an affair with an Italian countess, falls in love with one of the Queen's household.

OTHER REGIONS

Fiction

Lucca (2002)

Jens Christian Grøndahl

After a young actress is involved in a car crash in a provincial Danish town, her doctor tells her that she might never see again. Gradually, they begin to reveal their damaged pasts to each other.

Hamlet (1601/1602)

William Shakespeare

Perhaps not the first work that would spring to mind when thinking of Denmark, but *Hamlet* is, without doubt, one of the most famous plays set in the country. Prince Hamlet of Denmark is urged by his father's ghost to avenge his murder. To complicate matters, Hamlet's mother, Gertrude, has married Claudius, his father's brother and murderer, and the man who has assumed the throne. Hamlet pretends to be mad, even fooling his beloved Ophelia, while he schemes to avenge his father with tragic results. The play is set in Helsingor (Elsinore), north of Copenhagen, where tourists can visit many history sites.

🎬 http://www.gonomad.com/destinations /0607/helsingor.html (Helsingor)

ESTONIA

Fiction

Treading Air (1998)

Jaan Kross

In *Treading Air*, highly acclaimed author Jaan Kross charts protagonist Ullo Paerand's life, through the Second World War and the Soviet occupation of his country.

FINLAND

Fiction

The Kalevala (1835)

Compiled from the oral poetry of the Uralic languages of the first millennia from the Baltic region of Karelia (border of eastern Finland and Russia), *The Kalevala*, like the *Iliad*, *Odyssey* and *Aeneid*, is a great heroic poem. Recorded in the 1830s by Finnish scholar Elias Lonnart it inspired some of the work of the composer Sibelius.

🔍 Greece – Homer's *Iliad* and *Odyssey* (feature box); Italy – *The Aeneid* (feature box)

Wonderful Women by the Water (1994)

Monika Fagerholm

Much-respected novelist Monika Fagerholm's *Wonderful Women by the Water* follows the lives of glamorous mother Isabella, her friend Rosa and their families from the early 1960s to the 1970s.

The Summer Book (1972)
Tove Jansson

Better known perhaps to Western audiences for the beloved 'Moomin' series, Tove Jansson also wrote adult fiction. This novella is set on a small island in the Gulf of Finland, where six-year-old Sophia and her elderly grandmother spend a magical summer. It is a charming evocation of the growing bond between the two, despite the great differences in their ages. The island is based on one of the remote islands that Jansson and her family cultivated.

The 'Moomin' books

Seven Brothers (1870)
Aleksis Kivi

A Finnish classic, Kivi tells of seven brothers forced to fend for themselves when their mother dies. Untamed and unused to following authority, they scamper from mishap to adventure to mishap as they struggle to find their way through life. Kivi was a revered author and visitors can see his statue outside of the Finnish National Theatre in Helsinki.

The Unknown Soldier (1954)
Väinö Linna

Set during the Continuation War (1941–4) between Finland and the Soviet Union, this book tells the story of ordinary Finnish soldiers. Hailed as a classic, it shows the gritty realism of war.

The Year of the Hare (1975)
Arto Paasilinna

A cult book, Paasilinna's *The Year of the Hare* follows the story of Kaarlo Vatanen, a cynical journalist whose life changes when the car he's travelling in hits a hare. Fed up with his wife and his career, Kaarlo decides, after patching up the hare, to give it all up. He sells his boat and travels around the Finnish countryside – with his new-found friend, the hare – taking different jobs here and there and having a series of adventures.

FORMER YUGOSLAVIA

Fiction

The Bridge on the River Drina (1942–3)
Ivo Andric

Andric's chronicle of Visegrad, a town in the eastern part of Bosnia, near the Serbian border, focuses on the bridge over the river Drina, using it to show the history and changes in community mentality from the 16th century, when it was built, to the First World War, when it was destroyed.

http://www.ivoandric.org.yu/index.htm (author website)

Lie in the Dark (1999)
Dan Fesperman

Sarajevo detective Inspector Petric investigates murder in a country in which death and killing are all around him. But Petric has a job to do and it keeps him out of the army, so when the chief of Bosnia's Interior Ministry's special police force is killed and implicated in black market dealings, Petric has to investigate and finds himself entering a minefield. Fesperman's Petric is a man caught in the middle of war, his wife and daughter in exile in Germany, his own background half Muslim, half Catholic.

The Cellist of Sarajevo (2008)
Steven Galloway

Galloway's best-selling novel is set during the Siege of Sarajevo in the 1990s. Focusing on three people, a female sniper, a father and a belligerent neighbour, the characters are linked by a cellist who can be found playing *Adagio in G Minor*, every afternoon, in a crater where 22 people were killed during a mortar attack while waiting to get bread. He vows to play it for as many days as there were victims. The story is based on a real event in May 1992 when Vedran Smailovic, principal cellist of the Sarajevo Opera Orchestra, took up his bow and played for 22 days for the 22 friends and neighbours who had been killed in a mortar attack, despite the mortal danger to himself. Hailed as a hero, the cellist came to stand for courage, bravery and peace.

Made in Yugoslavia (2000)
Vladimir Jokanovic

Set in 1991, during the disintegration of Yugoslavia, the novel focuses on three friends in Osijek, northern Croatia, who are forced to face the reality of war and what their different ethnic backgrounds mean to their lives and their friendship.

🛜 http://www.sf.hr/osijek/osijek.html (Osijek website)

Ministry of Pain (2004)
Dubravka Ugresic

Focusing on the experience of people in exile, *Ministry of Pain* follows a Croatian literature teacher, Tanja Lucic, living in Amsterdam, who tries to teach Serbo–Croatian literature to a group of exiles. She says: 'I was, naturally, well aware of the absurdity of my situation: I was to teach a subject that no longer officially existed.' This book is a beautiful exploration of lost homelands and the experience of those in exile.

Non-fiction

The Fall of Yugoslavia (1996)
Misha Glenny

The third edition of Glenny's stunning book examines the factors that caused the disintegration of this former country. The complex historic, political and geographic background is examined, as well as the factors that resulted in one of the 20th-century's most brutal wars and genocide.

Black Lamb, Grey Falcon: A Journey Through Yugoslavia (1940)
Rebecca West

West's love letter to the region, 'the country I have always seen between sleeping and waking', was written on the cusp of the outbreak of the Second World War. West's book is far more than just a travelogue; it delves into the history of the area and is a snapshot of the politics of the time.

FRANCE

GENERAL

Non-fiction

Detour de France (2010)
Michael Simkins

Actor Michael Simkins spent 12 weeks journeying around France armed with just a smattering of French and with his wife's dire warnings of what would happen to him ringing in his ears. This memoir is the result. An amusing account of Simkins' dealings in and with France and the French, it is a very charming read.

Travels with a Donkey in the Cévennes (1879)
Robert Louis Stevenson

This entertaining account by Robert Louis Stevenson is based on the author's 1878 journey through the Cévennes accompanied by Modestine, a donkey, and a notebook. The book reveals as much about the landscape, the people and the customs of the country as about the author himself.

PARIS AND ENVIRONS

Fiction

Murder in the Marais (1999)
Cara Black

The first in the 'Aimée Leduc' series, *Murder in the Marais* introduces the half-French, half-American computer security investigator, who lives in a charming town house in the Île St Louis. A rabbi hires Aimée to decipher an encrypted photograph and deliver her findings to a woman living in the Marais, the historic Jewish part of the city, but everything changes when Aimée finds her dead. The 'Aimée Leduc' series is set in Paris, largely in the Marais, which San Franciscan-based Black finds the most fascinating area.

📶 http://www.carablack.com/ (author website)

🔍 *Murder in the Latin Quarter*

A Year in the Merde (2004)
Stephen Clarke

British author Stephen Clarke wrote *A Year in the Merde* while living in Paris, initially self-publishing it before it was picked up by a mainstream publisher and became a best-seller. An acerbic, bitterly funny and often unflattering look at the French through the eyes of protagonist Paul West, a Brit with a mission to set up an English tea room in Paris, *A Year in the Merde* gives the other side of the story about living in this beautiful city, such as where it's better to walk in the roads to avoid the mounds of dog poo on the pavements...

Maigret's Paris

Born in Liège, in Belgium, Georges Simenon used Paris as the location for his famous detective Jules Maigret, first introduced as a Chief Inspector in *The Strange Case of Peter the Lett* (1929). Over the next 42 years, Maigret appeared in more than 100 books and short stories.

In the Maigret books, the city is as much a character as the detective himself, as Maigret inhabits its cafes, working men's bistros and backstreets, but the Paris we see is a sanitized one, almost beyond recognition, seen through the eyes of a writer who was a visitor. Maigret fans can follow in the detective's footsteps, although the Paris of today is, for the most part, very different from the one often described in the books. The Les Halles that Simenon sketches for us, for example, is not the concrete shopping centre of today, but instead is the stomach of the city for Maigret. The lovely Places des Voges, with its beautiful geometric arches, as described by the writer, is still recognizable, however. The Brasserie Dauphine, where Maigret eats, didn't exist, but it is thought to have been based on the cafes that Simenon himself frequented, such as the Café Restaurant Aux Trois Marches, which was in the Rue de Harlay. The nearby Taverne Henri IV was also one of Simenon's local haunts; it is situated on the Pont Neuf, just minutes from Maigret's office at 36 Quai des Orfèvres on the Ile de la Cité. The tavern has framed photographs of Simenon and also of the French actor Yves Montand, who lived in the Place Dauphine.

📺 *Maigret* series (1992), starring Michael Gambon

🔍 *Simenon's Paris* by Georges Simenon (1970)

📶 http://www.stephenclarkewriter.com/index.php (author website)

🔍 *Merde Actually*, *Merde Happens* and *In the Merde for Love*

Les Misérables (1862)
Victor Hugo

Possibly one of the best-known books associated with the city, *Les Misérables* is a vivid portrait of the poor and dispossessed in the 19th century. Visitors to Paris can visit various monuments and places linked to the celebrated author, including the house where Hugo lived in the beautiful Place des Vosges, which is today a museum and research centre, and Avenue Victor Hugo. Hugo actually lived in the avenue (formerly named Avenue d'Eylau but retitled on the author's 80th birthday); it is here that a statue of the writer was located until it was destroyed during the Nazi bombing of the city.

➕ http://www.paris.org/Musees/Hugo/ (Maison de Victor Hugo)

The Phantom of the Opera (1910)
Gaston Leroux

Immortalized on film and at the theatre, Leroux's *The Phantom of the Opera* has thrilled audiences around the world. First published in 1910 as a serialization it originally didn't sell that well as a book. It follows the story of Christine, who is given a position in the chorus at the Paris Opera House. She believes that the Angel of Music, who her father told her he would send to her before he died, is speaking to her, but it is, in fact, Erik, a talented composer and musician. Erik is so disfigured that he hides behind a mask. He 'haunts' the building, living in its secret catacombs. He loves Christine but she is torn between Erik and another man, Raoul, who also loves her.

➕ http://www.operadeparis.fr/cns11/live/onp/ (Paris Opera House)

Arc de Triomphe (1946)
Erich Maria Remarque

Set in Paris in the winter of 1938, when the author spent time there himself, and apparently inspired by his love of actress Marlene Dietrich, *Arc de Triomphe* focuses on the many refugees who came to the city, fleeing the Germans. Dr Ravic stalks his enemy Nazi Haake around the city; he meets Joan one stormy night and embarks on a doomed love affair. The book was made into a film in 1948.

🎬 *Arch of Triumph* (1948), starring Ingrid Bergman, Charles Boyer and Charles Laughton

Quartet (1929)
Jean Rhys

Rhys's novel is set in the bohemian Paris of the 1920s and explores the tense and complex relationship between Marya, alone in the city after her husband is arrested, and the English couple who befriends her. Rhys apparently drew on her own affair with writer Ford Maddox Ford to write the book.

🔍 The Americas, Jamaica – Mrs Rochester's Jamaica (feature box)

🎬 *Quartet* (1981)

Perfume (1985)
Patrick Suskind

Jean-Baptiste Grenouille is born into the slums of 18th-century France, but is graced with a truly exceptional sense of smell. As a boy, he apprentices himself to the most prominent perfumer in the country, who teaches him the secrets of his trade. A true genius, Grenouille pushes himself to capture every essence that he can, until he smells one that he must have – whatever the cost. This lovely book is set mostly in Paris and Grasse.

🎬 *Perfume: The Story of a Murderer* (2006)

Non-fiction

A Moveable Feast (1964)
Ernest Hemingway

Published posthumously and edited by his widow, Mary, *A Moveable Feast* tells of Hemingway's time living in Paris in the 1920s as part of the American expat community. As a struggling writer, married to first wife, Hadley Richardson, he met and mixed with such people as James Joyce, Gertrude Stein, F. Scott Fitzgerald, Ezra Pound and Sylvia Beach, who ran the famous Shakespeare & Co. on the Left Bank. The Hemingway of this book is quite likeable as he plays with his son and his cat and gossips with friends in parks, restaurants and cafes around the city. It is possible to visit many of the places mentioned in the book and to follow in Hemingway's footsteps around Paris. Locations in the book include the Hôtel d'Angleterre, in the Saint-Germain-des-Prés district, where Hemingway stayed in Room 14. Hadley found their first apartment at 74 Rue de Cardinale Lemoine, between the Sorbonne and the Faculté des Sciences, and Hemingway's favourite restaurant

Remembrance of Things Past (A la recherché du temps perdu)

Possibly one of the most beautiful pieces of French literature ever written, Marcel Proust's epic seven-volume book is considered by some to be a masterpiece. Yet, the writer André Gide advised the publisher Gaumont not to publish the first volume (*Swann's Way*), leading Proust to self-publish; Gide later apologized to Proust for this grave mistake and offered to publish the subsequent volumes.

The novel, which is largely autobiographical, covers the period from 1820 to 1870 and features finely drawn characters, who attend soirées and discuss and analyse the times. It is largely based on the memories of Marcel, the narrator, who in a seminal moment in the book tastes a piece of madeleine that his aunt has dipped into her tisane. This triggers the host of memories that inform the book.

The first part of the book focuses on Marcel's life in Combray (Illiers-Combray, about 110 km/70 miles south-west of Paris) and focuses on three families: the Jewish Swanns, the aristocratic de Guermantes and Marcel's own. Proust spent his holidays as a child in Illiers (which became Illiers-Combray in 1971) and today visitors to the village often go to Mme Benoit's patisserie to sample a madeleine or two. The grey house of Proust's aunt Elisabeth Amiot (Tante Léonie in the book), which features in the book as the place where Marcel and his parents spend his holidays, is situated near the shop. Today it is a national monument and also the site of the Proust Museum. Visitors can see the magic lantern in the narrator's room and Tante Léonie's madeleine in her bedroom. About 10 minutes from the house, across the Loire River, lies the 2 ha (5 acre) garden in which Proust's uncle, Jules Amiot, recreated the Pré Catalan, named after an area in Paris's Bois de Bologne. This became the grounds of Tansonville, Swann's estate, in the book. The nearby medieval Château de Villebon, complete with formal gardens and moat, is the Château de Guermantes, country home of the Duchess of Guermantes, in Proust's book.

Le temps retrouvé (1999), starring Catherine Deneuve, Emmanuelle Béart and John Malkovich

http://www.retaworks.com/random_walk/random_htm/France/IlliersCombray/combray.htm (walk)

Swann in Love (1984), starring Jeremy Irons

in the beginning of his stay was just east of there, Pré aux Clercs, on the corner of Rue Jacob and Rue Bonaparte. Hemingway and friends hung out at Café Falstaff at 14 Rue Delambre, where he first met Scott Fitzgerald (the original bar was at 10 Rue Delambre, before Jimmy, the barman, moved to the Falstaff next door).

📶 http://www.slowtrav.com/france/paris/rl_hemingway.htm (walk taking in Hemingway's favourite haunts in Paris)

🏠 http://www.hotel-angleterre.com/hotel_angleterre_en.html (Hôtel Angleterre)

BRITTANY

Fiction

The Chouans (1829)
Honoré de Balzac

An early novel by Balzac, *The Chouans* combines the uprising in Fougères in 1799 with the love affair between aristocratic Marie de Verneuil and Chouan, Alphonse de Montauran. The Chouans were the French royalist rebels in Maine and Brittany.

Ninety-Three (1874)
Victor Hugo

The last of Hugo's novels, *Ninety-Three* opens in Brittany in 1793, where revolutionary forces are struggling to suppress the counter-revolutionary uprising of the Vendée. The revolutionaries are led by Gauvain, nephew of the Marquis de Lantenac, himself the leader of the Vendean guard. A dramatic examination of this terrifying period of French history, *Ninety-Three* is perhaps not as good as Hugo's earlier work, but it is an interesting read.

🔍 Paris – *Les Misérables*

Non-fiction

Over Strand and Field: A Record of Travel Through Brittany (1904)
Gustav Flaubert

Although much better known for his classic book *Madame Bovary* (1857), Flaubert also wrote about his travels around Brittany. The writer journeyed around Chateau de Chambord, Chateau de Clisson, Carnac, Quiberon, Quimper, Brest and Saint Malo, among other destinations.

🔍 Normandy – *Madame Bovary*

LOIRE

Fiction

Le Grand Meaulnes (1913)
Alain-Fournier

One of the great novels of France – and a personal favourite – this was the only completed work of Alain-Fournier. It is a romantic and enchanting story of the friendship between 15-year-old narrator François and 17-year-old Augustin Meaulnes, a mysterious but charismatic figure who arrives to shake up François's world.

🎬 *Le Grand Meaulnes* (1967)

Five Quarters of the Orange (2001)
Joanne Harris

Harris's book is set in the Loire Valley, near Angers, during the Nazi occupation of France. After the war a young woman returns to the village where she grew up, but no one realizes she is Framboise, the nine-year-old forced to leave the village with her mother, when she was accused of collaborating with the Nazis.

🔊 http://www.joanne-harris.co.uk/ (author website)

🔍 *Chocolat*

NORMANDY
Fiction

Madame Bovary (1857)
Gustave Flaubert

Flaubert's first novel and masterpiece opens in north-west France, where the young Charles Bovary is studying. After finishing medical school in Rouen, Bovary sets up practice in Tostes in Normandy, where he marries a widow, who dies. His second wife, Emma, dreams of a better, more sophisticated life and quickly becomes frustrated with her banal and provincial existence. Emma's attention begins to drift to other men and she borrows a large sum of money from a moneylender to finance her expensive habits. After failing tragically in love, Emma finds that she has only one way to deal with her many problems. Originally serialized in *La Revue de Paris* between 1856 and 1857, it was viewed as offensive to morality and religion and Flaubert was tried for obscenity, a charge of which he was acquitted. It became a best-seller soon afterwards.

🎥 *Madame Bovary* (1991)

Strait is the Gate (1909)
André Gide

Another favourite, *Strait is the Gate* is set in Normandy, where the narrator Jerome spends his summers at his uncle's home. There, he falls in love with his cousin Alissa, a love that she returns, but gradually things change and Alissa convinces herself that she must give Jerome up for his own salvation.

Arsène Lupin vs Sherlock Holmes: The Hollow Needle (2001)
Maurice Leblanc

Leblanc's witty and charming aristocratic gentleman thief, Arsène Lupin, in this book, is set against Sherlock Holmes. Visitors can go to the picturesque town of Etretat, nestled between tall alabaster cliffs, and see its lovely 19th-century villas. This is Arsène Lupin's town. It's also a beautiful location, which made it a popular resort with the artists Monet and Courbet and also with Maupassant.

🔊 http://www.etretat.net/office_de_ tourisme_etretat/pages/anglais_ accueil.php (tourist office)

Normandy Stories (1995)
Guy de Maupassant

Master of the short story, Guy de

Maupassant wrote about his beloved Normandy. This collection gathers together some of his most important work, detailing the land, people and society he loved. Visitors to Normandy can go to and stay in Maupassant's birthplace, Château de Miromesnil, Tourville-sur-Arques, which is situated in beautiful wooded parkland.

🏠 http://www.chateaumiromesnil.com (Château de Miromesnil)

Non-fiction

D-Day: The Battle for Normandy (2009)
Anthony Beevor

Beevor tells the story of D-Day in 1944, when the British launched one of the most important naval expeditions in history, the turning point in the Second World War. Master of detail, Beevor recounts this key piece of history from both sides, showing why we are right to celebrate its importance, but also showing that victory came at an enormous cost to all those involved. There are many tours operating in the area that visit key locations associated with D-Day. These include Pegasus Bridge and the Pegasus Museum, the Ranville British Cemetery, La Cambe German Cemetery, Point du Hoc and many of the beaches where the action took place such as Omaha Beach, where the cliffs are still pitted with shells and German bunkers.

🛜 http://www.overlordtour.com/ (one of several tours of the battlefields)

🔍 The Battle for Spain: The Spanish Civil War, 1936–1939

PROVENCE
Fiction

Super-Cannes (2000)
J. G. Ballard

Set in Eden-Olympia, a planned community, in the hills above Cannes, *Super-Cannes* is essentially a murder mystery. After a doctor goes on a shooting spree, killing 10 executives and then turning the gun on himself, young Dr Jane Sinclair is hired as his replacement and comes to live, with her middle-aged husband Paul, in the same house as her predecessor, with interesting results. Eden-Olympia is an elite business community, planned to turn Provence into the new Silicon Valley.

Tender Is the Night (1934)
F. Scott Fitzgerald

Fitzgerald presents a decadent view of the French Riviera through the eyes of wealthy Americans Richard 'Dick' Diver and his wife Nicole, based loosely on the real-life couple Sara and Gerald Murphy.

🎬 Tender Is the Night (1962), starring Jennifer Jones as Nicole and Jason Robards as Dick

The Murdered House (1999)
Pierre Magnan

Haunted by memories of his mother's brutal death, Seraphin Monge returns home after the war in 1920 to the place where his family was killed. He destroys the house, but as the stone crumbles, the secrets behind the murders are laid bare – with devastating results.

🔍 *Death in the Truffle Wood*

The Water of the Hills (1962)
Marcel Pagnol

Pagnol's two books, *Jean de Florette* and *Manon des Sources*, which make up this volume and which were immortalized beautifully in film, are set in the Provençal village of Les Bastides Blanches, based on La Treille, just east of Marseille. Pagnol was born in nearby Aubagne. La Bastide Neuve was the farmhouse holiday home that became the home of Jean de Florette and Pagnol is buried in the little cemetery. The Provençal landscape of olive groves and lavender fields, as described in detail in *The Water of the Hills*, hasn't changed that much and it is possible to imagine the landscape on which the hunchback Jean Cadoret pinned his dreams and the old-time prejudices that led Cesar Soubeyrand and his nephew Ugolin to try to thwart them. Visitors can go to many of the places key to Pagnol's Provence.

🎬 *Jean de Florette* and *Manon des Sources* (both 1986)

📶 http://www.walkaboutgourmet.com/Navigation/tours.htm (tour)

Bonjour Tristesse (1954)
Françoise Sagan

Initially seen as scandalous by French society when it was published in the

1950s, Françoise Sagan's *Bonjour Tristesse* is now a classic. The plot follows 17-year-old Cecile's plotting and scheming over one summer in the South of France. Used to the ways of her playboy father, who loves and leaves women, Cecile is faced with the prospect of change when her father meets Anne. Determined that the status quo won't be upset, Cecile does everything possible to disrupt her father's relationship with Anne with devastating results.

🎬 *Bonjour Tristesse* (1958), directed by Otto Preminger and starring Deborah Kerr, David Niven and Jean Seberg

Non-fiction

A Year in Provence (1989)
Peter Mayle

A guilty pleasure, *A Year in Provence* is Mayle's extremely entertaining account of doing what most people dream of – buying a derelict farmhouse and moving to France (with his wife) to do it up. Written with great affection and wit, Mayle's book follows the trials and tribulations of an English couple and their dogs as they deal with lazy builders, truffle hunters and the mistral in the medieval village of Menerbes in the Luberon. Mayle's book has sold millions of copies all over the world and inspired a huge increase in tourism to Provence.

📺 *A Year in Provence* (1993)

🔍 *A Good Year*

GERMANY

GENERAL
Fiction

In a German Pension (1911)
Katherine Mansfield

This collection of 13 short stories, written shortly after Mansfield visited Germany as a young woman, is essentially a series of sketches of German life and the psyche and character of the people. Mansfield captures perfectly the minutiae of the society of that time.

All Quiet on the Western Front (1926)
Erich Maria Remarque

Remarque served in the First World War and later wrote what was to become recognized as a classic account of the realities of war. Narrator 19-year-old Paul Bäumer is seduced by patriotic and nationalistic speeches. Along with some of his friends he enlists and ends up fighting in France on the German Front. There, he discovers that the idealism he has been fed is all lies and that there is little that is honourable or noble about war.

All Quiet on the Western Front (1930)

The Reader (1997)
Bernhard Schlink

Bernhard Schlink's lyrical book tells of collective guilt and loss during and after the Second World War (1939–45). In an unnamed city in West Germany in the 1960s, the teenage narrator, Michael Berg, embarks on a relationship with Hannah Schmitz, a woman in her 30s. Later, the ghosts from Hannah's past come back to haunt her, as does her work during the war. The Oscar-winning film version was shot in Berlin, Saxony, Cologne and Poland, among other destinations.

The Reader (2008), screenplay by David Hare and directed by Stephen Daldry

The Dark Room (2002)
Rachel Seiffert

Comprising three novellas, The Dark Room tells the stories of three people who in different ways are the victims and product of war: Helmut, a young disabled photographer, living in Berlin in the 1930s; Lore, the 12-year-old daughter of a high-ranking Nazi official, who in 1945, takes her siblings on a journey across zoned Germany to her grandmother in Hamburg; and Micha, a teacher living in modern-day Berlin, who begins to question his whole family's past when he discovers that his grandfather was in the SS.

Non-fiction

The Past Is Myself (1968)
Christabel Bielenberg

In 1934, Christabel Burton married a young German lawyer, Peter Bielenberg. On the couple's return to Germany, Peter, who was vehemently anti-Nazi, took a job at the Ministry of Economics in Berlin. The Bielenbergs became part of a group of dissidents that included Adam von Trott zu Solz, who was to become involved in the plot to overthrow Hitler. After the plot failed, von Trott was arrested and executed and Peter, as one of his friends, was imprisoned. Christabel was placed under house arrest with their children. Through a combination of deception, ineptitude and luck, Peter was released and managed to escape to the Black Forest where Christabel lived with the children. This is a very different insight into the German war machine from a very courageous woman who experienced it first-hand.

🎬 *Christabel* (1988); Dennis Potter's adaptation starring a young Elizabeth Hurley in the title role

BERLIN

Fiction

The Spy Who Came in from the Cold (1963)
John le Carré

Allegedly called the 'finest spy story ever written' by Graham Greene, *The Spy Who Came in from the Cold* follows British agent Alec Leamas, who is responsible for keeping the double agents under his care undercover and alive in early Cold War Berlin. Things start to go wrong when the East Germans begin murdering them and Leamas is given another role by his masters, that of a disgraced agent left out in the Cold in a bid to bring down East German intelligence.

Berlin and Len Deighton

Berlin is the perfect setting for espionage novels, particularly those set in the Cold War period. And no one, apart from John le Carré arguably, does this better than the writer Len Deighton, firstly with his iconic character Harry Palmer (as immortalized by actor Michael Caine in several films) and later in the 'Bernard Sampson' books. Palmer is the mysterious narrator who makes his appearance in Deighton's first novel *The Ipcress File* (1962). A working-class hero with a chip on his shoulder, Harry is an outsider in the British spy world of ex-public school boys and gentlemen's clubs. In the third novel, *Funeral in Berlin* (1964), he finds himself immersed in the Cold War proper, sent to the city to arrange the defection of a leading Russian scientist from the East to the West through a staged funeral. Harry has to deal with security chief Colonel Stok, who has his own personal agenda. The city looms large in the book, an obviously divided place in which the Wall, and its political connotations for the Cold War and the international community, is ever present. The legacy of the Second World War is still evident but Berlin now teems with international visitors who meet in its busy hotels and bars. This cosmopolitan atmosphere is even more obvious in the 1966 film of *The Ipcress File*. Visitors can see some of the locations featured, including Berlin Tempelhof Airport, where Harry first arrives, Swinemünder Brücke, the bridge on which the coffin crosses the border, Checkpoint Charlie (today a memorial museum), where Harry and Stok cross the border, and Hotel Am Zoo (Hotel Zoo Berlin), where Harry stays.

🎬 *The Spy Who Came in from the Cold* (1965), starring Richard Burton

Berlin Alexanderplatz (1929)
Alfred Döblin

A stream of consciousness novel in which Franz Biberkopf struggles to make a better life for himself, while living in the Berlin Alexanderplatz area.

🎬 *Berlin – Alexanderplatz* (1931; 1980)

Fatherland (1992)
Robert Harris

Set in a world in which Hitler won the war, this fast-paced thriller begins in 1964, just a week before the Führer's 75th birthday. When Xavier March, a detective, looks into the case of a dead body found near a lake in one of the city's richest suburbs, he uncovers more than he bargains for, a secret, which if revealed will change the course of history.

Goodbye to Berlin (1939)
Christopher Isherwood

Isherwood's celebrated book of interconnected stories is based on his experiences of living in Berlin. Set at the end of Weimar Germany in the hedonistic world of the 1930s, the central character, named after the author, lives with a host of colourful characters from Berlin's underworld – prostitutes, barmen and cabaret stars, including the most famous of them all, Sally Bowles. The characters live a frenzied life, which is drawing to a

close as the impact of the rise to power of the Nazis is felt on Germany and the microcosm of Berlin, in particular.

🎬 *Cabaret* (1972), starring Liza Minnelli

Berlin Noir Trilogy (1993)
Philip Kerr

Philip Marlowe transposed to Berlin, Kerr's Bernie Gunther is a wisecracking detective working in 1930s and '40s Germany. The trilogy comprises *March Violets*, set in 1936, *The Pale Criminal*, set in 1938, and *A German Requiem*, set after the war in 1947.

King, Queen, Knave (1968)
Vladimir Nabokov

Nabokov worked on the English translation of *King, Queen, Knave* himself, publishing it nearly 40 years after he originally wrote it. The book focuses on Dreyer, the owner of a Berlin department store, his 34-year-old wife, Martha, and his nephew, Franz, newly arrived from the German provinces to work for Dreyer. When Martha seduces Franz, the plot thickens...

🎬 *King, Queen, Knave* (1972)

HAMBURG
Fiction

A Most Wanted Man (2008)
John le Carré

In *A Most Wanted Man* le Carré focuses on Issa ('Jesus' in Chechen) Karpov, an illegal immigrant of half-Russian, half-

Chechen descent and a Muslim suspected of terrorism. Le Carré set the novel in Hamburg, where Mohamed Atta and other members of al-Qaeda planned the 9/11 attacks and which has since become of interest to American, British and German intelligence. Le Carré previously served as political consul in Berlin.

Africa, Kenya – *The Constant Gardener*

The Odessa File (1972)
Frederick Forsyth

Set in Hamburg in the 1960s, this well-researched thriller follows journalist Peter Miller, who begins to track down an alleged Nazi war criminal after the diary of a Jewish man falls into his hands. This describes the man's mental and physical torture at the Nazi's hands during the war. At the risk of his life, Miller discovers the secret organization ODESSA, a group of former SS officers who are infiltrating German politics, industry and society. He also discovers his own family skeletons.

The Odessa File, starring Jon Voight

MUNICH
Fiction

Six Graves to Munich (2009)
Mario Puzo

After being tortured by a group of seven Nazis towards the end of the Second World War (1939–45), Michael Rogan was left for dead. Years later,

still tormented by his injuries and the memories of that time, Rogan tracks down each of his torturers with extremely grim results.

The Book Thief (2007)
Markus Zusak

Set in Himmel Street in Munich during Nazi Germany, the story revolves around nine-year-old Liesel, sent to live with Hans and Rosa Hubermann. Liesel learns through the books that she steals and the words that she 'holds in her hands like clouds'. Zusak's fascinating (but very long) book is narrated by Death, who visits the book thief three times. Through Liesel, Zusak reveals to the reader some of the great kindnesses and atrocities committed, often by quite ordinary people, in this terrifying period in 20th-century history.

OTHER REGIONS
Fiction

The Lost Honour of Katharina Blum (1974)
Heinrich Böll

Nobel Prize winner Böll tells of a terrorist-obsessed country in the 1970s. An attack on yellow journalism, he shows how the hounding of Katharina Blum by the press ruins her life.

Die verlorene Ehre der Katharina Blum oder: Wie Gewalt entstehen und wohin sie führen kann (The Lost Honour of Katharina Blum, 1975)

The Blue Flower (1995)
Penelope Fitzgerald

Considered by many as Fitzgerald's masterpiece and the winner of several awards, *The Blue Flower* follows the life of the romantic poet and philosopher Friedrich ('Fritz') von Hardenberg, better known by his pen name Novalis, especially his relationship with 12-year-old Sophie von Kuhn in 18th-century Saxony.

Buddenbrooks (1901)
Thomas Mann

Written when Mann was just 24, this epic follows the decline of a wealthy 19th-century merchant family in the northern German town of Lübeck. Mann based the family on his own experience of growing up in a German merchant family in the town. Visitors can see the house at Mengstraße 4, where the Mann family lived, and the rooms described in the novel.

🎬 *Buddenbrooks* (2008)
✚ (http://www.historicgermany. com/3502.html (Buddenbrooks House)

Elizabeth and Her German Garden (1898)
Elizabeth von Arnim

An Englishwoman married to a German count, referred to as the 'Man of Wrath', Elizabeth describes with utter charm her endeavours to build a garden at her husband's estate in the Pomeranian wilderness. This is a charming account of aristocratic life in Germany in the last years of the 19th century. It is now a Virago classic.

GREECE AND THE ISLANDS

GENERAL
Fiction

Little Infamies (2002)
Panos Karnezis

Little Infamies is a series of short stories set in an unnamed Greek village. Focusing on ordinary people – a priest, a whore, a barber and a seamstress among them – Karnezis, with great skill and black humour, reveals the cruelties and infamous acts that people can commit.

Non-fiction

The Hill of Kronos (1980)
Peter Levi

Recently reissued, Peter Levi's *The Hill of Kronos* is a vibrant account of the Greece that he came to know and love through a lifetime of exploration, first as a scholar, later living in Athens in the days of the dictatorship and finally as a family man and poet.

Dinner with Persephone: Travels in Greece (1996)
Patricia Storace

Hailed as a travel classic, and possibly one of the best books about Greece, *Dinner with Persephone* is a love letter to the country. Poet Storace spent a year in Greece and this book is an evocation of the Greek psyche, past and present.

ATHENS

Fiction

The Late-Night News (1995)
Petros Markaris

The first book in the series featuring Inspector Costas Haritos, a CID chief based in central Athens, *The Late-Night News* opens with the murder of an Albanian couple. When the journalist investigating the murders is also killed, Haritos finds himself delving into the world of child trafficking. Markaris presents Athens in the winter, gridlocked with heavy traffic.

🔍 *Deadline in Athens*

Homer's *Iliad* and *Odyssey*

The epic poems *The Iliad* and *The Odyssey* are ascribed to the blind poet-singer Homer (although some experts argue that different hands penned these epics). Little is known about Homer, other than that he was perhaps an Asiatic Greek and that his birthplace might have been the island of Chios (also Khios) in the Aegean Sea; Smyrna, a seaport in western Turkey; Colophon, near Ephesus, Turkey; Rhodes, an Aegean island; Salamis, Cyprus; or Athens or Argos on the Greek mainland. He is believed to have composed/recited these works between 800 and 700BC. Homer's work was kept alive after his death through its recital by other poets and writers, who eventually wrote it down. In Homer's work, men mix with gods and honour and heroism are important. *The Iliad* opens in the ninth year of the Trojan Wars. After the Achaeans (Greeks) sack Chyrse, a town allied with Troy in the wars, Agamemnon, leader of the Achaean forces, insults the honour of Achilles, the Achaean's most heroic soldier. Achilles refuses to fight anymore but when the war turns against the Achaeans, Achilles, concerned about the fate of his forces, but too proud to fight under Agamemnon, allows his best friend Patroclus to wear his armour and fight in the war. When Patroclus is killed by Hector, the leader of the Trojan forces, Achilles, overcome with rage and grief, joins the battle once more, and in the ensuing fight fells Hector in battle. *The Odyssey* is much shorter than *The Iliad* and follows the epic journey of Odysseus to return home after the end of the Trojan Wars. Imprisoned on the island of Ogygia by Calypso, a nymph, Odysseus longs to return to his wife, Penelope, and son, Telemachus, in Ithaca, an island to the west of Greece. Battling with monsters, gods and men, Odysseus also worries about his wife's loyalty – when Agamemnon returned from the wars, he was murdered by Clytemnestra, his wife.

🎬 *Troy* (2004), starring Brian Cox as Agamemnon, Brad Pitt as Achilles, Sean Bean as Odysseus and Eric Bana as Hector

➕ http://www.literarytraveler.com/tours/greece_cruise_odyssey_tour.aspx (tourists can take a cruise featuring many of the places that Odysseus visited, including Troy and Ithaca)

➕ http://www.allaboutturkey.com/troy.htm (Troy is believed to be located in Hisarlik near Canakkale, Turkey)

🔍 Italy – *The Aeneid* (feature box)

My Brother Michael (1959)
Mary Stewart

Stewart set several of her books in Greece and on the islands. *My Brother Michael* takes place in Athens and mainland Greece, where protagonist Camilla Haven travels after a broken engagement. After lamenting that nothing ever happens to her, Camilla is mistaken for 'Simon's Girl' while sitting in a cafe in Athens and ordered to go to Delphi on a matter of life and death. There, Camilla discovers that Simon has no idea what's going on, but is in Greece to honour his brother, Michael, who died there during the war. A nostalgic look at Greece, *My Brother Michael* is also an old-fashioned thriller–romance.

🔍 *The Moon-Spinners* (1962), set in Crete

Z (1967)
Vassilis Vassilikos

Vassilikos is one of the nation's leading writers. Born in the northern Greek island of Thassos, Vassilikos has worked as a diplomat and journalist. One of his most critically acclaimed works is *Z* – the Greek letter 'zei' means 'he is alive', a slogan adopted by political activists in the 1960s and subsequently banned (like the book) by the military junta. A fictional account of real events *Z* looks into the 1963 assassination of Grigorios Lambrakis, a popular leftist member of the Greek Parliament, in Thessaloniki by members of the extreme right.

🎬 *Z* (1969)

➕ http://www.thassosisland.gr/en/villages/theologos (Thassos Island)

Non-fiction

92 Archarnon Street (2007)
John Lucas

An affectionate and candid account of the author's love affair with Athens and Greece, the book describes a city of infuriating traffic jams, petty bureaucracies, noisy tavernas and boisterous prostitutes, but also one full of people capable of great kindness and generosity.

Eurydice Street: A Place in Athens (2004)
Sofka Zinovieff

In the summer of 2001, Zinovieff accompanied her husband to Athens to take up a posting and *Eurydice Street* is the result of her time there. Part travelogue, part memoir, the book is an insightful look at Athenian life.

CEPHALONIA
Fiction

Captain Corelli's Mandolin (1993)
Louis de Bernières

Set during the early part of the Second World War on the island of Cephalonia, *Captain Corelli's Mandolin* is part history, part love story. When the Italians, under the command of the urbane Captain Antonio Corelli, occupy the island, life doesn't seem to change that much for the islanders. When Corelli is billeted with Dr Iannis and Pelagia, he and Pelagia almost inevitably fall in love. However, the difficulties of war and conflicts between friends, loved ones, the community and the invaders soon bring unwanted challenges to their affair. The 2001 movie was filmed on the island, particularly around Sami and Myrtos Beach.

🎬 *Captain Corelli's Mandolin* (2001)

➕ http://www.kefaloniatravel.com/ kefalonia_cephalonia_captain_corellis_ mandolin.html (film-related tours of the island)

CORFU
Non-fiction

The Corfu Trilogy (2006)
Gerald Durrell

Durrell's popular trilogy about growing up on the island of Corfu in the 1930s includes *My Family and Other Animals* (1956), *Birds, Beasts and Relatives* (1969) and *The Garden of the Gods* (1978). With great humour, Durrell recounts life as the youngest child of an eccentric family, who move to Corfu just before the outbreak of the Second World War. It's here that he discovers his emerging love of zoology, which results in the family home being filled with all manner of animals (including scorpions and bats). His great and abiding passion for the island is clear – something these books have passed on to generations of other people.

A House in Corfu: A Family's Sojourn in Greece (2002)
Emma Tennant

In the 1960s Emma Tennant's parents spotted a beautiful island and bay and decided to build a house there. *A House in Corfu* is the story of that house, Rovinia, and the family, including Maria, the cook, and her husband, Thodoros, who lived and worked there. It is also a testament to the changes that the island and its landscape have experienced since.

CRETE
Fiction

The Dark Labyrinth (1947)
Lawrence Durrell

After a major archaeological discovery in Crete of some intriguing caves, a group of English tourists, including a painter, a soldier and a spiritualist, come ashore from a cruise. Curious to learn more about the island, they become trapped in a labyrinth after their guide is killed in an accident. Durrell describes the Cretan landscape and mythology meticulously.

📶 http://www.lawrencedurrell.org/ (International Lawrence Durrell Society)

🔍 Cypress – *Bitter Lemons in Cypress*

The Island (2005)
Victoria Hislop

An epic novel, covering four generations of a family, *The Island* follows Alexis Fielding as she goes

Kazantzakis's Crete

Many people associate the beautiful island of Crete with the ebullient, passionate character of Alexis Zorba, as played by Anthony Quinn in the 1964 film *Zorba the Greek*. The creation of poet, philosopher and writer Nikos Kazantzakis, the book, on which the film is based, is a celebration of all things Greek – the people, landscape, culture and vitality; it is also based on the author's experiences of the island and those of his later life.

First published in Greek in 1946, the book was translated into English in 1952. A lyrical, poetic book, *Zorba the Greek* focuses on the friendship between a young British writer, the unnamed narrator, and Alexis Zorba. A man of the people, earthy and sensual, Zorba is someone who somewhat unconsciously lives his life to the full. He befriends the young man, who is his complete opposite in every way and navigates life through his intellect and careful reason. Zorba gradually teaches the man through example how important it is to grasp every minute as if it were his last and to celebrate the gift of life.

Karantzakis was born in Iraklion, the island's largest city, in 1883. After studying law in Athens and Paris, he fought in the Balkan Wars (1912–13) as a Greek volunteer. After the war, he travelled around Greece and lived in Switzerland for two years before returning to his native country in 1919, where he was appointed Director General in the Ministry of Welfare, working to repatriate the Greeks of the Caucasus. Disillusioned with politics, he spent time living and working in Germany and later Italy, before he returned to Crete, where he began working on *Odyssey: A Modern Sequel*, an epic poem of 33,333 verses, which took him 13 years to complete (1925–38), and which followed Odysseus's story from where Homer left off. Between 1925 and 1933, he travelled extensively, before returning to the Greek islands to settle on Aegina with Eleni, the woman who was later to become his wife. Kazantzakis spent most of the Second World War on the island, where he continued to write. In 1948, he moved to Antibes in the French Riviera. During his last years, he wrote the highly controversial *The Last Temptation of Christ* (1954), which was banned by the Roman Catholic Church and for which the Greek Orthodox Church tried to excommunicate him, and the autobiographical *Return to Greco* (1961), based on his experiences growing up in Crete and his later travels, which was published in English after his death. In 1957, while travelling with his wife, Kazantzakis became ill. He died in Germany, but his body was transported back to Iraklion, where it lay in state in the Cathedral of Saint Minas. Thousands of people gathered at his funeral and to witness his remains being interned at the Martinengo Bastion. Visitors can visit Kazantzakis's grave and read his epitaph: 'I hope for nothing, I fear nothing, I am free.'

🎬 Zorba the Greek (1964), starring Anthony Quinn as Zorba

➕ http://www.kazantzakis-museum.gr/index.php?level=0&id=623&lang=en (the Nikos Kazantzakis Museum in Myrtia, a village outside of Iraklion, gives an insightful overview of the author's world and writings. This is also a room dedicated to the author in the Historical Museum of Crete)

🔍 Homer's *Iliad* and *Odyssey* (box feature)

to Crete to find out more about her mother's past and heritage. Once there she discovers the former leper colony of Spinalonga and uncovers her family's secrets and their close connections to the island. Hislop evokes Crete after the war, examining the misconceptions and prejudices of the local community towards the afflicted lepers. She also depicts the civilization of Spinalonga – a prison essentially, but one with rules, morality and a working society.

🔊 http://www.victoriahislop.com/ (author site)

SPETSES
Fiction

The Magus (1965)
John Fowles

Set on Phraxos (based on the island of Spetses), Fowles's acclaimed novel follows Nicholas Urfe from London to Greece, where he has taken a job as an English teacher. Urfe's growing fascination with the island and its mysteries lead him to explore it. He meets the local 'magician' Maurice Conchis, one of the owners of a villa on the island. Through Conchis he encounters the twins Julie and June and finds himself subjected to a series of tests. Rejecting a reconciliation with his former girlfriend, who takes matters tragically into her own hands, Urfe finds himself facing a jury who judge his actions. The novel is partly based on Fowles's experiences of living on Spetses as a teacher in

the 1950s and it contains long passages about the island's flora and fauna.

🎥 *The Magus* (1968), starring Michael Caine and Anthony Quinn

🔊 http://www.breathtakingathens.com/ node/5000117 (Athens website)

🔍 Canada – *Fugitive Pieces*

GREENLAND
Fiction

No One Thinks of Greenland (2003)
John Griesemer

Griesemer's book is set six years after the Korean War in Qangattarsa, Greenland, where Corporal Rudy Spruance is sent by mistake. He ends up in a secret military hospital, where he meets a host of comic characters, including Irene, the alluring mistress of his commanding officer. The book was made into a movie but retitled *Guy X*.

🎥 *Guy X* (2005), starring Jason Biggs and Natascha McElhone

Cold Earth (2009)
Sarah Moss

A debut novel, which has been very well received, *Cold Earth* is a thriller but also a book about survival. When a group of archaeologists on a dig in Greenland discover that an epidemic has hit the outer world and they are cut off, they fight to survive a winter, for which they aren't equipped, with the knowledge that their loved ones far away might all be dead.

Greenlanders (1988)
Jane Smiley

Set in the 14th century, Smiley's epic saga tells of a small Nordic settlement on the island and its struggle for survival as the climate changes and the once healthy green land becomes colder and darker. With meticulous detail, Smiley reconstructs the life of farmer Asgeir Gunnarsson and his community, the mythology and witchcraft, the feuds and the harsh climate and famines that make it so difficult for them to exist.

HUNGARY

BUDAPEST
Fiction

Fateless (1975)
Imre Kertész

Nobel Prize winner Kertész's semi-autobiographical *Fatelessness* examines a 15-year-old Jewish boy whose life in Budapest is turned upside down when he is transported to the concentration camps. Kertész was himself sent to Auschwitz in 1944 and then on to Buchenwald.

OTHER REGIONS

They Were Counted (1999)
Miklós Bánffy

First published in 1934, Bánffy's book examines aristocratic life as seen through two Transylvanian cousins at the end of the Austro–Hungarian empire. Bánffy creates a romantic world of shooting parties, gaming tables and wealthy society in Budapest, set against the plight of the Romanian mountain peasants and the poverty of other areas. Bánffy's writing has been compared to Trollope.

🔍 *They Were Found Wanting; They Were Divided*

Under the Frog (1992)
Tibor Fischer

In *Under the Frog*, Tibor Fischer presents a charming comic account of Pataki and Gyuri, who travel across post-war communist Hungary between 1944 and 1956 with a basketball team.

🔍 *Good To Be God*

Embers (2002)
Sándor Márai

Considered by many to be Hungary's finest writer, Sándor Márai wrote in 1949, 'the world has no need of Hungarian literature'. *Embers*, written in 1942, has only recently been translated into English. Although Márai considered it one of his lesser novels, *Embers* is a very interesting read, part detective novel and part exploration of a world that no longer exists. The protagonist, Henrik, invites Konrad, a friend whom he has not seen in four decades, to his home, a castle below the Carpathian Mountains.

His mission is less to catch up with Konrad than to conduct an investigation into why Konrad betrayed him so badly all those years ago.

Century in Scarlet: the Epic Novel of the 19th-century Revolution (2001)
Lajos Zilahy

Zilahy's classic tale of two brothers fighting on opposing sides in 1848 revolutionary Europe mixes fictional characters with real-life ones, such as Tsar Nicholas I. Through vivid descriptions of political events and of places such as Budapest and Vienna, Zilahy evokes Europe at a time of historic upheaval.

ICELAND

REYKJAVIK

Fiction

Tainted Blood (Jar City, 2007)
Arnaldur Indridason

Originally published as *Jar City* in the UK, this book quickly established Icelandic author Arnaldur Indridason as a major international writer. Indridason's protagonist Inspector Erlendur Sveinsson is often compared to Henning Mankell's detective Kurt Wallender. *Tainted Blood* opens in Reykjavik, where most of the 'Erlendur' books are set, in a flat in which a man

An Independent People: Halldór Laxness's beloved Iceland

Nobel Prize winner Halldór Laxness is one of Iceland's most revered writers. The author of several novels, plays and short stories, Laxness was born in 1902 in Reykjavik, but was brought up in the countryside. Laxness travelled as a young man, chiefly in Europe and the United States, and in his mid-20s converted to Catholicism, something he wrote about in *Under the Holy Mountain* (*Undir Helgahnúk*, 1924). He later became interested in socialism, about which he also wrote in his novels. In 1930, Laxness settled again in Iceland. The following decade proved to be Laxness's most prolific writing period during which he produced three novel cycles, focusing on Iceland and its people: *Salka Valka* (1932); *Independent People* (1934–5); and *The Light of the World* (1937–40). *Independent People* arguably won Laxness his Noble Prize. It is certainly one of the most celebrated of the author's novels. Set in a remote part of Iceland, the book follows the bleak, relentlessly hard life of farmer Bjartur of Summerhouses. It is 'the story of a man who sowed his enemy's field all his life, day and night. Such is the story of the most independent man in the country.' Visitors to Iceland can gain some insight into Laxness's life and thinking by going to Gljúfrasteinn, Laxness's home for more than half a century. Situated about 20 minutes out of Reykjavik, towards Thingvellir National Park, Gljúfrasteinn is now a museum and its impressive gardens are open to the public, who can go on one of several highly recommended walks that the author himself used to take while writing one of his famous books.

🛜 http://www.gljufrasteinn.is/cat.html?super_cat=6&cat=16 (Gljúfrasteinn)

is found murdered. Through dogged determination, Erlendur and his colleagues link the man's death to a rape that took place more than 25 years earlier and to the national Genetic Research Centre. Erlendur is a bleak character, haunted by ghosts from his past and dealing with his dysfunctional relationships with his children. The books featuring Erlendur all address important social subjects and are set in the dark underbelly of the city. Through these books, rather like in Ian Rankin's 'Rebus' series, the reader discovers a Reykjavik not usually seen by outsiders.

🎬 *Mýrin (Jar City*; 2006)
🔍 *Silence of the Grave*

101 *Reykjavik* (1996)
Hallgrímur Helgason
Named after the downtown district of Reykjavik in which it is set, Helgason's popular comic-drama follows the life of protagonist Hlynur Bjorn. Unemployed, almost 30 and living with his mother, Hlynur spends his days surfing the Net, downloading cyberporn and wandering the city's streets and his nights at the K-Bar. Hlynur's life, as he knows it, is threatened when his girlfriend becomes pregnant and he becomes obsessed by his mother's friend, who turns out to be her lover as well. The 2001 film of the book features many of 101's best sites, including Kaffibarrin, the central Reykjavik bar (coincidentally owned by writer/director Baltasar Kormakur and his soundtrack composer and Blur frontman Damon Albarn). Other memorable sites include

Hallgrimskirkja, the controversial modern cathedral that dominates the city skyline and which Hlynur sees as he lies down to die, Inuit-style, in the snow, and the principal shopping street, Laugavegur, the setting for the final scene.

🎬 *101 Reykjavik* (2001)

Last Rituals (2008)
Yrsa Sigurdardóttir
Yet another Icelandic thriller set in the capital, Reykjavik, *Last Rituals* has attorney Thóra Gudmundsdóttir as its protagonist. When a German student is found dead with an elaborate symbol carved into his chest, the victim's mother contacts Thóra to ask her to help solve the case. Forced to work with German investigator Matthew Reich, Thóra uncovers a world of black magic and witchcraft that dates back centuries in her country's history. Sigurdardóttir presents a more old-fashioned type of detective novel than that of the 'Erlendur' novels, but through the plot the reader gains insight into Iceland's history and culture, particularly the witch-hunts that took place in the 1600s.

🔍 *My Soul To Take* (2009), the second Gudmundsdóttir novel

Non-fiction

Dreaming of Iceland: The Lure of a Family Legend (2004)
Sally Magnusson
The daughter of commentator Magnus Magnusson, Sally invited her father to

return with her to the land of his birth to visit the places where he grew up and about which he had told her stories (namely around Akureyri and Húsavík). This book is about that trip and reveals a lot about Magnus Magnusson, the man, and also the culture, history and family that shaped him.

IRELAND (EIRE)

DUBLIN
Fiction

More Pricks than Kicks (1934)
Samuel Beckett

Beckett set this tragicomedy in the city of his birth and drew on his own experiences of studying at Trinity College Dublin to create the central character Belacqua Shuah, a student of modern languages there. The book comprises 10 stories, following the life, loves and death of Shuah. Beckett named Belacqua after a figure in Dante's *Inferno*.

Dublin 4 (1982)
Maeve Binchy

Acclaimed author Maeve Binchy sets the four stories in this early collection in the fashionable Southside of Dublin. As with her later books, Binchy concentrates on the minutiae of her characters' lives, portraying everyday life in Dublin through their very different perspectives. The stories feature a woman hosting a dinner party at which her husband's mistress is present, a country girl coming to grips with living in the city, an unmarried pregnant student and a photographer trying to relaunch his career while dealing with his drink problem.

Christine Falls (2006)
Benjamin Black

The pen name of Irish author John Banville, Benjamin Blacks sets *Christine Falls*, for the most part, in 1950s' Dublin. The plot centres on Quirke, a pathologist, who tries to find out why his brother-in-law obstetrician has altered the cause of death on a woman's records. Black meticulously recreates the Dublin of this era through the characters, the locations they inhabit and the plot itself. Quirke's Dublin is a city full of secrets, in which the Church is a brooding, all-powerful force. The characters drink their way around the city and local hot spots, such as Jammet's, one of the leading restaurants at the time (now defunct) feature. Quirke's old drinking companion, Barney Boyle, is based on real-life character and writer Brendan Behan.

The Barrytown Trilogy (1992)
Roddy Doyle

Doyle's trilogy follows the lives of a fictional working-class Irish community, as seen through a central family, the Rabbittes, who speak Dublinese. Although most of Doyle's characters suffer great economic hardship and face great adversity, they retain their humour, resilience and even a certain pride throughout. *The Commitments* follows Jimmy Rabbitte, Jr, as he puts together a local band, who sing Motown; they become a success in Dublin and then other factors intervene; *The Snapper* focuses on Sharon Rabbitte's pregnancy following her rape and how the family copes with it; and *The Van* follows Jimmy, Sr, as he and a friend set up a fish and chip business. Barrytown is based on Kilbarrack, where Doyle grew up.

🔍 *The Commitments* (1987);
The Snapper (1990);
The Van (1991)

🎬 *The Commitments* (1991), adapted by Alan Parker

The Country Girls (1960)
Edna O'Brien

O'Brien's first novel tells of Kate and her friend, Baba, both from difficult homes, who are expelled from their convent boarding school and travel to the big city, Dublin, to experience life. There they find freedom and excitement but both yearn for true romance. Kate yearns for 'Mr Gentleman' and Baba, her alter ego, defies convention, flouting the authority of the Church, parents and accepted social convention. The novel caused great outrage in Ireland when it was published. Copies were burned in Limerick and the novel was finally banned there. O'Brien wrote two further books following Kate and

Joyce's Dublin

Think of Dublin: think of James Joyce. From *Dubliners* (1914) and *Ulysses* (1922) to *Finnegans Wake* (1939), Joyce's novels are full of the city. *Ulysses*, probably Joyce's most famous novel, focuses on central character Leopold Bloom as he walks around Dublin. Joyce once said that he wanted to 'give a picture of Dublin so complete that if the city one day suddenly disappeared from the earth it could be reconstructed out of my book.' And many a tourist has tried to follow the trail left by Bloom as he traverses Dublin by foot, horse-drawn carriage and tram, covering an estimated 29 km (18 miles).

The book opens with Stephen Dedalus (familiar to readers from *A Portrait of the Artist as a Young Man*, 1916) and Mortello Tower in Sandycove, where today the James Joyce Museum is located (http://www.jamesjoyce.ie/); the book also features 7 Eccles Street, where the Blooms live, and Glasnevin Cemetery, where Bloom goes to a funeral. The cemetery is the resting place of many famous Irish people, including Charles Stewart Parnell, Michael Collins and Brendan Behan.

Today, people around the world celebrate Bloomsday on 16 June, the day on which Bloom takes his walk. This is also the date on which Joyce first walked out with Nora Barnacle, the woman who was to become his wife. Visitors to the city can take one of the many Joyce walks available. They can also eat at Dublin's most famous literary pub, Davy Byrnes in Duke Street (www.davybyrnes.com), which Joyce and other literary luminaries frequented. The pub is mentioned in both *Ulysses* and *Dubliners*.

Baba, *The Lonely Girl* (1962) and *Girls in Their Married Bliss* (1964).

📺 *The Country Girls* (1983)

At Swim-Two-Birds (1939)
Flann O'Brien

When Flann O'Brien published his novel, the comic masterpiece *At Swim-Two-Birds*, he managed to get a copy to France to the ailing James Joyce. Joyce allegedly said, 'That's a real writer with a true comic spirit... A really funny book.' O'Brien's novel weaves many different tales together combining fictional characters such as the university student narrator who is writing a book featuring the long-suffering novelist Dermot Trellis, himself writing a Western, and figures from Ireland's past such as Finn MacCool. Graham Greene was among the early fans of the novel, saying that its comic charge evoked 'the kind of glee one experiences when people smash china on the stage.'

Non-fiction

My Left Foot (1954)
Christy Brown

A gruelling autobiography, written by the author and artist when he was just 22, *My Left Foot* is an honest account of his life growing up in Crumlin, a working-class suburb of Dublin, in the 1930s and '40s.The author, who suffered from cerebral palsy, was viewed as intellectually backward when he was a child, as he couldn't speak. His mother persevered

and one day Brown famously began to write with a piece of chalk clutched between the toes of his left foot.

🎬 *My Left Foot* (1989), Jim Sheridan's classic film starring Daniel Day-Lewis as Brown

OTHER REGIONS

Fiction

The Sea (2005)
John Banville

Banville's lyrical novel follows art historian and recent widower Max Morden, who returns to the seaside town of Ballyless, where he spent his summers as a child, after the death of his wife. Here he looks back on his life with his late wife and further back to a summer spent with the Graces in Ballyless, where we discover that something happened that summer... Banville was brought up in Wexford.

The Last September (1929)
Elizabeth Bowen

Anglo–Irish author Elizabeth Bowen has been hailed as one of the great writers of the 20th century. *The Last September* is set in 1920, in County Cork, where Sir Richard Naylor and his wife, Lady Myra, have their country home. Their lives and those of their social group are set against the impending end of British rule in southern Ireland.

🎬 *The Last September* (1999), starring Michael Gambon and Keeley Hawes

Troubles (1970)
J. G. Farrell

Set in the Majestic Hotel, a 300-room hotel on the coast of County Wexford that is falling into rack and ruin, Farrell's book details the end of British Rule in the south, the rise of Sinn Fein, and the Troubles. As Edward Spencer, the proprietor, struggles to go on as English tourism dwindles and many of his guests don't have the resources to pay their bills, Major Brendan Archer, scarred by the war, arrives to reacquaint himself with his fiancée. As the hotel falls into disrepair, the danger from Irish insurgents becomes more evident.

📺 *Troubles* (1988), two-part adaptation starring Ian Richardson

🔍 India – *The Siege of Krishnapur*

The Butcher Boy (1992)
Patrick McCabe

Set in Clones, County Monaghan, McCabe's black comedy, *The Butcher Boy*, follows 11-year-old protagonist, Francie Brady, as he moves from wayward child to dangerous and violent adult. Careering around the town with his best mate, Joe, Francie gets into increasingly more trouble. McCabe, who was shortlisted for the Booker Prize, draws on his own experiences of growing up in Clones.

🎬 *The Butcher Boy* (1997)

Amongst Women (1990)
John McGahern

A national best-seller and runner up to the Booker Prize, *Amongst Women* is set on a farm in rural Ireland, where the aged Michael Moran, formerly an officer in the Irish War of Independence in the 1920s, lives. Moran has to come to terms with his past, his brutal tyranny of his two sons and three daughters as they grew up and his life after the war, one in which he finds himself displaced, living a life of quiet desperation.

The Heather Blazing (1992)
Colm Tóibín

A judge in Ireland's High Court in Dublin, Eamon Redmond, seems to have it all, admired by his friends for his successful career and his happy marriage and lovely children. Every summer the family stays in a beautiful house on the coast at Ballyconnigor in Wexford, south-east Ireland. This is where Eamon grew up, and he begins to reflect on his life and past as he realizes how unconnected to people he really is. Tóibín paints the Irish coast vividly through Eamon's love for Wexford, the place he considers his home.

🔍 *The South*

Fools of Fortune (1983)
William Trevor

Once referred to as Ireland's answer to Chekhov, William Trevor has set many of his novels in and around Ireland. *Fools of Fortune* depicts the Troubles as seen through the eyes of Willie Quinton and his cousin. Willie and his mother's lives are blighted when they are the only survivors of a fire, intentionally started by the Black and Tans after an informer's body is found on the Quinton estate.

🔍 *Mrs Eckdorf in O'Neill's Hotel* (1969), set in Dublin

ITALY

GENERAL
Non-fiction

D. H. Lawrence and Italy (2007)
D. H. Lawrence

This collection draws together Lawrence's writings on Italy: *Twilight in Italy* (1916) on the people of Lake Garda; *Sea and Sardinia* (1921); and *Sketches of Etruscan Places* (originally *Etruscan Places*, 1932).

Italian Hours (1909)
Henry James

The American writer Henry James loved Italy and visited it on several occasions from the early 1870s to 1909. Many of his articles were published in American magazines and several were collected together and published as *Italian Hours*. Featuring essays on culture, politics and the nature of travel itself, James writes evocatively of a country in the midst of great change.

The Dark Heart of Italy (2003)
Tobias Jones

In 1999, Jones moved to Italy and after four years of living there produced *The Dark Heart of Italy*, his musings on the Italian people, culture and politics. Through Jones's prose we are introduced to a country where soccer, language, cinema and religion coexist with terrorism, paranoia and Berlusconi's rather extreme brand of politics. Condé Nast described it as: 'the book to take on your Italian holiday'.

An Italian Education (1996)
Tim Parks

Parks moved to Italy a few decades ago and has written several books on the country, including one on football and Verona. The book opens in Pescara, where Parks (along with many Italians) visits the beach with his family during the summer, and gives the reader an affectionate insight into Italy and Italian family life as Parks and his children experience it first-hand.

📶 www.timparks.com (author website)

ROME
Fiction

Cabal (1992)
Michael Dibdin

Cabal forms part of Michael Dibdin's successful detective series featuring Venetian-born detective Aurelio Zen, an investigator in Rome's Criminalpol.

Zen originally appeared in 1988 in *Ratking*. *Cabal* opens dramatically at St Peter's Basilica in Rome, where subsequently Zen is called in to investigate a murder at the Vatican. Using all of his skill to liaise between the Vatican Curia and the Rome Police, Zen has to deal with another murder, the interference of his own mistress in the investigation, a centuries-old cabal and medieval manuscripts in the Vatican Library before the case takes him to the city of Milan, where the novel climaxes.

✚ www.vatican.va (The Vatican)

I, Claudius (1934)
Robert Graves

Graves's celebrated novel follows the life of Roman Emperor Claudius and the history of the Julio–Claudian dynasty and Roman Empire, from Julius Caesar's assassination in 44BC to Caligula's assassination in AD41. In *I Claudius*, the protagonist is a nobleman, who watches the political intrigues and sexual debauchery of Ancient Rome from the sidelines. Dismissed by many as a stammering fool, Claudius records the details of his time. Graves owes much of his detail to Plutarch, Tacitus and Seutonius. This is a great introduction to an extremely rich part of history. Graves wrote a sequel, *Claudius, the God*, in 1935. The BBC later produced an award-winning adaptation of both books.

▣ *I, Claudius* (1976)
🔍 Majorca – *A Woman Unknown* by Lucia Graves (his daughter)

VENICE
Fiction

Don't Look Now and Other Stories (1971)
Daphne du Maurier

Although perhaps better known for Cornish novels such as *Rebecca* and *Jamaica Inn*, Daphne du Maurier was a prolific short-story writer. Some of her stories were wonderfully and terrifyingly adapted into movies by leading directors – Alfred Hitchcock (*The Birds*) and Nicolas Roeg (*Don't Look Now*) among them. The story *Don't Look Now*, published in the collection originally titled *Not After Midnight*, focuses on the death of a child and how the parents deal with it – or not. Opening just outside Venice, where John and Laura have gone after the death of their daughter Christine, the couple encounter two sisters, one of them blind but endowed with psychic power. She tells the couple that their daughter is present in Venice, much to Laura's delight and John's growing scepticism. The acclaimed film adaptation picks up on the darkness of du Maurier's story. Fans can visit some of the locations featured in Roeg's adaptation. For example, the church that is being restored in the film is San Nicolo dei Mendicoli, one of the oldest in Venice, and the restaurant in which John and Laura first encounter the sisters is Ristorante Roma, near the Ponte Scalzi.

🎦 *Don't Look Now* (1973), starring Julie Christie and Donald Sutherland and directed by Nicolas Roeg
🔍 United Kingdom –Daphne du Maurier's landscape (feature box)

Death in Venice (1925)
Thomas Mann

Possibly the work most associated with the city, Thomas Mann's novella *Death in Venice* follows the decline of aging German writer Gustav von Aschenbach after he travels to Venice to find inspiration. There, he encounters and becomes obsessed with Tadzio, a young Polish boy. The writer follows the boy and his family around the city, and even when cholera sweeps across Venice, he cannot leave. Luchino Visconti made the book into a beautiful film, starring Dirk Bogarde. Visitors can stay in the same hotel as von Aschenbach, the Grand Hôtel des

---

Donna Leon's Venice

Commissario Guido Brunetti, the civilized and urbane hero of Donna Leon's successful crime series set in Venice, first made his appearance in *Death in La Fenice* in 1992. Since then, Brunetti's razor-sharp mind, wit and humanity have brought him millions of fans around the world. Translated into more than 20 languages, the Brunetti books are popular not just for Leon's insightful plots, which deal with everything from immigration, prostitution and illegal adoptions in Italy to corruption and murder in the canal ways, but also for their in-depth knowledge, descriptions and obvious love of Venice and the Venetian way of life. Brunetti's world (and Leon's, too, as she has lived there for more than 20 years) is the narrow alleys and wide squares of the Cannaregio district. The reader follows the commissario as he walks (for the most part) around a city that he knows intimately, along the *calles* to the Rialto, from his office in the Questura to Ponte Dei Greci, and beyond. At the beginning of each Brunetti book is a detailed map that shows the major locations mentioned in the plot. This allows the reader to follow Brunetti as he has coffee or a glass of wine at a local bar or eats the special dish that his beloved wife, Paola, a university professor but also a fine cook, prepares for him and their two children for lunch or dinner. In *The Girl of His Dreams*, Leon explores the relationship between the 'Rom', who live on the fringes of mainstream Italian society, and ordinary Venetians, after the body of a young girl is found floating in the Grand Canal and nobody comes to claim her. The book also deals with corruption in the Church, fraudsters, blackmail and extortion, set against the beautiful backdrop of the city.

Through her character of Brunetti, Leon allows the reader to experience a Venice at odds with the tourist world that most people associate with the city. It is a small provincial town, 'where gossip [is] the real cult and where, had it not been at least a nominally Christian city, the reigning deity would surely have been rumour' *(Death in La Fenice)*.

🔍 *Guido Brunetti's Venice* (2009)

Bains on the Lido. Some of the book's action also takes place around the maze of canal streets beside La Fenice, where Von Aschenbach follows Tadzio.

🎬 *Death in Venice* (1971), starring Dirk Bogarde and directed by Luchino Visconti

🏠 http://desbains.hotelinvenice.com (Hôtel des Bains)

FLORENCE AND TUSCANY
Fiction

A Room with a View (1908)
E. M. Forster

A Room with a View is a social comedy set in prim, restrained and class-conscious Edwardian society. The heroine, Lucy Honeychurch, meets socially unacceptable but attractive George Emerson when she faints after witnessing a murder in a Florentine square. Back in England, Lucy becomes engaged to a suitable, socially acceptable man, but must decide whether to follow her head or her heart. Turned into an Oscar-winning film by the Merchant–Ivory team, *A Room with a View* features many beautiful scenes of Florence and the Tuscan countryside. Pensione Bertolini in the novel was filmed in the Hotel degli Orafi, near the Arno. Visitors can also go to Piazza Santissima Annunziata, which Judi Dench and Maggie Smith's characters visit in the film, and the monument to Dante in the Church of Santa Croce, Piazza Santa Croce 16, where Lucy

(Helena Bonham Carter) is hassled by locals. The knife scene was filmed at Piazza della Signorina.

🎬 *A Room with A View* (1986)

🔍 India – *A Passage to India*

🏠 http://www.hoteldelgliorafi.com (Hotel degli Orafi)

The English Patient (1992)
Michael Ondaatje

This award-winning novel by Michael Ondaatje is set in 1944, towards the end of the Second World War, when the forces have all but withdrawn from central Italy, leaving behind destruction and desolation in their wake. Hana, a young Canadian nurse, exhausted by the war, nurses her last patient, a man burned beyond all recognition, who recalls bits and pieces of his life and dreams. Into this comes Kip, a young Sikh, who has spent most of the war risking his life to dismantle bombs, and Caravaggio, a thief. The book focuses on these four characters as they play out their drama in the Villa San Girolamo. Most people probably know the book through Anthony Minghella's compelling film adaptation starring Ralph Fiennes, Juliet Binoche and Kristin Scott-Thomas. Minghella used the Hôtel des Bains on the Venice Lido for the scenes that take place in Cairo's famous Shepheard's Hotel, where spies, officers, diplomats and explorers, among others, met; it was destroyed in the 1950s. He also used the Monastero di Sant'Anna, near Pienza, to recreate the place where Hana, Kip, Caravaggio and the English patient spend their time.

The English Patient (1996)

http://desbains.hotelinvenice.com
(Hôtel des Bains)

UMBRIA

Fiction

My House in Umbria (1991)
William Trevor

After a terrorist bomb goes off on a train, Mrs Delahunty, a romance writer living in Umbria, invites three of the survivors to stay with her. Together, the General, an elderly Englishman, Aimee, an 8-year-old girl, and Otmar, a young German man recover from their injuries and losses. Having escaped a sordid background, including prostitution, Mrs Delahunty weaves fact with fiction as she imagines the lives of the three people who have come to live with her and, gradually, begins to remember her past. Matters are complicated when Aimee's only surviving relative, a seemingly cold American, comes to claim her back.

My House in Umbria (2003)

Ireland – *The Fools of Fortune*

NAPLES

Fiction

The Bay of Noon (1970)
Shirley Hazzard

A Virago modern classic, Hazzard's novel is set in Naples. Jenny arrives in the city seeking adventure and an escape from her former life, only to encounter a much bigger adventure through getting to know Giaconda, a beautiful author, and then her lover, Gianni, and Justin, a marine biologist.

Treasure of Naples (1949)
Giuseppe Marotta

Viewed as a classic, but sadly out of print (although available in second-hand bookshops), the book is also known by its more literal title *Neapolitan Gold*. It is a collection of short stories, a series of vignettes of Neapolitan life, portraying the heat, dust, passion and violence of the place. Marotta, who was a journalist and film critic, helped the great Cesare Zavattini adapt some of the stories into a film, starring two great icons of Italian cinema, Sophia Loren and Eduardo de Filippo.

L'oro di Napoli (1954), directed by Vittorio de Sica

The Volcano Lover (1992)
Susan Sontag

In this lush historical novel, Sontag evokes the life and times of Sir William Hamilton ('the Volcano lover'), British diplomat and, perhaps more famously, the cuckolded husband of Emma Hamilton, Lord Nelson's mistress. Set mostly in Naples, from the 1760s to 1800, Hamilton is appointed ambassador to the Kingdom of the Two Sicilies and the story, which is divided between Hamilton, his wife and Nelson,

Andrea Camilleri's beloved island

Since *La forma dell'acqua* (1994) was first published in English as *The Shape of Water* in 2002, Andrea Camilleri's 'Inspector Montalbano' novels have gained millions of fans around the world and have been translated into many different languages. Set in Sicily, *The Shape of Water* introduces the charming detective Salvo Montalbano, who lives and works in the fictional southern coastal town of Vigàta. A combination of Columbo and Philip Marlowe, Montalbano is a fascinating character, moral, streetwise, yet honest in the face of great corruption. He deals with local criminals with humour but with a determination that usually enables him to solve his crime in the end, although sometimes loosely within the framework of the 'law'. Vigàta is based on the author's native birthplace Porto Empedocle, which has subsequently changed its name to Porto Empedocle Vigàta to honour Camilleri. Donna Leon has said that Camilleri's novels 'breathe out the sense of place, the sense of humour and the sense of despair that fills the air of Sicily'. And certainly Camilleri's Sicily is drawn from his own experience. Visitors to Sicily can view the villa where Camilleri's mother used to live and the author's house (although he resides in Rome for most of the year). They can also eat some of the dishes that gastronome Montalbano dines on at the San Calogero trattoria, which actually exists in Porto Empedocle Vigàta. Sicily Tours runs a literary tour to visit the places featured in the books and another tour that focuses on the locations featured in the television adaptation of the books around Ragusa Ibla, a baroque inland town that is UNESCO heritage-listed in the south-east of the island.

📺 *Il commassario Montalbano* (1999)

📶 http://www.sicilytourguides.net (tours)

---

moves from his marriage to Emma to her grand passion with Nelson.

Non-fiction

Gomorrah: Italy's Other Mafia (2006)
Roberto Saviano

Written by Neopolitan Saviano, *Gomorrah: Italy's Other Mafia* exposes the gritty underworld of Naples. Saviano describes a city overrun by the mafia and the centre of Italy's cocaine trade.

🎬 *Gomorra* (2008)

SICILY

Fiction

The Leopard (1958)
Giuseppe Tomasi di Lampedusa

Published in 1958, a year after Prince Giuseppe Tomasi di Lampedusa's death, this unfinished novel was instantly hailed as a masterpiece. Set in 19th-century Sicily, around the time of Italy's Risorgimento (1860), Lampedusa based his protagonist, Fabrizio Corbero, Prince of Salina, or 'The Leopard', on his grandfather. Through Lampedusa's beautifully written prose, the reader witnesses the decline of the local aristocracy, as seen through the rise to eminence of the fabulously wealthy former peasant Don Calogero Sedara. While the prince fails to adapt to the changing times, his favourite nephew, Tancredi, decides to confirm his own position in the new Sicilian society by marrying Sedara's daughter. Lampedusa claimed that Donnafugata in the novel is actually Palma Montechiaro and the palace at Donnafugata is 'one and the same as the one at Santa Margherita.' Visitors can take a Donnafugata tour to visit some of the places mentioned in the classic novel.

Il gattopardo (*The Leopard*; 1963) is Luchino Visconti's masterpiece, starring Burt Lancaster and Claudia Cardinale

www.sicilytourguides.net (tours)

The Day of the Owl (1961)
Leonardo Sciascia

Most people think of the mafia when they think of Sicily. Sciascia's *The Day of the Owl* (*Il giorno della civetta*) was the first novel to really evoke the reality of the Sicilian mafia. Sciascia (incidently a friend of writer Andrea Camilleri's) was inspired to write the novel (really a novella) after the assassination of a communist trade unionist. Set in Sicily, it follows the story of a young policeman from the north investigating a man's murder. He encounters silence, suspicion and the local mafia boss, who gives him a quick lesson on the difference between good and evil. Sciascia's books have received great critical

acclaim for their depiction of the mafia, Sicilian society and culture. The writer Gore Vidal once commented: 'What is the mafia? What is Sicily? When it comes to the exploration of this particular hell, Leonardo Sciascia is the perfect Virgil.'

Italy – *The Aeneid* (feature box)

To Each His Own (1966), Sciascia's highly acclaimed crime novel

CAPRI
Fiction

South Wind (1917)
Norman Douglas

Douglas's classic and much-acclaimed novel *South Wind* is based on the author's experiences of living on the island and delves into Capri's hedonistic society, of which Douglas was so much a part. A roman-à-clef, the book takes its name from the south wind, which 'blows constantly during the spring and summer. Hardly less constantly in autumn. And, in winter, often for weeks on end.' The 2009 edition of the book features an introduction by the writer Jan Morris.

Lunch with Elizabeth David (1999)
Roger Williams

Mixing history, fiction and fact, Williams's entertaining novel is partly set on the island of Capri, where the protagonist, Eric Wolton, is summoned in 1951 by his one-time seducer, the charming writer Norman Douglas, to attend a farewell lunch with his entourage (including Graham Greene and Gracie Fields) for the cookery writer Elizabeth David.

Non-fiction

Greene on Capri: A Memoir (2001)
Shirley Hazzard

Novelist Shirley Hazzard first encountered Graham Greene in the late 1960s in a cafe in Capri. This memoir is an affectionate account of Hazzard's friendship with the writer. *Greene on Capri* is also a beautiful evocation of the island, its romance and charm.

🔍 *Lunch with Elizabeth David*

SARDINIA
Fiction

Bakunin's Son (2008)
Sergio Atzeni

A Sardinian writer of some repute, Sergio Atzeni wrote in Italian but used many of the colloquialisms and phrases of his island. At present, only *Bakunin's Son* has been translated into English, although there are French translations of many of his other books. In this novel, a son tries to find out more about the life of Tullio Saba, his father, by interviewing the people who knew him. The book spans a time of great political change, from the early 20th century onwards, and the protagonist follows his father

---

The Aeneid

The celebrated first-century BC epic poem *The Aeneid* is considered to be Virgil's masterpiece. At the beginning of *The Aeneid*, we see Aeneus, son of the Trojan mortal Anchises and the goddess of love, Venus, sailing away from Troy after the sack of the city. One of the few survivors of the Trojan Wars, he leaves his land with a handful of Trojan citizens, including his father and his son, for Italy, where he has been told great fortune awaits him. After several adventures and his father's death, Aeneus lands in Carthage, North Africa (modern-day Tunisia), where he falls in love with Dido, the queen. Dido understands his loss, as she was herself driven from her homeland by her brother, Pygmalion, who murdered her husband. For a while, Aeneus is happy to stay in Carthage with Dido, until he is reminded that a greater glory awaits him. Sacrificing his love for Dido, who kills herself after he leaves, Aeneus sails away. His journey takes him to the Underworld, where his father shows him the future heroes of Rome to demonstrate why his journey is so important, to Sicily and finally to mainland Italy, where he must undergo further battle to achieve his ends.

Virgil (70–19BC) looked back to Homer's two epic works, *The Iliad* and *The Odyssey*, as the 12 books of *The Aeneid* sweep through Roman history from the birth of Rome to Augustus. Visitors to Italy can visit Virgil's place of birth in Mantua and his burial place in Naples, near the entrance to the Grotta Vecchia, a tunnel that was constructed during the rule of Augustus to connect Naples to other cities.

as he moves through the various stages of his life.

Reeds in the Wind (2008)
Grazia Deledda

Nobel Prize winner Grazia Deledda wrote 33 novels and several collections of short stories, most set on the island of Sardinia. In *Reeds in the Wind*, Deledda focuses on the Pintor sisters, the descendants of noble landowners. Deledda presents their story against the rugged backdrop of her beloved island, detailing the folk culture, festivals and magnificent but unforgiving landscape of Sardinia.

🔍 *They Were Found Wanting*

LATVIA
Fiction

Headcrusher (2005)
Garros-Evdokimov

An international best-seller, *Headcrusher* is a fast-paced thriller in which Vadim, a PR person in Latvia's biggest bank, spends most of his time playing a violent cybergame called *Headcrusher*. When his boss discovers him doing this, fantasy and reality merge as Vadim embarks on a killing spree.

The Dogs of Riga (2001)
Henning Mankell

Inspector Wallander doesn't always stay in Sweden... In the early 1990s, after a life raft is washed up with two well-dressed but very dead men on it, Wallander discovers that they are of East European origin. In the course of his investigation, Wallander is forced to travel to Riga in Latvia, where he finds a country on the verge of democracy, but with police surveillance, corruption and gangs still very much at the fore.

🔍 Sweden – Kurt Wallander's Sweden (feature box)

NETHERLANDS

AMSTERDAM
Fiction

Love in Amsterdam (1962)
Nicholas Freeling

Crime writer Nicholas Freeling is probably best known for his novels featuring Amsterdam detective Piet van der Valk, who first made his appearance in *Love in Amsterdam*. In this novel van der Valk investigates a seemingly straightforward crime, in which a young woman is murdered with a gun belonging to her ex-lover. However, he claims not to have seen her for years... Featuring local slang, fast-paced plots set in and around the city's cafes, bars and canals and an extremely unorthodox hero, the 'Van der Valk' series was an international hit. When Freeling killed his hero off in 1972, he was inundated with complaints from angry fans and

263 Prinsengracht

Practically everyone has heard of Anne Frank and many people have read her diary. Although born in Frankfurt, Germany, Anne Frank spent the most significant part of her young life in hiding in her father's office building at 263 Prinsengracht in central Amsterdam. After the rise of the Nazis to power in 1933, the Franks decided it was no longer safe to live in Germany. Otto Frank, Anne's father, set up a business in Amsterdam and the family moved to the city, where they felt safe until the Nazi invasion of the Netherlands in 1940, and the subsequent persecution of Jewish people. In 1942, after her mother was notified that she would be sent to a work camp, the family went into hiding in a secret part of a building owned by Otto Frank's company; the Van Pel family also joined them there. Earlier in 1942, on Anne's 13th birthday, she had received a diary as a present and had begun to record the events that were to affect her and her family. She continued this practice while she was at Prinsengracht, meticulously recording the life of a Jewish family in hiding. When the hiding place was discovered in August 1944, Anne and her family were sent to Westerbork and from there to Auschwitz–Berkenau. Anne and Margot were sent on from there to Bergen–Belsen. It was here that Anne died of typhus. Her diary was later given to her father after her death. Published as *The Diary of Anne Frank*, it has been translated into most languages and has been an international best-seller since publication. The Anne Frank House, in Prinsengracht, where Anne and her family spent so much time, has been open since 1960 as a museum; it contains fragments of letters and other memorabilia relating to the Franks' life and holds special exhibitions.

📶 http://www.annefrank.org/content.asp?pid=1&lid=2 (The Anne Frank House)

several countries refused to publish his books.

📺 *Van der Valk* (1970–2)

The Coffee Trader (2004)
David Liss

In Liss's novel, protagonist Miguel Lienzo, a Portuguese Jew, is persuaded to invest in coffee, a new strange commodity, by a lovely Dutch widow. Lienzo is one of the many Portuguese Jews living in Amsterdam in 1659 who lost everything when they fled the Inquisition. Determined to make money, Lienzo realizes that that the stakes are so high

that he really cannot trust anyone. He must also make sure that his enemy, Parido, doesn't catch wind of his investment.

The Apothecary's House (2005)
Adrian Mathews

Set in modern-day Amsterdam, Paris-based writer Mathews's book is part detective fiction, part exploration of the serious subject of art looted by the Nazis. When an elderly woman comes to the Rijksmuseum demanding her painting back, Ruth, an art historian, starts to investigate the truth of the claim. As she delves deeper she is threatened, her boat on Bloemgracht canal is vandalized and she finds herself involved in a world she never knew existed.

 Rijksmuseum
(http://www.rijksmuseum.nl/)

Tulip Fever (1999)
Deborah Moggach
Set in Amsterdam in the 1630s, Moggach's novel centres on the young Sophia, married to an elderly rich husband, Cornelis, to whom she's beholden. Cornelis decides to commission a portrait of Sophia by the painter Jan van Loos. The painting also includes a tulip, from which (like so many other men) he has made a great deal of money. Moggach meticulously creates a vivid portrait of the emerging city, its extreme wealth, its society and, of course, the passion for one flower and its bulbs...

🔊 http://www.deborahmoggach.com
(author website)

The Assault (1982)
Harry Mulisch
The Assault examines the weighty issue of culpability and innocence. At the end of the Second World War, after seeing his family shot when they are wrongly implicated in the death of the Chief of Police, a Nazi collaborator, Mulisch's protagonist Anton moves from Haarlem to Amsterdam to be with his uncle and aunt. An intense and powerful book, the plot is based on a real incident.

🎬 *The Assault* (1986)

OTHER REGIONS
Fiction

The Girl with the Pearl Earring (1999)
Tracy Chevalier
Weaving the story behind Johannes Vermeer's painting *The Girl with the Pearl Earring*, Chevalier creates Griet, the daughter of a tile painter, who goes to work in the Vermeer household in 17th-century Delft. A Protestant, Griet is a lovely young girl, the very opposite of the Catholic Catharina, Vermeer's wife, who is immediately suspicious of her. Vermeer (1632–75) recognizes some artistic talent in the young girl and teaches her in secret about colour palettes and how to make paints. Matters are complicated further when the great artist's patron insists that Vermeer paint Griet as his next commission. Chevalier's detailed accounts of the artistic process, the colours, culture and society of Delft at the time help conjure up this small town. The book was turned into a highly successful film starring Colin Firth as Vermeer and Scarlett Johansson as Griet.

🎬 *The Girl with the Pearl Earring* (2003)
🔊 http://www.tchevalier.com (author website)

In Babylon (1997)
Marcel Möring
A best-seller in the Netherlands and winner of several awards, *In Babylon* is an entertaining family saga that spans Eastern Europe, Holland and the United States. When Nathan

Hollander and his niece are stranded in the Dutch house of his late uncle, Herman, during a blizzard, Nathan begins to tell her about her ancestors, a family of clockmakers. Möring's book was highly acclaimed.

NORWAY

OSLO

Fiction

The Half Brother (2003)
Lars Saabye Christensen
Living in Oslo in the 1960s, Barnum and Fred are half-brothers. Barnum is a screenwriter while Fred, conceived during the rape of their mother, lurks in the shadows. Leading very separate lives, they are brought together again at their mother's deathbed. *The Half Brother* was a best-seller and a literary sensation in Norway.

Death in Oslo (2009)
Anne Holt
In 2005 the first US female president chooses Norway for her first state visit. Unfortunately, she has a secret and when she vanishes from a secure, locked bedroom, the Norwegian police and FBI have to work together to find her.

The Redeemer (2009)
Jo Nesbø
Hailed by Michael Connelly as his favourite hero, Oslo-based detective Harry Hole is the troubled protagonist of crime writer and musician Jo Nesbø's series of novels. In *The Redeemer*, an assassin realizes that he's killed the wrong man but becomes increasingly desperate as Harry and his team investigate and begin to close in on him. Nesbø uses local places in his novels, including the Schroeder restaurant (Waldemar Thranes Gate 8), which is a local haunt, serving cheap Norwegian food. Harry lives in Sofie Gate in the east part of Bitlett, Oslo, near where the author once lived.

🛜 http://www.jonesbo.co.uk/jonesbo.asp (author website)

OTHER REGIONS

Fiction

Don't Look Back (2003)
Karin Fossum
Introducing the no-nonsense character Inspector Sejer, *Don't Look Back* is set in a village near Kollen Mountain. The sleepy town is disturbed when a young girl's body is found in a lake at the top of the mountain and it's shown that still waters run deep.

Dreamers (1904)
Knut Hamsun
Hamsun's classic novel is set in a remote Norwegian fishing village, where Ove Rolandsen, the telegraph operator and local Casanova, hatches a series of madcap plans to make

his fortune. He lands himself in trouble when he decides to manufacture glue from fish waste. Nobel Prize winner Hamsun was one of the most influential writers of the 20th century, revered by such authors as Rebecca West and Isaac Bashevis Singer.

Out Stealing Horses (2004)
Per Petterson

Set in a remote part of Norway, near the Swedish border, as Trond, a man in his 60s, looks back to the summer in 1948 that changed his life when he and a friend borrowed some horses. Essentially a coming-of-age story, Petterson's love for the landscape and evocative descriptions of the forest and seasons bring the Norwegian countryside to life.

Kristin Lavransdatter (1920–22)
Sigrid Undset

Nobel Prize winner Sigrid Undset is believed to have largely won the award for her trilogy *The Wreath* (*Kransen*, 1920), *Wife* (*Husfrue*, 1921) and *The Cross* (*Korset*, 1922) set in 14th-century rural Norway. The heroine of the books, Kristin Lavransdatter, sacrifices her values, morals and faith for love and when she eventually marries, she realizes that she and her husband cannot make each other happy but that this is her destiny.

The Ice Palace (1963)
Tarjei Vesaas

For some people, Tarjei Vesaas's *The Ice Palace* comes close to being a perfect novel. Revealing Vesaas's profound respect and love for his country's landscape, the book is set in a remote Norwegian village, where two young girls, Siss and Unn, build a profoundly deep friendship. When Unn disappears, Siss is devastated. She struggles to retain her memories of her friend. Unn's fascination with a strange frozen waterfall, the Ice Palace, also haunts the novel. Vesaas's understated style has won many fans, including the novelist Doris Lessing. Vesaas also wrote in his native Nyorsk.

POLAND

Fiction

Death in Danzig (2004)
Stefan Chwin

Chwin's beautiful novel, set in 1945 Danzig (Gdansk), is a book about people and a town in transition as the Germans move out and Poles move back in. A time of chaos for Danzig, Chwin manages to present beautifully realized characters that give the town a sense of life, survival and courage.

The Tin Drum (1959)
Günter Grass

Grass's macabre yet funny novel established him as a writer of international renown. The protagonist, Oskar Matzerath, decides, aged three, clutching his new drumsticks and toy drum, just to 'stop' as he is – and so he does, 'for many years, I not only stayed the same size, but clung to the same attire.' Bitter and impassioned, Oskar scathingly shows us the madness of people during war and the cruelty of the Nazi era.

🎬 *Die Blechtrommel* (*The Tin Drum*, 1979)

Poland (1983)
James A. Michener

A typical Michener epic, *Poland* spans 800 years of history and follows three families from 1241 to the early 1980s, setting history against their changing and evolving lives.

Satan in Goray (1935)
Isaac Bashevis Singer

Singer's account of the Jews of Goray, recovering after the horrific massacre of Chmelnik in the 1640s, was originally published in instalments in a literary magazine in 1935, before being published in book form. As Goray recovers from being gutted, Sabbatai Zevi arrives claiming to be the Messiah and the isolated village falls prey to a period of extreme messianic fever. It is an interesting study of religious mania set in this brutal period of history.

Defiance (1983)
Nechema Tec

Tec tells the true story of Tuvia Bielska, who headed a group of Jewish resistance fighters that rescued more than 1,200 Jews, hiding them in the forests of Belorussia, during the Second World War. A story of great courage, bravery and survival, Tec's book reveals one of the largest efforts by Jews to save other Jews during the war.

🎬 *Defiance* (2008), starring Daniel Craig and Liev Schreiber

House of Day, House of Night (2002)
Olga Tokarczuk

A best-seller in Poland, Tokarczuk's *House of Day, House of Night* is a collection of linked narratives set in Nowa Ruda, a small Polish village near the Czech border, as seen by a woman moving to the village with her husband. The village, set in an area of shifting borders and identities, has been Czech, German and Austro–Hungarian in the past.

PORTUGAL

LISBON
Fiction

Tragedy of the Street of Flowers (2001)
Eça de Queiroz

Published to celebrate the centenary of the author's death, *Tragedy of the Street of Flowers* was an unfinished manuscript. Although largely unknown outside of Portugal, Eça (as he is known in his native country), is considered the nation's greatest novelist and was celebrated by authors as varied as Zola and V. S. Pritchett.

Visitors to Lisbon can find a statue of him at the southern end of the Bairro Alto, a few steps down the Rua do Alecrim. Eça is best known for his brilliant satirization of the decadence of the bourgeoisie and aristocracy in late 19th-century Lisbon. At the heart of the novel is the cosmopolitan beauty Genoveva de Molineux, whose appearance in Lisbon society throws it into a fever of speculation. It also draws the protagonist Vitor da Silva slowly into an incestuous relationship with the mother who had abandoned him as a child.

The Book of Disquiet (1992)
Fernando Pessoa

Hailed as a masterpiece by authors John Lanchester, George Steiner and Paul Bailey, this book by one of Portugal's leading writers was published posthumously. Described as a 'factless autobiography', through notebooks and fragments it details the life of a Lisbon bookkeeper, Bernardo Soares. Pessoa himself described it as the 'saddest book ever written'.

🔍 *The Year of the Death of Ricardo Reis*

The Year of the Death of Ricardo Reis (1984)
José Saramago

Probably best known in the West for the novel *Blindness* (which spawned the film of the same name starring Julianne Moore, 2008), Saramago is a Nobel Prize winner. This book, like many of his others, experiments with different styles and challenges the reader. The Ricardo Reis of the title is actually a heteronym of the writer Fernando Pessoa and the book involves Reis, newly returned from Brazil, embarking on many conversations with his old friend Pessoa while they walk the streets of Lisbon. This has led to the book being referred to as the 'Portuguese *Ulysses*'. Set in the 1930s, the novel's backdrop is the Spanish Civil War (1936–9), war with Europe, fascism and many other key political events of the time.

🔍 *The History of the Siege of Lisbon* (1989) is also set in the city

🔍 *The Book of Disquiet*; Ireland – Joyce's Dublin (feature box)

The Last Kabbalist of Lisbon (1998)
Richard Zimler

Written in the tradition of Umberto Eco's *The Name of the Rose*, Zimler's book is set in early 16th-century Lisbon. Part detective story, part history, it explores what happened to the Jews living in Portugal after Isabella and Ferdinand's expulsion of the Jews from Spain. The Portuguese king, encouraged by the Spanish to follow suit, embarked on a policy of forced conversion to Christianity, which culminated in the massacre of the Portuguese Jews in 1506. It is during this massacre that Berekiah Zarco, a young manuscript illustrator, finds the naked dead body of his uncle Abraham, a well-known kabbalist, in a secret cellar room. He sets out to discover what happened and suspects that his uncle was betrayed by someone he knew; someone in his intimate circle.

ROMANIA

Fiction

Balkan Trilogy (1981)
Olivia Manning

Based on Manning's experiences of living in Romania with her husband, *The Great Fortune* (1960), *The Spoilt City* (1962) and *Friends and Heroes* (1964) tell of Guy and Harriet Pringle as they live first in Romania and then escape to Greece during the Second World War. In the first book, the newly married Pringles arrive in Bucharest, a country on the cusp of war, full of strange characters and with a society still trying to cling on to the decadence of the past; in *The Spoilt City*, set in 1940, the Pringles find their position in Bucharest, ever more precarious as it becomes increasingly obvious that the Nazis might invade at any moment; and the third book finds Harriet in Athens waiting for Guy who is still in Bucharest. Manning's books were very well received on publication and Anthony Burgess referred to her as one of the best female novelists of her generation.

📺 *Fortunes of War* (1987)

The Land Of Green Plums (1996)
Hetar Müller

A group of students struggle for some semblance of normality at the height of Ceausescu's reign of terror. Müller's account breathes life into what it was like to live under a dictatorship.

RUSSIA

GENERAL

Fiction

Doctor Zhivago (1957)
Boris Pasternak

Pasternak's epic novel, generally recognized as one of the greatest Russian books of the 20th century, was first published in translation in Italy in 1957, but was banned in the Soviet Union for three decades because of its alleged 'nonacceptance of the Socialist Revolution'. The novel opens in 1903, when the mother of Yuri Zhivago (the 'Dr' of the title) dies. After his father commits suicide, Yuri is brought up by the Gromeko family in Moscow. A talented poet, Yuri decides to study medicine at the University and later marries Tonya with whom he has a child, Sasha. During the First World War, he meets Lara, a young woman, who he has encountered twice before – when attending an attempted suicide and when Lara tried to shoot a lawyer, Komarovsky. Lara has travelled west to find her missing husband Pasha, a young soldier, leaving their daughter in Yuriatin, Lara's birthplace in the Urals. Although attracted to Lara, Yuri returns to Moscow to his family after the Revolution, but famine drives them from the city to Varyniko, Tonya's father's old estate, which is now a collective. Yuri and Lara are reunited again in Yuriatin, the nearest town to the estate, and begin an affair. Yuri eventually decides to break off the affair and confess everything to his wife, but is captured by the partisan army who conscript him as a medical officer. After his release, he travels back to Yuriatin to find Lara, but through further difficulties the couple is separated again. Yuri returns to Moscow, where he eventually dies. Lara turns up at his funeral. Partly autobiographical, Yuri is based on Pasternak and Lara, most likely, on his lover, Olga Ivinskaya. The book was turned into an award-winning film by director David Lean.

📽 *Dr Zhivago* (1965), starring Omar Sharif (Yuri), Julie Christie (Lara), Geraldine Chaplin (Tonya)

Anna Karenina (1875–77)
Leo Tolstoy

The wife of a prominent but unaffectionate St Petersburg government official and mother of a young son, Anna Karenina has a typical upper-middle class existence, until she meets Count Vronsky, a young officer of the guards. The couple fall in love and begin an affair but when Anna asks for a divorce, her husband refuses. After giving up everything, even her young son, Anna and Vronsky become social outcasts. Finally, Vronsky's interest begins to wane and he leaves her, but Anna, still a social pariah, has few options left to her and decides to take her life tragically into her own hands. Set predominantly in St Petersburg, where the Karenins live, Tolstoy's book also moves further afield into the Russian countryside, to Moscow and even Italy.

📽 There have been many film and television adaptations, but the 1935 film starring Greta Garbo is probably the best known

➕ http://www.ibiblio.org/sergei/Exs/YasnayaPoliana/yp1.html (Tolstoy's estate, Yasnaya Poliana, situated in Tula, is open to visitors)

Non-fiction

A People's Tragedy: The Russian Revolution, 1891–1924 (1997)
Orlando Figes

This hugely impressive book is a meticulously researched and captivating account of one of the most important events of the 20th century, the Russian Revolution. Proposing that the revolution occurred from 1891 to 1924, Figes examines the tragic circumstances that led to the demise of the nobility in Russia and the horrific brutality of the revolution itself, which led to the dehumanization of the great majority of the people. Figes brings individuals to life, drawing on personal papers and histories to illustrate the magnitude of the effects of the Revolution on the people. This is not only a fascinating read, but also a great insight into this turbulent period of Russian and world history.

Putin's Labyrinth (2008)
Steve LeVine

Journalist LeVine's examination of Vladimir Putin could easily form the basis of a spy novel. He provides a penetrating analysis of modern Russia under the repressive rule of yet another autocrat and looks at the 'state-sponsored' deaths of Putin's critics, such as the inspiring journalist Anna Politkovskaya. LeVine draws on his own experiences of living and working in Russia for more than a decade to give an informed and compelling look at Russia today.

ST PETERSBURG AND ENVIRONS

Fiction

Petersburg (1913–14)
Andrei Bely

Although born in Moscow, Russian symbolist poet and writer Andrei Bely is perhaps best known for his novel *Petersburg*, which has often been compared to Joyce's *Ulysses* as the city becomes a character in itself. The book, set over two days in 1905 St Petersburg, is a story of betrayal and conspiracy in pre-Revolutionary Russia and follows a group of radicals as they plan the assassination of tsarist bureaucrat Senator Apollon Apollonovich Ableukhov. The senator's son, Nikolai, is given the task of murdering his father, but the plan deteriorates into farce. In order to get the language of the time right, Bely studied Gogol and Pushkin in particular and the city he presents mixes reality with myth and hallucination. It is one of straight lines laid on top of 'cosmic infinity'. Vladimir Nabokov called the book one of the four greatest of the 20th century.

🔍 Ireland – Joyce's Dublin (feature box)

The Master of Petersburg (1994)
J. M. Coetzee

Coetzee imagines Dostoyevsky returning in disguise to St Petersburg from exile in Dresden to investigate the death of his stepson, Pavel. As the middle-aged writer struggles to find the truth behind Pavel's suicide and rediscover his stepson in the process, he becomes obsessed with the boy, moving into his room, taking his landlady as his lover (as his stepson had done?) and tracking every part of Pavel's life. He discovers as he does so a world of conspiracy and intrigue led by the murky figure of Sergei Nechaev.

🔍 Life and Times of Michael K

The Siege (2001)
Helen Dunmore

As Hitler's troops prepare to lay siege to the imperial city of St Petersburg, the Levin family fight for love and survival. Dunmore's beautiful book is a carefully researched and detailed portrayal of a formerly majestic city under siege and the people who struggle on in times of war.

🔍 The Betrayal

Fathers and Sons (1862)
Ivan Turgenev

Fathers and Sons is essentially a study of the complexities of the relationships between older and younger generations. The book's central character, nihilist and medical student Yevgeny Bazarov, has been described as 'the first Bolshevik' in Russian literature. Bazarov travels with his friend, Arkady, to stay at Arkady's father's estate, just outside St Petersburg. Arkady's father, Nikolai Petrovich Kirsanov, his mistress and his brother, Pavel, live on the estate and represent the old order, while Arkady and Bazarov represent the new order, which rejects the social and political norms of their elders. Although Turgenev is highly regarded in his native Russia, hostile reviews of *Fathers and Sons* arguably led the author to leave his homeland. He died in France, but requested that he be buried in St Petersburg, where his remains lie in Volkov Cemetery. Visitors can see Turgenev's grand statue created by Yan Neiman and Valentin Sveshnikov, who used Turgenev's death mask when sculpting the writer's face.

[+] The first Turgenev Museum in Moscow, a building in Ostozhenka Street rented by Turgenev's mother, and where the writer lived and worked during his stays in Moscow between 1840–50, will open in 2011

[Q] *Sketches from a Hunter's Album* about Turgenev's travels through Russia, satisfying his passion for hunting

Crime and Punishment – Dostoyevsky's St Petersburg

Possibly one of the best-known pieces of Russian literature, *Crime and Punishment* is synonymous with the city of St Petersburg. The impoverished protagonist Raskolnikov is affected by the city, which plays a central role in the novel and in directing the actions of the book's characters. Living in a cramped room, Raskolnikov is as oppressed at home as he is by the outside city. When Raskolnikov plans and commits murder, he justifies it by claiming that society would be better off without his victim, who is a parasite. Visitors to the city can see many of the locations featured in this book. Tuchkov Bridge, which crosses the Malaia (Little) Nev and is the bridge that Raskolnikov crosses on his way to the islands; the Nicholas Bridge, which spans the Neva River and connects central St Petersburg with Vasilievskii ostrov (island), is where Raskolnikov throws away a 20-kopek coin that was given to him by a sympathetic woman who took pity on his shabby appearance; and at the entrance to Grivtsova Pereulok from Haymarket Square is the place where Raskolnikov overhears the fateful conversation informing him that his victim, the pawnbroker, would be alone in her apartment. Visitors can also view the author's various homes, including his last apartment at 5 Kuznechnyi Pereulok, on the corner of Dostoevskogo Ulitsa (number 2), formerly Iamskaia Ulitsa, today a museum, where he lived from 1878 to 1881 and wrote *The Brothers Karamazov*. Dostoyevsky is buried at the Tikhvin Cemetery (Tikhvinskoe kladbishche) at the Alexander Nevsky Monastery (Aleksandro-Nevskaia Lavra).

[+] Dostoyevsky Memorial Museum – http://www.saint-petersburg.com/ museums/dostoyevsky-memorial-museum.asp

Non-fiction

Literary St Petersburg (2007)
Elaine Blair

Much of Russian literature is set in and around the city of St Petersburg. Blair's book focuses on 15 writers, who lived, worked and/or set their books in this magnificent location. The writers include: Anna Akhmatova, Fyodor Dostoyevsky, Nikolai Gogol, Vladimir Nabokov, Alexander Pushkin, Leo Tolstoy and Ivan Turgenev. Each entry features a biographical sketch and some analysis of the author's relationship to the city, the locations he or she visited, such as the square in *Crime and Punishment* where the murderer-hero asks for forgiveness.

MOSCOW AND ENVIRONS

Fiction

The Master and Margarita (1940)
Mikhail Bulgakov

Bulgakov's satirical masterpiece has the Devil living in Moscow, disguised as Professor Woland. With his entourage of strange characters, including a talking black cat, he causes havoc in Moscow. Woland searches for the Master, a resident in a psychiatric hospital, after his novel, based on the repressive regime of Pontius Pilate and its condemnation of Jesus in Jerusalem, was savaged. Margarita, the Master's mistress, sells her soul to Woland in exchange for the writer's release. The novel was highly critical of Soviet society between 1920 and 1940 and did not appear in its full form until 1973. Visitors to Moscow can take a bus tour of Bulgakov's haunts in Moscow and see where Bulgakov lived when he wrote the novel, next door to Bulgakov House, which is today a gathering place for artists.

➕ http://www.mn.ru/lifestyle/20100118/55403412.html (tour)

➕ http://www.inyourpocket.com/russia/Moscow/Sightseeing/Writer-s-museums/Bulgakov-House_39392v (tour)

The Russia House (1989)
John le Carré

Master of espionage le Carré this time gives us further intrigue and suspense in Russia. Barley Scott Blair, a middle-aged publisher, regularly attends book fairs in Moscow. When a beautiful woman, Katya, tries to get a typescript to Barley (in fact a breakdown of Soviet nuclear capabilities and atomic secrets), it falls into the hands of British Intelligence. Barley finds himself manipulated into working with them to find out if the document is authentic.

🎬 *The Russia House* (1990)

Darkness at Noon (1940)
Arthur Koestler

Set during the Moscow Trials against Stalin's opponents during the Great Purge of the 1930s, Koestler's novel explores the brutality of politics. The protagonist,

Nicolas Rubashov, an old guard Communist, waits out his days in prison, victim of an unnamed government that has arrested and incarcerated him for crimes he has not committed.

Child 44 (2008)
Tom Rob Smith

This best-selling crime novel opens in Moscow in the early 1950s, when secret policeman Leo Demidov, a young veteran of the war, finds himself involved in the case of a four-year-old child, who officially died in a train accident. The boy's father, a fellow officer, believes he was murdered. Transferred to a provincial office, Demidov discovers similar cases and the existence of a serial killer preying on young children. Demidov soon finds himself torn between obeying the state in which he believed and stopping a ruthless killer.

Boris Akunin – a literary Russian Frankenstein

Akunin's detective books, set mostly in late 19th-century Russia and featuring the elegant detective Erast Fandorin, have sold more than 20 million copies around the world. Akunin (the pseudonym of Grigory Chkhartishvili) started writing the books in the 1990s for the emerging Russian middle classes. At the time, he claims, there were only two types of Russian literature – classic heavyweights written by the masters, such as Tolstoy, or pure pulp – and so he began to write detective novels to fill that gap.

Erast Fandorin made his first appearance in *The Winter Queen*, a novel set in pre-Revolutionary tsarist Moscow, a place vividly described as full of international intrigue, danger and romance. At this point a young, naive detective, poor but from an aristocratic background, Fandorin, through bitter experience and personal loss, emerges to become the cool-headed, attractive, highly intelligent detective of the later novels. Akunin describes his character as very 'un-Russian', in fact 'Anglo–Japanese' – a British gentleman (in style and manners), a Russian intellectual (although this is often underplayed) and a Japanese samurai (as his moral code and reasoning gained during his time as a diplomat in the East shows). Fandorin also has the most extraordinary luck and he can't lose when he's placing a bet, a fact that stands him in extremely good stead in several of the novels. In the tradition of all good detectives, Fandorin has a faithful sidekick, his loyal, yet comic Japanese assistant and servant Masa (introduced in *The Death of Achilles*).

The Fandorin books are beautifully researched and historically accurate, telling not just a good yarn but also depicting Russia and, in many cases, other parts of Europe, at this politically volatile time. Fast paced, with often quite complicated plots, the books also evoke the Russian landscape and the cities of Moscow and St Petersburg, in particular. Akunin's eye for detail enables the reader to easily imagine the culture and politics of late 19th-century Russia and Europe. The 'Fandorin' books are the best of their genre.

http://www.boris-akunin.com (featuring information on the 'Fandorin' novels and the 'Sister Pelagia' series also written by Akunin)

SIBERIA

Fiction

The Kitchen Boy: A Novel of the Last Tsar (2003)
Robert Alexander

The question of what happened to Tsar Nicholas II and his family in their last days has informed the plots of many books, plays, films and television plays – *The Kitchen Boy* provides yet another explanation. Set in Yekaterinburg, on the Siberian side of the Ural Mountains, where the Romanovs were exiled in Ipatiev House, Alexander recounts their last days. Blending fact with fiction, the book is narrated by an elderly widower, Misha Semyonov, now living in America. As death approaches, Misha decides to reveal his past to his granddaughter – he is none other than Leonka, the kitchen boy who vanished from the house where the Romanovs were held captive, apparently just hours before they were shot. Misha reveals that he carried messages between the tsar and the band of men the tsar hoped would rescue them and that he witnessed the executions of the family. But does he know what happened to Tsarevich Alexei and his sister Grand Duchess Maria, the two people whose bodies were never recovered?

➕ http://www.the-trans-siberian.com/tsr/tsr02/ (Trans-Siberian Railway, The Romanov Triangle tour, from Moscow to Siberia)

Kolyma Tales (1980)
Varlam Shalamov

Shalamov's stories of life in the labour camp of Kolyma, in north-east Siberia, are based on his personal experiences. Born in 1907, Shalamov was first arrested as a student in 1929 for an unknown crime and sent to a camp in Solovki for three years. He was later arrested again and sent to Kolyma, although he didn't begin writing his stories until after he was released from prison in 1951. The stories mix fact and fiction and largely draw on the relationships between the prisoners and the officials, doctors, and other people who live and work in the camps. Visitors to the region can travel along the Kolyma Highway (the road of bones), today a World Heritage Site, built entirely by forced labourers, whose bones were often added to building materials. Several of the Gulag sites along the route are museums.

➕ http://www.worldheritagesite.org/forums/index.php?action=vthread&forum=6&topic=231 (Kolyma Highway)

One Day in the Life of Ivan Denisovich (1962)
Aleksandr Solzhenitsyn

A book that shocked the Western world when it was first published in translation in the early 1960s, *One Day in the Life of Ivan Denisovich* revealed the stark brutality of life in Stalin's concentration camps. Drawing on his own experiences of more than a decade in the Gulag, Solzhenitsyn provides not just a compelling and harsh portrayal of the Siberian camps, but also an indictment of Russian politics and society at the time.

Non-fiction

In Siberia (1999)
Colin Thubron

Respected writer Thubron embarked on a 24,140 km (15,000 mile) journey to discover Siberia, 'Russia's Elsewhere', which occupies about one-twelfth of the Earth's landmass. Travelling mostly by bus and train, with the occasional hitchhike, steamship and plane journey thrown in, Thubron visits the neglected and emptied prison camps, 'planned' cities, scientific towns and other areas for which Siberia is so famous. While Siberia has always served as Russia's prison, it has also been a haven for men and women seeking safety, such as the Cossacks. And, as Thubron also witnesses first-hand, Siberia is a place of unimaginable beauty, with large areas of unspoiled wilderness.

Shadow of the Silk Road

SPAIN

GENERAL

Non-fiction

The Buried Mirror: Reflections on Spain and the New World (1999)
Carlos Fuentes

Surveying five centuries of Hispanic culture and history, politician and writer Carlos Fuentes seeks to discover and portray a prevailing vital spirit that still exists today but finds its roots in Spain. This is an essential guide to understanding the Iberian peoples and the conflicts and divisions of modern Spain and Latin America.

As I Walked Out One Midsummer Morning (1969)
Laurie Lee

In 1934, Laurie Lee walked away from his life in England and went to Spain without knowing a word of Spanish. For a year he traipsed around the country, moving from region to region, encountering a people and a nation on the outbreak of one of the bloodiest civil wars in modern history and a beautiful countryside, about both of which he wrote so lyrically more than 30 years later. Following on from the autobiographical *Cider with Rosie*, Lee's trilogy concludes with *A Moment of War*.

United Kingdom, Gloucestershire – Cider with Rosie

Ghosts of Spain: Travels Through a Country's Hidden Past (2006)
Giles Tremlett

Tremlett evokes the heart of a culturally and historically rich country with great love and warmth. Part history, part travelogue and part journalistic enquiry, this book gives the reader a great overview and understanding of Spain and its people. Examining the ghosts of the country's past, Tremlett asks such questions as, 'Why do the Catalans hate Madrid?' and 'Were the 2004 Islamist bombers harking back to a Moorish past?' He takes readers on his voyage of discovery, introducing them to a range of different people and places, from a roadside brothel and a royal residence to a garish hotel in Benidorm, and through doing so reveals his love of the country.

MADRID

Fiction

The Spanish Game (2006)

Charles Cummings

The Spanish Game is the third book featuring former MI6 agent Alec Milius. Alec has made a home and a new life in Madrid, where he is now working alone, but still susceptible to intrigue. After a politician disappears in mysterious circumstances, Alec decides to investigate and finds that the world is a very different place when he is not attached to an official agency. Described as the natural heir of John le Carré, Cummings sets up an intriguing and suspenseful book, set against the backdrop of Madrid.

🌐 http://www.charlescumming.co.uk/
home.htm (author website)

The Fencing Master (1988)

Arturo Pérez-Reverte

Set in a sweltering city on the eve of Spain's September Revolution in 1868, Pérez-Reverte's *The Fencing Master* tells of Don Jaime Astarloa, the greatest fencing master in Madrid, who teaches his art to an ever-dwindling group of students in the age of the pistol. Everything changes when Don Jaime is visited by the beautiful but mysterious Adela de Otera, who asks him to teach her in secret a very difficult sword thrust. Although Don Jaime baulks at teaching a woman, Adela's knowledge of fencing leads her to teach him and she soon reveals herself to be an excellent pupil.

🎬 The Fencing Master (*El maestro de esgrima*, 1992)

Winter in Madrid (2006)

C. J. Samson

A spy thriller, a love story and so much more, *Winter in Madrid* is set in 1940, when the once-majestic city lies ravaged after the Spanish Civil War (1936–9) and Franco considers entering into a pact with Hitler. Into this scene enters Englishman Harry Brett, a man sent to spy reluctantly on his old schoolmate, Sandy Forsyth, a businessman with apparently shady connections. Brett also meets Sandy's girlfriend Barbara, who still pines for her lost love, Bernie Piper (also one of Brett's former schoolmates). Bernie, a passionate Communist, disappeared during the war, but is actually interned in a camp. This is a fascinating evocation of Madrid (and Spain) just after the end of civil war and at the beginning of the Second World War.

Non-fiction

A Load of Bull: An Englishman's Adventures in Madrid (2007)
Tim Parfitt
In the 1980s, Parfitt was sent, as a young journalist, to Madrid to help launch Spanish *Vogue*. He was meant to stay six weeks and ended up staying nine years. Now living in East Anglia, Parfitt wrote this memoir because he was fed up with reading regional books based on Brits living abroad. This book is a about the challenges of living in a foreign city, and what shines through is Parfitt's love for Spain (and Madrid in particular). After the initial challenges of adapting to a much slower pace of life, in personal and business terms, Parfitt fell in love with the city.

SEGOVIA
Fiction

For Whom the Bell Tolls (1940)
Ernest Hemingway
Based on Ernest Hemingway's experiences in Spain before and during the Spanish Civil War (1936–9), this book, hailed by some as a masterpiece, takes place just outside Segovia in the mountains and dense forest of the Spanish Sierra. Robert Jordan, an American International Brigadist with expert knowledge of explosives, is assigned to blow up a bridge to coincide with an attack on Segovia itself. Hemingway intended his book to portray the reality behind the 'good fight' of the Loyalists in the war; according to reviews of the time, he largely succeeded.

📽 *For Whom the Bell Tolls* (1943), starring Gary Cooper and Ingrid Bergman

🔍 *The Sun Also Rises*; Cuba – *The Old Man and the Sea*; USA, Florida – *To Have and to Hold*

Non-fiction

Don Quixote's Delusions: Travels in Castilian Spain (2002)
Miranda France
Award-winning travel writer Miranda France spent a year in Spain in 1987, when the country was still emerging from its years of being ruled by a dictator. Eleven years later she returned to travel around Madrid, Segovia, Toledo, Salamanca and other places in central Spain. Through her travels and the characters whom she meets, France discovers that *Don Quixote* is a work of genius and its protagonist a symbol of the country itself. France believes the book does much to explain the Spanish character today.

BARCELONA AND CATALONIA
Fiction

Don Quixote (Part I, 1605; Part II, 1615)
Miguel Cervantes
A Spanish classic, *Don Quixote* is a comic satire following the adventures of a middle-aged farmer wishing to emulate the journey of a chivalrous knight. He swears allegiance to a local farm girl, Dulcinea del Tobosa, and sets out on an expedition astride his

trusty steed Rosinante with his squire Sancho Panza. After a catalogue of disasters and comic interactions with other knights he eventually returns home having been persuaded to abandon his ridiculous quest. Cervantes's book has inspired many people to visit Spain, not least to follow in the footsteps of Don Quixote. Several travel companies run tours visiting key sites in the book or in the author's own life, such as Alcalade Henares, where Cervantes was born, and Lagunas de Ruidera, where Don Quixote and Sancho visit.

🔊 http://www.spainexchange.com/
spain_tours/donquixote_route.php
(Don Quixote's Route, one of many
such tours)

A Dead Man in Barcelona (2008)
Michael Pearce
The fifth book in Michael Pearce's successful 'Dead Man in...' series is set at the turn of the 20th century in Barcelona. Sandor Seymour of Scotland Yard's Special Branch is called to the city to investigate the death of an Englishman two years earlier during the 'Tragic Week' – when Catalonian conscripts bound for Spanish Morocco to take part in an unpopular war rebelled against the Royalists. During the crackdown by the Spanish government, Sam Lockhart, an Englishman based in Gibraltar, was arrested and died. Seymour has to find out why. Pearce's novel is rich in setting and historical context.

🔍 Egypt – *The Girl in the Nile*

The Shadow of the Wind (2004)
Carlos Ruiz Zafón
This international best-seller caught the imagination of millions of readers around the world. Set in the back streets of Barcelona, during Franco's dictatorship, the book centres on Daniel Sempere's obsession with a lost book called *The Shadow of the Wind*. Daniel first discovers it as a 10-year-old boy in the Cemetery of Forgotten Books and is intrigued by both the book and its unknown author Julián Carax. So begins an investigation that leads him to discover life in pre-war Spain and the realities of war and also to cross paths with Laín Coubert, a man dedicated to eradicating Carax's work completely. Visitors to the city can take a walking tour to see some of the locations mentioned in the book, including the *calle* in which the Sempere bookshop is set.

🔊 http://www.barcelona-on-line.es/
marketing/SombraDelViento/eng.asp
(tour)

Tattoo (1975)
Manuel Vásquez Montalbán
Award-winning author and poet Manuel Vásquez Montalbán set his popular detective series featuring Pepe Carvalho in his native Barcelona. The 'Pepe Carvalho' books run from the end of Franco's rule to just beyond the Olympics. Carvalho is an ex-policeman and a former Marxist; he is also a gourmet whose stomach rules his life (Vásquez Montalbán was an acknowledged gastronome

who wrote two cookery books). In *Tattoo* Carvalho is hired to find out the identity of a decomposed body, which is pulled from the sea. His investigation brings him into close contact with drug dealers and prostitutes and takes him to Amsterdam in his bid to find out who John Doe is and what he's involved in. Carvalho has attracted many fans, and visitors to the city can go to the Raval district, which begins near Las Ramblas, where much of the action takes place. Cross the Carrer Ferran and a row of arches reveals the entrance to the Plaça Reial. Bar Glaciar, which appears in the books, is located below one of the arches. The Casa Leopoldo restaurant on Carrer Sant Rafael 23 also features in Montalbán's novels as one of Pepe Carvalho's haunts. Because food is such an important part of Carvalho's psyche, the Boqueria Market, the largest market in Spain, constantly appears in the books, and Carvalho is (like his creator was) a regular at Bar Pinocho, which is located within the market.

Non-fiction

Homage to Catalonia (1938)

George Orwell

Homage to Catalonia is based on George Orwell's experiences of war and betrayal while serving as an infantryman on the Republican side in the Spanish Civil War (1936–9). Orwell depicts what he perceived as a betrayal of the worker's revolution by the Spanish Communist Party, as supported by the Soviet Union, and of his own injuries, sustained in May 1937, during that war. It is an honest account of the journalist's experiences and a very good history of Spain at the time and the battle between communism and fascism in Europe.

🛜 http://www.george-orwell.org (George Orwell website, includes complete works online, biography, photos and essays on the author)

THE NORTH

Fiction

The Sun Also Rises (1926)

Ernest Hemingway

Hemingway was fascinated by Spain and set many of his books, both fiction and non-fiction in the country. Bullfighting also interested him and he set part of his novel *The Sun Also Rises* in Pamplona and the surrounding hills of Navarre in northern Spain. Set in the 1920s, the novel depicts the lost generation of expats living in Europe and moves between France and Spain, where the main protagonists Jake Barnes and the woman whom he loves, Lady Brett Ashley, go to watch the bulls run in the Festival of San Fermin. Visitors can drink and eat in Café Iruña on Plaza del Castillo, where Jake and his friends drink. They can also stay at Hemingway's favourite hotel, Gran Hotel La Perla (La Montoya in the book), where his favourite room 217 is now renumbered as 201. A bust of Hemingway can be found near the

Plaza de Toros on Paseo Hemingway. The village of Burguete, about an hour from Pamplona, and the river Irati have also become tourist attractions, as they feature in the book in a passage where Jake and Bill fish for trout in a secret spot, which Hemingway never revealed.

🎬 *The Sun Also Rises* (1957), starring Ava Gardner and Tyrone Power in the lead roles

🔍 *Death in the Afternoon*, Hemingway's non-fiction account of bullfighting

🏠 Gran Hotel La Perla (http://www.granhotellaperla.com/)

The Carpenter's Pencil (1998)

Manuel Rivas

Focusing on love and survival during war, the story opens with Dr Daniel Da Barca returning from exile in Mexico and being interviewed by a journalist about his experiences during the Spanish Civil War (1936–9). Condemned to death in 1936, the doctor was saved unknowingly by Herbal, a Falangist guard, who stepped in to save him. Herbal once murdered an artist who sketched prisoners in Santiago de Compestela and he kept the artist's pencil (originally a carpenter's pencil) as a keepsake. The ghost of the artist seems to whisper in his ear, thus becoming his conscience. Herbal is in love with Da Barca's lover, Marisa, and helps her to follow the doctor through his various Spanish prisons. A beautiful piece of prose, Rivas's book was originally written in his native Galician and received critical acclaim after it was translated.

THE SOUTH

Fiction

Shadows of the Pomegranate Tree (1992)

Tariq Ali

The first in the *Islam Quartet* by political commentator Tariq Ali, *Shadows of the Pomegranate Tree* is set in the period just after the fall of Granada in the 15th century, as witnessed by a Muslim family trying to decide how to survive. Ximenes de Cisneros, a fanatical inquisitor, attempts to obliterate Moorish culture, the most infamous event being the burning of Moorish books. Muslim families who had lived in the region for generations were offered the options of assimilation, exile or death. In this beautifully evocative book, Ali manages to portray much of the atmosphere of the time and focuses on a period of Islamic and Spanish history that has been little written about.

🔍 *The Islam Quartet – Shadows of the Pomegranate Tree*; *The Book of Saladin*; *The Stone Woman*; *A Sultan in Palermo*

Non-fiction

Family Life: Birth, Death and the Whole Damn Thing (1996)

Elisabeth Luard

As a young ex-debutante wife (of then 'King of Satire' Nicholas Luard) in London, Luard decided to take her family to the wilds of Andalusia in southern Spain. *Family Life* is Luard's moving book about her life during that time and it gives the reader a great insight into the Spanish psyche, culture and regional cuisine (recipes are scattered through the book). Luard is better known today as a cookery writer.

Driving Over Lemons: An Optimist in Andalusia (1999)
Chris Stewart

An enchanting and funny account of Chris Stewart's life in the Alpujarras mountains. When occasional Genesis drummer and sometime sheep farmer Chris Stewart visits Andalusia and falls in love with the Alpujarras, he decides to move there after purchasing a bargain home – after a while he realizes why it was so cheap.

MAJORCA
Non-fiction

A Woman Unknown: Voices from a Spanish Life (1999)
Lucia Graves

Daughter of writer Robert Graves, Lucia grew up from the age of three on the island of Majorca, where her father moved to the village of Deya. Graves had moved there on the recommendation of Gertrude Stein who described it as 'a paradise, if you can stand it.' After being educated in Switzerland, London and Oxford, Lucia married musician Ramn and settled in Spain. This book is an intimate account of Spain and Majorca and of Lucia's relationship with her father.

SWEDEN

GENERAL
Non-fiction

Letters Written in Sweden, Norway and Denmark (2009)
Mary Wollstonecraft

Reissued by Oxford University Press (2009) to celebrate the 250th anniversary of the great feminist's birth, this collection of letters was written just after the author tried to commit suicide for the first time and while she was travelling with her baby and nursemaid through Scandinavia on a mission to find a stolen boat of silver. First collected in book form in 1796, Wollstonecraft's letters to her lover, Gilbert Imlay, include vivid descriptions of her voyage, and of the people, landscape and places she encountered and visited. They also provide insight into her thoughts on revolutionary Europe and the workings of her mind at the time.

STOCKHOLM
Fiction

Missing (2003)
Karin Alvtegen

Sybilla is one of Sweden's dispossessed, those nameless, faceless people who are ignored by society; that is until a businessman pays for her meal and room in the Grand Hôtel and is found dead the

Kurt Wallander's Sweden

Readers of modern detective fiction have become increasingly aware of the plethora of very good, very erudite Scandinavian literature in this genre. Perhaps one of the most famous and successful exponents of such books is Swedish writer Henning Mankell, the creator of middle-aged detective Kurt Wallander. The books have been published in more than 30 countries, sold more than 25 million copies and spawned both Swedish and English television adaptations of the books, filmed at Ystad Studios.

The first Wallander novel, *Faceless Killers*, was published in 1991. In the books published in the almost two decades since then, readers have gained a deep insight into Wallander's family life and work. Although Wallander travels to other parts of Sweden, the books are primarily located in Ystad, the city in which the inspector lives and works – in real life, a seemingly fairly tranquil medieval city.

Located in the southern province of Skåne, Ystad was already a popular destination for tourists wanting to visit its historical sites and lovely beaches, but now it attracts a different type of visitor, one eager to stand outside the row of half-timbered houses that housed one of Mankell's serial killers (*One Step Behind*, 1997) or stay at the Hotel Continental, where Wallander frequently has dinner. They can visit the main square where a dead body was discovered near an ATM at the beginning of *Firewall* (1998), eat at Wallander's favourite pizzeria, Bröderna M, or have a Wallander herring sandwich or cake at Fridolfs Konditori, his favourite cafe. They can also visit his home at 10 Mariagatan (although it's the entrance to 11C that is often seen on television). The city offers a tour to enable fans to walk in Wallander's footsteps, or, for those who prefer to go it alone, the tourist office offers a map. Similarly, the Ystad Studios offer visitors a chance to look at material related to the Swedish adaptations.

Mankel's books also feature detailed and loving descriptions of the countryside outside of Ystad, such as Hagestad Nature Reserve near Löderup, where a murderer strikes in *One Step Behind*, or Löderup, on the eastern tip of Skåne, where Wallander's artist father lives.

🛜 http://www.inspector-wallander.org/guide/sweden/index.html (fan site, featuring information on Ystad)

🏠 http://www.hotelcontinental-ystad.se/en_index.asp (Hotel Continental)

➕ www.brodernam.se (Bröderna M)

➕ www.cineteket.se (Ystad Studios)

➕ Map www.ystad.se

next day. When another person is murdered in a similar fashion, Sybilla suddenly becomes news.

🏠 http://www.grandhotel.se/in_english/default.asp (Grand Hôtel Stockholm, one of Stockholm's finest hotels)

The Girl with the Dragon Tattoo (2005)
Stieg Larsson

Part of the *Millennium* trilogy, published in Europe between 2005 and 2007, the highly acclaimed *The Girl with the Dragon Tattoo* was originally called *Men Who Hate Women*. Larsson, who died after he finished the three books, was a well-known journalist, particularly famous for his fight against racism and fascism. *The Girl with the Dragon Tattoo* is a long, sprawling book that covers a lot of ground and several weighty themes – financial fraud, murder, abuse and racism among them. Disgraced journalist Mikael Blomkvist is asked by wealthy Henrik Vanger to look into the disappearance of his beloved great-niece Harriet on the family estate on (the fictitious) Hedeby Island, on the Norrland coast of Sweden, 36 years earlier. Each year, Henrik receives a gift, a mounted flower, as a reminder of Harriet. He is determined to find out what happened to her and if a family member killed her. Blomkvist begins to investigate and finds himself under investigation as well by Vanger to see if he's up to the job; the person surveying him is the unlikely tattooed girl of the title and the two form an unusual alliance to discover the truth. Visitors to Stockholm can take a tour to see some of the places mentioned in the book, including Bellmansgatan Street, where Blomkvist lives, and Goetgatan Street, where the magazine for which Blomkvist works, is based.

🎬 *Män som hatar kvinnor* (Men Who Hate Women, 2009)

📶 http://www.stieglarsson.com/ (author website)

➕ http://www.stadsmuseum.stockholm. se/museet.php?artikel=109&sprak= english (Millennium Tour, Stockholm City)

🔍 *The Girl Who Kicked the Hornets' Nest; The Girl Who Played with Fire*

Gregorius (2004)
Bengt Ohlsson
This award-winning re-imagining of Söderberg's Doctor Glas (*see overleaf*) sees the love triangle between Glas, Gregorius, the pastor, and his wife from Gregorius's viewpoint. Beautifully written, it captures Gregorius's longing and loneliness and explores the nature of love itself.

Roseanna (1968)
Maj Sjöwall and Per Wahlöö
The writers of a 10-book series featuring Swedish detective Martin Beck (written between 1965 and 1975), Maj Sjöwall and Per Wahlöö are generally considered to have put Swedish crime fiction on the map. The first in the series, *Roseanna*, was published in 1965 in Swedish and in English three years later, although all the books have recently been reissued. In the book we meet the melancholic Beck when he is called in to investigate the body of an unknown woman, found in the Göta Canal. Through dogged determination and detailed and solid police work, Beck links the woman back to a cruise ship, and gradually her identity and the mystery behind her death unravel. All of the 'Beck' books were turned into films, the most famous of which starred Walther Matthau (*The Laughing Detective*, 1973), although Martin Beck became Jake Martin and the story was relocated to San Francisco.

Doctor Glas (1905)

Hjalmar Söderberg

This classic book by playwright, short-story writer and novelist Hjalmar Söderberg shocked Swedish society when it was first published in 1905. It wasn't published in English until 1963. Set in Stockholm, the book takes the form of a journal in which Dr Tyko Gabriel Glas reveals his dark and sometimes comic innermost secret thoughts. Glas falls in love with the wife of an elderly pastor and plots to kill him. He also ponders over some extremely controversial moral dilemmas for the time, on such subjects as abortion and euthanasia. Through Glas's diary entries we see his boredom and cynicism and also the hypocrisy of Swedish society at the time.

🎬 *Doktor Glas* (Swedish, 1942)
🔍 *Gregorius*

OTHER REGIONS
Fiction

Hanna's Daughters (1998)

Marianne Fredriksson

First published in Sweden in 1994, Fredriksson's award-winning best-seller was first translated into English in 1998. Set in the grand isolation of the Scandinavian lakes and mountains, the story follows Anna who has returned home to visit her mother, Johanna. As she wanders through the house, she recalls scenes from her childhood, including of her silent grandmother, Hanna. A story of three generations of women, through diaries, letters and photographs, Anna begins to piece together not just her mother's but her grandmother's past.

SWITZERLAND
Fiction

Hotel du Lac (1984)

Anita Brookner

Winner of the 1984 Booker Prize, Brookner's novel follows Edith Hope, who finds herself washed up at the Hotel du Lac, in Switzerland, after embarrassing her friends. At the hotel, she finds a whole host of characters who make her realize what she wants from life.

🎬 *Hotel du Lac* (1986)
🔍 *Strangers*

Her Lover (1995)

Albert Cohen

First published in 1968 as *Belle de Seigneur*, Cohen's novel is set in 1930s' Geneva. When Solal, the Under Secretary General of the League of Nations, becomes increasingly disillusioned with the political and social world in which he operates, he turns to Ariana, the wife of a dull colleague, for solace. André Brink described this as the 'most beautiful love story ever told.'

TURKEY

ISTANBUL
Fiction

The Towers of Trebizond (1956)
Rose Macauley

The last novel of travel writer and novelist Rose Macauley, *The Towers of Trebizond* won several awards when it was published. Seen as largely autobiographical it focuses on a group of lively and eccentric travellers on their way from Istanbul to Trebizond (Trabzon on the Black Sea coast of north-east Turkey). The group includes a High Anglican clergyman and his friend, Aunt Dot (Dorothea ffoulkes-Corbett), 'a woman of dreams', who was allegedly based on Macauley's friend, the writer Dorothy L. Sayers.

Visitors can travel from Istanbul to Trabzon by boat.

➕ http://istanbultraveltours.com/sf-articles-of-Boat_Ferry_Travel_in_Istanbul-aid-29-tp-30_17.htm (boats run from May to September from Istanbul to Trabzon)

The Prophet Murders: A Hop-Ciki-Yaya Thriller (2008)
Mehmet Murat Somer

A refreshingly different, rather frothy look at Istanbul, Murat Somer's *The Prophet Murders* is firmly placed in the subculture of the city, the transvestite club scene. The narrator, Burcak, is a transvestite and the owner of one of the clubs. She is seriously disturbed when a series of murders start to upset her life, her business and the community. Murat Somer says 'Most tourists come and visit the historical sights of Istanbul, but we have very modern

---

Thumbprint (2004)

Friedrich Glauser

Hailed as the Swiss Simenon, Friedrich Glauser's life was almost as dramatic as his plots. Troubled by psychiatric problems and addicted to morphine, he spent much of his life in and out of mental asylums and also prison (for forging prescriptions); he also spent two years in the Foreign Legion. Just days before his wedding, he died, aged 42. Glauser left behind five elegantly written books, featuring Sergeant Studer and drawing on the author's experiences, including his time as a mental patient. *Thumbprint* introduces Studer, who is called in to investigate the death of a salesman in Gerzenstein forest on the Swiss–French border. Although seemingly straightforward, nothing is, of course, as it initially seems and Studer's investigation threatens the very ordered façade of Swiss society. Subsequent books in the series, all reissued by Bitter Lemon, include *In Matto's Realm* (2005), *Fever* (2006), *The Chinaman* (2007) and *The Spoke* (2008). Their locations include Bern and Basel.

🎬 *Thumbprint* (1939)

parts and the life is completely different there. I wanted to put in my novel the places where the tourists don't go.'

Belshazzar's Daughter (1999)
Barbara Nadel

The first in the crime series that features Inspector Ikmen, *Belshazzar's Daughter* examines the torture and murder of an elderly Jewish man, a crime that sends shock waves through Istanbul. Nadel's books have often been referred to as travelogues, so detailed are their descriptions of the city's geography and architecture.

🔍 *Death by Design*

My Name is Red (1998)
Orhan Pumuk

Nobel Prize winner Orhan Pumuk is one of Turkey's most celebrated authors. When *My Name is Red* was published in 1998 it quickly became the fastest-selling book in Turkish publishing history. Set in 16th-century Istanbul at the end of Sultan Murad III's reign, the book is part detective novel and part homage to the country's rich history and art. When the sultan secretly commissions an illustrated book, in a style that is deemed an affront to Islam, the artists involved are not allowed to know the identity of their patron. When one of them disappears, presumed dead, all kinds of passions and petty jealousies rise to the fore, and questions are asked about the morality of the

project and the reason behind the man's disappearance.

📶 www.orhanpumuk.com (author site)

The Flea Palace (2004)
Elia Shafak

Shafak's highly acclaimed book focuses on the residents of the Bonbon Palace, a once grand residency built by a Russian émigré at the end of the Tsarist period, but now a sadly rundown block of flats. Shafak uses the structure of *A Thousand and One Nights* to present stories within stories.

Non-fiction

The Bridge: A Journey Between Orient and Occident (2008)
Geert Mak

Mak's thoughtful and beautifully written travelogue brings to life an Istanbul that spans both the East and the West through the Galata Bridge, which crosses the Golden Horn. Linking the Sultan Ahmet district, where Topkapi Palace and Hagia Sophia lie, to Pera, the European shore, the bridge may not perhaps possess the grandeur or beauty of other such European structures, but Mak presents it as a microcosm of Turkey itself. Mak allows us to hear the stories of the people who live on, work and visit the bridge and through them, we gain a vital insight into Turkey's history, culture and society.

🔍 Europe, General – *In Europe: Travels Through the Twentieth Century*

The Orient Express: murder and intrigue

Perhaps one of the most popular books set on the train is Agatha Christie's *Murder on the Orient Express* (1932), in which Belgian detective Hercule Poirot pits his wits against a group of seemingly unconnected travellers, one of whom (at least) is involved in the heinous crime of murder. As Poirot travels from Stamboul (Istanbul) to London in the company of his friend M. Bouc, one of the passengers, Ratchett, is found dead, having been stabbed 12 times. As the train careers across Europe, through clever deduction, Poirot realizes that Ratchett is, in fact, a man called Cassetti, who several years ago kidnapped and killed the three-year-old daughter of a wealthy couple. He concludes that one of two things occurred: either everyone on the train is complicit and actually took part in the murder, or a stranger boarded the train and killed Ratchett. Knowing the truth, Poirot suggests to his friend what really happened...

The train also formed the setting for British writer Graham Greene's *Stamboul Train* (1932), arguably the book that made Greene's name. A gripping spy thriller, the plot unfolds as the train speeds across Europe, from Ostend to Constantinople (modern-day Istanbul), a journey which, a couple of years after the book's publication, became impossible to make due to shifting political alliances and the outbreak of war. The passengers of *Stamboul Train* join and leave the train at the various points at which it stops – Ostend, Cologne, Vienna, Subotica and Constantinople. Many authors have made use of a train journey as a frame for their plot, but perhaps there is no more luxurious, romantic or dramatic train than the Orient Express.

Murder on the Orient Express (1974), starring Albert Finney, Ingrid Bergman, Vanessa Redgrave and a host of other stars

http://www.orient-express.com/web/vsoe/vsoe_a2a_home.jsp (Orient Express)

Istanbul: Memories and the City (2008)
Orhan Pumuk

Essentially a love letter to his city, this book by one of the greatest living Turkish writers of our age presents a side to Istanbul, the old town, that most tourists never see. Pumuk says, 'To savour Istanbul's backstreets, to appreciate the vines and trees that endow its ruins with accidental grace, you must, first and foremost, be a stranger to them.' Among the destinations that Pumuk focuses on are the Galata Bridge, Eyup, where the holiest mosque in Istanbul is located, and the Bazaar District.

OTHER REGIONS
Fiction

On Freedom Street (2008)
Yesho Atil

On Freedom Street follows Mehmet, one of 10 children brought up without a father in a village in the mountains, to Adana, Turkey's fourth largest city, on the eastern Mediterranean coast. In this beautifully written book, Atil tells of love, loyalty and the importance of women in Turkish families.

Birds without Wings (2004)
Louis de Bernières

This book originated from a visit that the author paid to a deserted town in south-west Turkey. 'It used to be a mixed community, as described in the book more or less, and they obviously had a wonderful way of life, quite sophisticated. The town was finally destroyed by an earthquake in the Fifties, but it really started to die when the Christian population was deported,' the author said. In the book the town is called Eskibahce and is situated on the coast of south-west Anatolia; in reality it is called Kayaköy. De Bernières's book moves from the end of the Ottoman Empire, when Christians and Muslims lived peacefully together, through to the First World War (1914–18) when nationalist fervour increases and communities are torn apart.

🔍 Greece – *Captain Corelli's Mandolin*
🔍 *The Troublesome Offspring of Cardinal Guzman*

Memed, My Hawk (1955)
Yashar Kemel

Described as a masterpiece, *Memed, My Hawk* made the author an international name. The Memed of the title is brought up as the serf of a vindictive overlord, from whom he plans to escape with the girl he loves. His plan is foiled when his master captures the girl. Memed, who finds his way to the mountains, becomes a bandit hero, a Turkish Robin Hood, fighting against corruption and evil for the benefit of ordinary Turks. The book is set in the Chukurova plain in south-central Turkey.

🔍 *They Burn the Thistles*

Non-fiction

My Grandmother: A Memoir (2008)
Fethiye Cetin

Cetin grew up in Maden, where her grandmother was a respected Muslim woman. It was not until much later, when her grandmother asked Cetin for her help in tracking down some relatives, that she discovered her grandmother had endured great brutality and loss as a child. Born a Christian Armenian, in 1915 she had witnessed most of the men in her village being slaughtered. The womenand children were then forced to leave their homes on what was to become a death march. Rescued by a Turkish captain, who later adopted her, Cetin's grandmother survived the Armenian genocide. A gut-wrenching and important memoir on what is still a contentious part of 20th-century history.

🔍 Middle East – *The Great War for Civilization: the Battle of the Middle East*
🔍 *A Shameful Act*

UNITED KINGDOM

GENERAL
Non-fiction

Notes from a Small Island (1995)
Bill Bryson

After living in Britain for 20 years, and before his departure back to the United States, American writer Bill Bryson embarked on a journey across the island, from Lands End to John O'Groats. Bryson travelled mostly by public transport, and this book is a humorous but loving portrayal of his experiences of the country and its people. In 2003, in a poll organized for World Book Day, *Notes From a Small Island* was voted the book that best represents England, ahead of George Orwell's 1984!

🔍 *I'm a Stranger Here Myself* (1999), on Bryson's reunion with the land of his birth

ENGLAND

GENERAL
Fiction

A Dance to the Music of Time (1951–75)
Anthony Powell

Comprising 12 books, Anthony Powell's highly acclaimed series – better known under the title *A Dance to the Music of Time* – follows a group of people from 1914 to 1971. The books are a detailed look at English social history over five crucial decades in the 20th century, beginning with the First World War. The books, which draw upon Powell's experiences, feature, among other things, detailed descriptions of Bohemian London during that period, including the Ritz Hotel in Piccadilly, where Powell used to go to meet friends. Powell was inspired by Nicolas Poussin's painting *A Dance to the Music of Time* (found in the Wallace Collection, London), featuring Father Time playing music to which the Four Seasons dance. Powell made his main characters dance to time's tune.

📀 *A Dance to the Music of Time* (1997)
🔍 Wallace Collection (www.wallacecollection.org)

Brideshead Revisited (1945)
Evelyn Waugh

Waugh's nostalgic tale portrays England between the two world wars, through the eyes of Charles Ryder, a middle-aged army officer who finds himself near Brideshead, the home of his old friend Sebastian Flyte. Ryder recalls his life in Oxford in the early 1920s and his involvement with Flyte's fabulously wealthy aristocratic Catholic family. The England that Waugh presents, through scenes predominantly set in Brideshead, London and Oxford, is one of privilege and decadence, but it is also a country of great extremes – the fantastic wealth represented by Sebastian Flyte's family is set in contrast to the poverty experienced by the masses. The reader also gets a sense of the larger political and social events of the time, such as the 1926 General Strike, for which Ryder returns to England from France, the Spanish Civil War (1936–9), in which Sebastian's sister, Cordelia, works as a nurse, the rise of fascism and the outbreak of war in 1939. In 1981, ITV broadcast an award-winning adaptation of the book, featuring Jeremy Irons as Ryder and Anthony Andrews as Sebastian. This was mostly filmed at Castle Howard in Yorkshire.

- 🎬 *Brideshead Revisited* (2008)
- 📺 *Brideshead Revisited* (1981)
- ➕ www.castlehoward.co.uk (Castle Howard)
- 🔍 *Vile Bodies*

Non-fiction

Hidden Treasures of England: A Guide to the Country's Best Kept Secrets (2009)
Michael McNay

A lavishly illustrated guide to the best-kept secret places in England – be it a Roman villa in Lullingstone, Kent, or the Victorian murals in Manchester Town Hall. Aimed at the visitor who wants to get off the beaten track, this book is arranged geographically and provides detailed information on landmarks that are often forgotten or overlooked.

LONDON
Fiction

Hawksmoor (1985)
Peter Ackroyd

A dark and skilfully written book, *Hawksmoor* moves between the 18th and 20th centuries, interweaving the lives of the two protagonists – brilliant Satanic architect Nicholas Dyer, commissioned to build seven new London churches (Spitalfields, Wapping, Limehouse, Greenwich, Lombard Street, Bloomsbury and Moorfields) in the aftermath of the Great Fire, and Nicholas Hawksmoor, a detective investigating a series of murders, each committed within the grounds of one of Dyer's churches more than 200 years later. Ackroyd blends fact with fiction, cleverly changing time, events and place to create his world. Nicholas Hawksmoor, the detective, is named after the real-life 18th-century architect who, like the fictional Dyer, studied under Christopher Wren. *Hawksmoor* includes some extremely evocative descriptions of London during the plague, the rebuilding of the city after the Great Fire and of the churches themselves. Ackroyd lovingly describes London, present and past, in many of his works, including the novels *The Great Fire of London* (1982), *The House of Doctor Dee* (1983), set mainly in Clerkenwell in East London, and *Dan Leno and the Limehouse Golem* (1994), again set in London's East End.

- 🔍 Iain Sinclair's *Lud Heat* (1975), which also looks at Nicholas Hawksmoor's churches and which is often said to have inspired Ackroyd's *Hawksmoor*

Brick Lane (2003)
Monica Ali

Brick Lane in East London is historically synonymous with the Jewish and Asian communities who came to settle there in the late 19th and 20th centuries. A bustling area, famous in recent years for its curry houses, bangra and late-night bagel shops, Brick Lane has also become known for the artists and musicians who live and work there. The area has become a popular stop for tourists on their way to Columbia Road Flower Market or Spitalfields. In this book, Monica Ali tells the story of Nazneen, a young Bangladeshi girl who, after an arranged marriage, is forced to leave her native country, family and community to live with her new, much older husband in an inner-city London tower block. Nazneen's new life and environs are shown through the eyes of an outsider who speaks very little English, is married to a stranger and is very much isolated. Her world and ideas change when she meets the charismatic Karim.

🎥 *Brick Lane* (2007), starring Tannishtha Chatterjee, Satish Kaushik and Christopher Simpson and directed by Sarah Gavron

London Fields (1989)
Martin Amis

Amis's book was apparently originally titled *The Death of Love*, but published as *London Fields*. Although Amis describes London streets and green spaces, there is a conflict between the imagined locations of his plot and the real landscape of London – London Fields is, in reality, a green space in Hackney, East London, but the book is mostly set in West London. The park, in which protagonist Sam, a dying New York writer, walks with various other characters, is Hyde Park and the famous Portobello Road also features in the book. Set in 1999, just before the millennium, *London Fields* shows a city in moral, social and political decline in the last days of the 20th century. A film of the book is currently in production, directed by Michael Winterbottom and due for release in 2010.

🎥 *London Fields* (2010)

Twenty Thousand Streets Under the Sky: A London Trilogy (1935)
Patrick Hamilton

Set in 1930s' London, Patrick Hamilton's trilogy –*The Midnight Bell* (1929), *The Siege of Pleasure* (1932) and *The Plains of Cement* (1934) – evokes the quiet desperation of the people who work in, and frequent, the Midnight Bell, a seedy pub on the Euston Road. Hamilton, who is probably better known to many as the writer of *Rope* and *Gas Light* (both turned into acclaimed films), brings the grimness and reality of a rundown part of Central London to life, weaving his story around his three main characters: waiter Bob, barmaid Ella and prostitute Jenny. They spend their evenings in Soho, drinking in bars and clubs around Wardour Street, take coffee in

Hampstead and drive around Chiswick, where Jenny works at the beginning of *The Siege of Pleasure*, which also features Hammersmith Broadway. Hammersmith is also the location of the pub, where Jenny moves from being a housemaid to a prostitute; some people believe that the description is based on the pub called Edwards, on the Broadway – a very different place from the one featured in Hamilton's book. Writers such as J. B. Priestley, Graham Greene, Martin Amis and Doris Lessing have admired Hamilton's writing.

📺 *Twenty Thousand Streets Under the Sky* (2005)

🔍 *Hangover Square: A Story of Darkest Earls Court* (1941), which brings to life the grimy pubs of Earls Court just before the outbreak of the Second World War

Sherlock Holmes: The Complete Stories (1996)
Arthur Conan Doyle

Probably one of the most famous addresses in literary London is 221b Baker Street. There, on the first floor, world-famous detective Sherlock Holmes and his companion, Dr John H. Watson, solved many of the most heinous crimes ever committed in Victorian society. The creation of Sir Arthur Conan Doyle, Holmes first appeared in *A Study in Scarlet* (1887), and the stories were published in *Strand* magazine from 1891. Most were set in and around London, or at least featured 221b Baker Street, and many have detailed descriptions of London

society and the criminal underworld of the late 19th century. Conan Doyle's stories have been turned into many radio, play, television and film adaptations, and Holmes has been played by leading actors from William Gillette on the stage in 1899 to Basil Rathbone, Jeremy Brett, Rupert Everett and Robert Downey, Jr, in the 20th and 21st centuries. Holmes's house in Central London has been turned into a museum where visitors can study personal effects such as his deerstalker, magnifying glass and pipe.

🎥 A selection: *The Hound of the Baskervilles* (1939), starring Basil Rathbone; *Sherlock Holmes* (2009), starring Robert Downey, Jr, with Jude Law as Dr Watson

📺 Again a selection: *Sherlock Holmes* (1984–94), starring Jeremy Brett; *Sherlock Holmes and the Case of the Silk Stocking* (2004), starring Rupert Everett

➕ www.sherlock-holmes.co.uk (The Sherlock Holmes Museum)

🏠 Park Plaza Sherlock Holmes, 108 Baker Street, London W1 – in the same street as Holmes's house, but *not* the house in which Sherlock Holmes resided

Bridget Jones's Diary (1996)
Helen Fielding

A runaway success for author Helen Fielding, the Bridget Jones books began as columns published in the 1990s in the *Independent* newspaper. Bridget represents the fears, failures and triumphs of many 30-something single women and she therefore struck a chord with the millions who flocked to buy Fielding's books. Bridget is a flawed (but strangely

Dickens' London

Many writers have set their novels in London, but none perhaps more evocatively or successfully than the novelist Charles Dickens (1812–70). Although Dickens was born in Hampshire, he spent much of his early childhood in London and Kent; his family moved to the poverty-stricken area of Camden, North London, when he was 10. The defining moment of Dickens's life came two years later when his father was sent to the Marshelsea debtors' prison in Southwark, South London, where the whole family temporarily resided. Aged 12, Dickens was forced to leave school to work in a factory. Although his father was eventually released from prison, this experience of poverty, prison and debt informed much of Dickens's later writing. In *Little Dorrit* (1855–7), for example, much of the action takes place in the Marshelsea (which was located in Borough High Street), in which William Dorrit is incarcerated for many years, and Mr Micawber in *David Copperfield* is imprisoned for debt in the King's Bench in Southwark (which also features in *Nicholas Nickleby*, 1838–9).

Much of Dickens's vision of London is based on the long walks (sometimes up to 32 km/20 miles) that he regularly took around the city. Vivid descriptions of the smells, sounds, people, market life, gangs and prisons litter Dickens's books, giving the reader an insight into what it was really like to live in Victorian London – a place of great wealth fuelled by the Industrial Revolution but, at the other end of the spectrum, heartbreaking poverty and disease. Dickens's books also allow us to see the effects of industrial change on the cityscape. The coaching inns described in *The Pickwick Papers* (1836–7), for example, give way to the descriptions of how London is affected by the coming of the railroads in *Dombey and Son* (1846–8). Dickens's books are so detailed that most of them have been easily adapted for radio and television and turned successfully into films.

Today, there are many city walks based on Dickens's London, and it is possible to visit his last surviving home, 48 Doughty Street. He lived there for two years, from 1837, producing the last pages of *The Pickwick Papers* and writing *Oliver Twist* (1837–9) and *Nicholas Nickleby* while living there. The house is now a museum. (http://www.dickensmuseum.com).

realistic) comic hero – a woman who spends her time dreaming of Mr Right (Mr Darcy!), worrying about her weight, smoking and drinking too much and gossiping in trendy London locations with her friends. In Fielding's newspaper column, Bridget's playground is predominantly West London: she shops at such places as Graham and Greene (Elgin Crescent, off Portobello Road) and Harvey Nichols (Knightsbridge) and her locals include the Pharmacy in Notting Hill (defunct), the famous media hangout 192 (192 Kensington High Street, now Luna Rossa), Café Rouge on Portobello Road, and the private members club the Groucho in Soho. However, in the two highly successful films, featuring actor Renée Zellweger in the starring role, Bridget was relocated to Borough, South London, and was seen in such places as the Globe Pub on Borough High Street, Borough Market, the ICA and Tate Modern.

🎞 *Bridget Jones's Diary* (2001); *Bridget Jones: The Edge of Reason* (2004)

📶 http://uk.visitlondon.com/city_guide/maps_guides/movie_maps.html (movie map)

The London Novels (1957–60)
Colin MacInnes

MacInnes set many of his books in London. Probably most famous is his trilogy – *City of Spades* (1957), *Absolute Beginners* (1959) and *Mr Love and Mr Justice* (1960) – also known as *The London Novels*. MacInnes's stylized pop dialect and detailed descriptions of Soho, Brixton and Notting Hill, in particular, successfully bring to mind the underworld and alternative culture of late 1950s' London. In the books, we experience London first-hand through the eyes of the main characters, who inhabit smoky Soho jazz bars, rub shoulders with criminals and comment on the emerging and changing youth culture, while roaming London's streets against a background of great social change, caused partly by increased immigration and racial tension.

🎞 *Absolute Beginners* (1986)

Hackney:
That Rose-Red Empire (2009)
Iain Sinclair

Sinclair has written many books, both fiction and non-fiction, about London.

He is obsessed by the city, its history and culture. In this 'documentary fiction', the reader is introduced to various characters, ordinary and famous, who live, work and pass through the East London borough of Hackney, including the writer Joseph Conrad, actor and director Orson Welles and political figures Tony Blair and Lenin.

Non-fiction

London: The Biography (2000)
Peter Ackroyd

Perhaps there's no one better placed to write a 'biography' of London than the author Peter Ackroyd, who pays homage to the city in many of his works. He envisages the city as a 'living organism' in 'the form of a young man with his arms outstretched in a gesture of liberation.' This is no ordinary history of London, but rather Ackroyd gives the city life through his exploration of themes such as drink, sex, lost rivers, theatre, crime and crowds. Most interestingly perhaps, Ackroyd weaves London's history with its present, stating, for example, that the London Eye has its precursor in the 17th century at Bartholomew's Fair. This is an ambitious book but an essential read for anyone living in or intending to travel to the city.

🔍 London – *Hawksmoor*

📶 http://www.timeout.com/london/ (Time Out London website)

BRIGHTON AND SUSSEX
Fiction

Brighton Rock (1938)
Graham Greene

Probably one of Greene's most famous books, *Brighton Rock* is a fast-paced thriller, describing in cinematic detail the seedier side of the seaside town in the 1930s. Featuring one of the most famous opening lines in crime literature ('Hale knew, before he had been in Brighton three hours, that they meant to murder him.') the book is essentially a fight between good and evil, as represented by the two main characters, Ida Arnold, Hale's 'guardian angel', and Pinkie Brown, a young sociopath. In *Brighton Rock*, Greene presents a town full of menace, troubled by gang warfare, slightly grim, slightly grimy, certainly a city with an edge. In 1947, a stylish film noir version of the book was released to great acclaim.

🎬 *Brighton Rock* (1947)

➕ http://www.brightonwalk.co.uk/ (visitors to the city can see many of the locations featured in the film)

The West Pier (1952)
Patrick Hamilton

The first book in Patrick Hamilton's 'Gorse Trilogy', *The West Pier* introduces psychopath Ralph Emerson Gorse. Set mostly in and around Brighton's seafront, the book was described by author Graham Greene as the best ever written about the city. Like Hamilton's other books, it focuses on the darker side of the city and society, portraying the people who usually tend not to have a voice – prostitutes, criminals, the dispossessed.

🔍 London – *Twenty Thousand Leagues Under the Sky*

Regency Buck (1935)
Georgette Heyer

No section on Brighton would be complete without some nod to the Regency era when the town became such an important holiday destination for the ton, the fashionable upper echelons of English society. Many writers have used the city as a backdrop to a fine romance or thriller with varying degrees of success, but perhaps none more successfully or popularly than the prolific writer Georgette Heyer. *Regency Buck* is predominantly set in Brighton and follows the fortunes of heiress Judith Taverner and her brother Peregrine during the year of their guardianship under the 5th Earl of Worth. Blending fact with fiction, Heyer's fictional characters mix easily with historic figures, such as Beau Brummell and the Prince Regent. Heyer not only gives a detailed portrayal of the Regency period, with accurate descriptions of dress, dance, social customs and Brighton, but also successfully sustains interest by blending the different genres of history, romance and suspense in this very entertaining read.

➕ www.visitbrighton.com/site/ maps-guides-and-interactive/ walking-tours (tours)

Dead Simple (2006)
Peter James

Sometimes compared to Ian Rankin's Rebus, Detective Superintendent Roy Grace of the Sussex Police is the creation of award-winning writer Peter James. Set in and around Brighton, the books reveal the underbelly of Brighton society. Grittily real, the plots were created after James shadowed the Sussex Police and visited the city morgue. *Dead Simple* follows the fortunes of successful Michael Harrison, who seemingly has everything and is days away from marrying the woman of his dreams. After a stag night prank goes horribly wrong, Harrison finds himself buried in a coffin, with all but one of the people who know he's there dead or incapacitated. Detective Superintendent Grace is called in and uses all of his powers and local resources, including a clairvoyant, to find Michael. James, who says he wishes he had written *Brighton Rock*, lovingly portrays the town, revealing the darker elements that exist beneath the surface.

In 2008, James took some lucky readers on the Roy Grace tour of Brighton, visiting locations featured in his books, including the building where the superintendent has his office, the main police station and to Shoreham, where Grace lives. Included in the tour was the 'Grace' police car, which James sponsors for the local constabulary.

📶 http://www.peterjames.com (author site)

🔍 *Dead Like You*

KENT
Fiction

Darling Buds of May (1958)
H. E. Bates

Set in the Kentish Weald, full of oast houses, orchards and farms, the book is the first of five that follow the lives of the Larkin family. Based partly on Bates's experiences of living in Kent with his wife in a granary in Little Chart, the books present a charming view of Garden England during the 1950s. The 1990s' television series was filmed in Pluckley (once voted the 'most haunted village in Britain'), Tentedene and Folkestone. Buss Farm, the Larkins' house in the series, just outside Pluckley, opens its doors every year for a classic car rally. The Black Horse in the village also doubled as Pop Larkin's favourite pub in the series. A lesser-known fact is that the book was also turned into a Hollywood movie called *The Mating Game* (1959), starring Debbie Reynolds and Tony Randall.

🔍 *The Darling Buds of May* (1958); *A Breath of French Air* (1959); *When the Green Woods Laugh* (1960); *Oh! To be in England* (1963); *A Little of What You Fancy* (1970)

🎬 *The Mating Game* (1959)

📺 *Darling Buds of May* (1991–3), starring David Jason and a very young Catherine Zeta-Jones

Great Expectations (1861)
Charles Dickens

Set in Kent and London, the book traces protagonist Pip's life from his early days as an orphan and his strange encounter with an escaped convict in a cemetery in the northern Kent marshes (based on Cooling Marshes, 8 km/5 miles north of Rochester) to his visits with the strange Miss Havisham and her ward Estella in Satis House 'up town' and his move to London after receiving a mysterious legacy. Dickens loved Kent; he spent his early childhood in Chatham and his last years in and around Rochester, and the Kent landscape appears in many of his books. He often stayed at the Bull Inn (the Royal Victoria and Bull Inn) in Rochester, which features in the opening pages of *The Pickwick Papers* and is renamed the Blue Boar Inn in *Great Expectations*. Visitors can also see Satis House in Rochester, although it was the name of the house and not the house itself that features in *Great Expectations*.

🎬 *Great Expectations* (1946), David Lean's classic version, starring John Mills as Pip; *Great Expectations* (1998), modern Hollywood version, starring Ethan Hawke and Gwyneth Paltrow

📶 http://www.walksoflondon.co.uk/ (there are a number of walking tours of Dickens's Rochester and Kent, including several featured on Richard Jones's London Walking Tours)

Last Orders (1996)
Graham Swift

Although the book opens with a group of men gathered together to honour their dead friend and drinking pal Jack Dodds in Bermondsey, London, it moves to the Kent town of Margate, where Ray, Lennie and Vic, and Jack's foster son, Vince, drive to carry out Jack's last orders and scatter his ashes off the pier. A beautiful and moving book, *Last Orders* follows the characters as they recall their lives and their friendship with Jack, and each other, over the years.

🎬 *Last Orders* (2001)
🔍 East England – *Waterland*

OXFORD AND OXFORDSHIRE
Fiction

Restless (2006)
William Boyd

Former Oxford lecturer Boyd creates an interesting tale of espionage, intrigue and deception in this book set in Oxford. Single mother Ruth lives a humdrum life in Oxford until her mother, Sally Gilmartin, hands her a memoir detailing her life in the Second World War (1939–45). Ruth quickly discovers that her mother's real story is very different from the one she had grown up with and that Sally is, in fact, Eva, a Russian émigré and former spy. Part love story, part thriller, *Restless* also details Ruth's mundane existence as a postgraduate student in Oxford.

Enigma (1995)
Robert Harris

Based on the true story of the code breakers who lived and worked at Bletchley Park in Oxfordshire during the Second World War, *Enigma* blends fact with fiction. For many years Bletchley Park, or Station X, as it was known, and the men and women who heroically worked behind the scenes to end the war, remained a secret but in the last years of the 20th century their story began to be told. Set in 1943, *Enigma* focuses on a burnt-out young code breaker, who through trying to find out what happened to his girlfriend, the lovely Claire Romilly (who has disappeared), finds himself drawn deeper and deeper into a world of espionage, murder and intrigue.

🎬 *Enigma* (2001)

➕ www.bletchleypark.org.uk/ (visitors can to go Bletchley Park to find out about the history of the house and to learn about and view an Enigma machine)

🔍 Germany – *Fatherland*

The Oxford Murders (2005)
Guillermo Martínez

Narrated by a South American student, *The Oxford Murders* merges mathematical theory with a plot that pays more than a nod and a wink to Sherlock Holmes. After receiving a message, Seldom, a mathematician of some repute at Oxford, discovers the body of a woman. He joins forces with the nameless narrator to try to discover the identity of the serial killer who is murdering people in the city and leaving a series of mathematical symbols at each scene.

🎬 *The Oxford Murders* (2008)

Northern Lights (1995)
Philip Pullman

The first book in Pullman's gripping trilogy, *His Dark Materials*, opens in Oxford, but the mood and feel is more reminiscent of the 19th century. Jordan College is the greatest of all the Oxford colleges, where the world's brightest minds meet, and it is here that Lyra lives. When her uncle, Lord Asriel, comes back to Oxford to visit her, the adventure begins and Lyra and her friend, Will, are taken to worlds that they could never have imagined.

🎬 *The Golden Compass* (2007)

➕ http://www.oxfordcity.co.uk/ (explore the Oxford of Lyra and Will and some of the locations featured in *Northern Lights*, such as Christ Church, Exeter College and Radcliffe Square)

🔍 *His Dark Materials – Northern Lights* (*The Golden Compass* in the United States); *The Subtle Knife*; *The Amber Spyglass*

🔍 *Lyra's Oxford*

Gaudy Night (1935)
Dorothy L. Sayers

Oxford-born novelist Sayers set this novel in the fictional Shrewsbury College, a thinly disguised Somerville College, where Sayers herself studied. Although termed a 'Lord Peter Wimsey novel', *Gaudy Night* features Wimsey's great love Harriet Vane in the role of protagonist. After a series of vindictive crimes occur at the college, Vane calls on Lord Peter Wimsey to help her stop the culprit. Covering a lot of ground, the book sketches such

Inspector Morse's Oxford

Oxford is associated with so many literary figures, but it is hard to think of the city without conjuring up the image of Colin Dexter's Detective Chief Inspector Endeavour Morse. The 'Morse' books first hit the bookshops in 1975 with the publication of *Last Bus to Woodstock*. Now numbering 13, they feature the detective and his slightly stolid sidekick Lewis as they roam the city and the surrounding countryside solving the many crimes – often murders – that seem to litter that region.

Morse is a complex character: an intellectual and a loner, he is notoriously blunt, sometimes prickly, often bad-tempered and is not afraid of upsetting his superiors. In his own time, Morse listens to opera, particularly Wagner, and he loves a pint. He is often found in one of the many pubs located in his beloved Oxford, such as the Eagle and Child, on Wellington Place, the Bear Inn, on the corner of Alfred and Blue Boar Streets (mentioned in *Death is Now My Neighbour*, 1996), and the Turf Tavern (*Daughters of Cain*, 1994), sited in a passageway off Bath Place. The city provides a haunting and vivid backdrop for the 'Morse' books, which often feature Oxford colleges and the world of academia. (Morse himself studied at St John's for two years before leaving.) Brasenose becomes Lonsdale College in the books. Oxford's lovely architecture and waterways (the Oxford Canal, the Cherwell and the Thames) also give the books a grand setting. The Ashmolean Museum, the Pitt Rivers Museum, the Radcliffe Camera and Blackwell's Books are among the locations mentioned in such books as *The Daughters of Cain*. Oxford University Press (which is located in Jericho) makes an appearance in *The Dead of Jericho* (1981).

Today, visitors can take advantage of one of the many walking tours that focus on the 'Morse' novels and the television series, which will enable them to walk – and drink – in the footsteps of their favourite tragic hero.

📺 *Inspector Morse* (1987–2000), starring John Thaw in the title role

📶 http://www.visitoxford.org/see-tours.asp (tours)

themes as the role of women in academia and Sayers draws on her own scholarly background to give a detailed overview of life in the Oxford colleges and university politics.

📺 *Gaudy Night* (1987), starring Harriet Walter as Harriet Vane

📶 www.sayers.org.uk (Dorothy L. Sayers Society)

🔍 *Lord Peter: the Complete Lord Peter Wimsey Stories*

CORNWALL

Fiction

Zennor in Darkness (1993)
Helen Dunmore

This book is set during the First World War, as the men of Zennor and St Ives are being conscripted and the region is full of gossip and suspicion. Into this come the novelist and pacifist D. H. Lawrence and his wife, Frieda, who move to Zennor, a tiny hamlet, in 1915 to escape war-torn London. Dunmore contrasts the beautiful, rambling landscape of Cornwall with the obscenity of war. She weaves fiction with historical fact, such as the growing anti-German feeling in Cornwall and the suspicion that the Lawrences' stay there evoked, which led to Lawrence's expulsion from the county.

📶 www.cornwall-calling.co.uk/gazetter-cornwall/zennor.htm (Zennor)

➕ www.theheritagetrail.co.uk/notable%20houses/dhlawrence%20house.htm (8a Victoria Street, Eastwood, Nottinghamshire, where Lawrence was born, now a museum)

The Wind in the Willows (1908)
Kenneth Grahame

A vision of pastoral England, The Wind in the Willows, Kenneth Grahame's much-loved children's book, features Mole, Rat, Toad and Badger. Rescued from obscurity by A. A. Milne, who adapted it for the stage in 1929, the book is based on a series of letters that the author wrote to his son in 1907, while staying at the Greenbank Hotel, in Falmouth. The hotel overlooks the Fal estuary, and the countryside around Falmouth and Fowey is believed to have inspired Grahame. Toad Hall is thought to be based on the lovely Fowey Hall Hotel.

🏠 www.greenbank-hotel.co.uk/ (Greenbank Hotel, Falmouth); www.foweyhallhotel.co.uk/ (Fowey Hall Hotel, Fowey)

Ross Poldark (1945)
Winston Graham

Although Winston Graham wrote more than 40 novels (including Marnie, which Alfred Hitchcock turned into a successful film), he is probably best known for his 12 books focusing on the Poldark family and set in Cornwall in the late 18th to 19th centuries. Written between 1945 and 2002, the first book begins with the return of tired and embittered soldier Ross Poldark from America to his beloved Cornwall, only to find that Elizabeth, the woman he loves, is promised to another.

🔍 The 'Poldark' series – Ross Poldark; Demelza; Jeremy Poldark; Warleggan; The Black Moon; The Four Swans; The Angry Tide; Stranger from the Sea; The Miller's Dance; The Loving Cup; The Twisted Sword; Bella

📺 Poldark (1975)

📶 www.poldark.org.uk/ (Winston Graham and Poldark Literary Society)

➕ www.poldark.org.uk/museum.html (Perranzabuloe Folk Museum, Perranporth, where visitors can learn more about the author and the inspirations for Poldark)

The Shell Seekers (1987)
Rosamunde Pilcher

Cornish-born Rosamunde Pilcher wrote the highly successful romance The Shell Seekers at the age of 63. Set in London and Cornwall, it follows the story of Penelope Keeling as she looks back on her family and life from the Second World War onwards. The title is taken from the name of one of her father's

Daphne du Maurier's landscape

Millions of readers and cinema goers have been captivated by the vision of Daphne du Maurier's Cornwall, as depicted in such books as *Jamaica Inn* (1936), *Rebecca* (1938) and *Frenchman's Creek* (1941). Although born in London in 1907, du Maurier spent much of her adult life in Cornwall and she drew inspiration for her books from the landscape, particularly that of the southern part of the region, which is full of lovely coves and beaches, pretty villages and inlets.

In 1926, du Maurier's parents bought Ferryside, situated in Fowey on the Bodinnick side of the river, and it was here that she set her first novel *The Loving Spirit* (1931), drawing on the local shipbuilding community for inspiration. She met her future husband, Major Frederick 'Tommy' Browning as a result of the novel when he sailed down to meet her after reading it. Her historical romance *Frenchman's Creek* was inspired by an inlet of the same name on Helford River, where the Brownings spent their honeymoon in 1932, and the author's inherent love of that countryside comes through in the book. It was Menabilly, however, the 17th-century estate west of Fowey, which she leased from 1943 until 1969, that inspired some of the most famous houses in her books, including Manderley, Max de Winter's imposing family home in *Rebecca*. Kimarth, the house she leased after Menabilly, was the inspiration for the *House on the Strand* (1969). *Jamaica Inn* was written after du Maurier stayed at the inn of the same name and Bodmin Moor inspired her plot of smugglers and intrigue.

Du Maurier's rich descriptions of Cornwall and her use of landscape to support or impose a certain mood on her characters or plot have meant that many of her books have been easily adaptable to film. Alfred Hitchcock famously adapted *Jamaica Inn* (1939), *Rebecca* (1940) and the 1953 short story *The Birds* (1963). Nicholas Roeg adapted the 1971 short story *Don't Look Now*, set predominantly in Venice, Italy, into a cult film in 1973.

Today, visitors can take part in all kinds of activities to discover du Maurier's Cornwall. These include a cruise that sails from Fowey via Helford, visiting Tywardreath village and St Andrew's Church, which feature in *House on the Strand*, walking along Polridmouth, one of the inspirations for the beach that features in *Rebecca*, visiting Jamaica Inn (http://www.jamaicainn.co.uk) or simply going to one of the events held at the annual du Maurier festival in May (http://www.dumaurierfestival.co.uk/index.php).

Venice – *Don't Look Now and Other Stories*

---

paintings. The television adaptation was filmed at Lands End, Lamorna Cove and Marazion.

The Shell Seekers (1989), starring Angela Lansbury and Sam Wanamaker; *The Shell Seekers* (2006), starring Vanessa Redgrave and Maximilian Schnell

The Camomile Lawn (1984)
Mary Wesley

Set in the summer of 1939 in Cornwall (as are many of Wesley's novels), *The Camomile Lawn* follows the story of five young cousins gathered at their Aunt Helena's house for

The Agatha Christie Mile

Visitors to Torquay can follow the Agatha Christie Mile, which takes in 10 landmarks that relate to the author, who was born in Torquay. Each is marked with a particular plaque. They include the Imperial Hotel, renamed the Majestic in such books as *Sleeping Murder*, *Peril at End House* and *Body in the Library*; Beacon Cove, where the author bathed; the Torquay Museum, where there is an exhibition about Christie; the Grand Hotel, where the author spent her honeymoon; the Princess Pier, where she skated, one of her favourite past times; and the Pavilion, where she attended many concerts. Many of Christie's books feature Devon-inspired locations; for example, *Why Didn't They Ask Evans?* is believed to be set in Watcombe.

their last summer together before the outbreak of war. The house in which they stay has a camomile lawn that stretches down to the cliffs above the sea. The book moves between Cornwall and London.

🖥 *The Camomile Lawn* (1992), starring Felicity Kendal, Paul Eddington and Jennifer Ehle

🔍 *Wild Mary: A Life of Mary Wesley*

DEVON

Fiction

Sense and Sensibility (1811)
Jane Austen

Drawing on her happy memories of holidays in Devon, Austen used the village of Upton Pyne, north of Exeter, as the main setting for Barton Valley in her first novel *Sense and Sensibility*. It is here that Elinor, Marianne and Margaret Dashwood and their mother go to live after their father's death and the inheritance of his estate by the son of his first marriage. Austen peppers the book with nearby locations: among them are the village church and

Dawlish, a small fishing village on the south Devon coast of which Austen was particularly fond, having visited it with her parents in 1802. In the book, the younger Mr Ferris is heard to say that it is surprising to him 'that anybody could live in Devonshire without living near Dawlish.' Dawlish is also the birthplace of Dickens's *Nicholas Nickleby*.

📶 www.devon-online.com /towns/dawlish/dawlish.html (Dawlish)

Dead Man's Folly (1956)
Agatha Christie

Hercule Poirot receives a call from his friend, detective writer Ariadne Oliver, who is staying at Nasse House and helping with a local charity event. Her intuition tells her that something is not quite right and Poirot journeys down to help out. Like other Christie books, *Dead Man's Folly* draws on the author's native Devonshire countryside for its location. Nasse House is based on Christie's own beloved Greenway House, situated on the river Dart, and the real-life boathouse and river both feature in the book. The house makes another appearance as Alderbury in *Five Little Pigs*.

📶 www.agathachristie.com/ (author society)

➕ www.nationaltrust.org.uk/main/ w-vh/w-visits/w-findaplace/ w-greenway/w-greenway-history.htm. (Greenway House, in which Christie lived from 1938 to 1959)

The Hound of the Baskervilles (1902)
Arthur Conan Doyle

The first chapters of this novel, based on a real legend about the hound that roams Dartmoor, appeared in *Strand* magazine in 1901. *The Hound of the Baskervilles* immediately grabbed public attention as it featured the popular detective duo, Sherlock Holmes and his sidekick Dr Watson, solving yet another deadly crime. The plot revolves around Sir Henry Baskerville, who has recently inherited the Baskerville estate on the Devon moors, following the death of his uncle who was found with the footprints of a giant hound near his body. Sought out by Dr James Mortimer, they are informed about the Baskerville curse, which dates back to the 17th century when a demonic hound allegedly killed one of Sir Henry's ancestors. Holmes and Watson travel from London to Dartmoor to help and another evil plot is foiled. The book includes descriptions of such moorland places as Princetown and Bellever Tor; Fox Tor Mires seems the likely inspiration for Grimpen Mire. Similarly, Hayford Hall or Brook Manor, both near Buckfastleigh, may have been the inspiration for Baskerville Hall, as could Baskerville Hall Hotel in Hay-on-Wye.

🎬📺 There have been several film and television adaptations, including the classic 1939 version starring Basil Rathbone as Holmes and Nigel Bruce as Watson and the 2002 television version starring Richard Roxborough and Ian Hart

🔍 *The Hound of the Baskervilles: Hunting the Dartmoor Legend*

Tarka the Otter (1927)
Henry Williamson

After witnessing first-hand the horrors of the First World War, Henry Williamson escaped from London to rebuild his life in Georgham, North Devon. Caring for an orphaned otter cub helped Williamson begin to see the world through new eyes. His experiences and the countryside and wildlife of Devon inspired him to write *Tarka the Otter* about a cub born beside the river Torridge between Bideford and Torrington.

➕ www.beautiful-devon.co.uk/tarka-trail.htm (visitors can see Williamson's house in Georgham, identifiable by its Blue Plaque, and follow the 290 km/ 180 mile Tarka Trail in North Devon)

DORSET
Fiction

Persuasion (1818)
Jane Austen

Persuasion follows the fated love affair between Anne Elliot and Captain Frederick Wentworth. The book moves between Somerset, Bath and Lyme Regis, where Wentworth's close friends, Harville and Benwick, lodge. Lyme was the seaside resort closest to the part of Somerset where the Musgroves (Anne's sister and brother-in-law) lived and is a natural location for them to visit. In contrast to the stuffy world of Bath, Lyme is set up as a place where Anne can be herself. Here she looks 'remarkably well; her very regular, very pretty features, having the bloom and freshness of youth restored by the fine wind which had been blowing on her complexion, and by the animation of eye which it had also produced.' Jane Austen drew on her own experience of visiting Lyme Regis with her family in the summer of 1804. She wrote of walking on the Cobb, which features significantly in *Persuasion*, visiting the Assembly Rooms and dancing. Many Austen fans visit Lyme Regis as a result.

🔍 Bath – In the footsteps of Jane Austen (feature box)

Hardy's Wessex – mixing fact with fiction

The countryside around Thomas Hardy's beloved Dorchester in Dorset provided the setting for many of his books. Hardy, who was born in 1840 in Higher Bockhampton, Dorset, lived in London briefly before ill health made him return to his home county. There, while working as an architect, he began to concentrate on writing. Success came with *Far From the Madding Crowd* (1874), a novel set in Weatherby (based on Puddletown, near where he grew up), in which he refers to the fictional region of Wessex, an area that appears in many of his books. A financial success, the book gave Hardy the means to concentrate on writing full time.

In creating Wessex, Hardy mixes fictional places with real ones, but at its heart is the unspoilt landscape of Dorset, at the time a relatively untouched, poor region, yet to be linked by the railway to the outside world. Wessex appears in his other books, and villages and towns near to him often make an appearance under different names: In *The Return of the Native* (1878), Black Heath becomes Egdon Heath and East Egdon is Affpuddle, near Dorchester. In Hardy's 1886 novel, *The Mayor of Casterbridge*, the town of the title is actually Dorchester. First serialized in 20 segments in the *Graphic*, it was later turned into a book. Parts of the original manuscript are on view at the County Museum in Dorchester. Beaminster and Bere Regis became Enminster and Kingsbere in South Wessex. *Jude the Obscure* (1895) is set in North Wessex (made up of Oxfordshire and Berkshire). Wiltshire becomes Mid-Wessex, Hampshire is Upper Wessex, and Devon and Cornwall are West Wessex and Outer Wessex respectively.

Hardy sketched many maps of his locations while writing and some can be viewed online http://www.st-andrews.ac.uk/~bp10/wessex/evolution/maps/). Visitors to the area can go to any number of places associated with Hardy, including Hardy's Cottage in Higher Bockhampton, where he wrote *Far From the Madding Crowd*, and Max Gate, the Dorchester home that he designed and in which he lived for 43 years until his death in 1928. Both are now owned by the National Trust (http://www.nationaltrust.org.uk).

🔍 *Thomas Hardy's Vision of Wessex* (2003) by Simon Gatrell

The French Lieutenant's Woman (1969)
John Fowles

Set initially in Lyme Regis, where Fowles also lived, the opening of the book features the narrator describing the town. The story revolves around the obsessive relationship between Charles Smithson and the mysterious Sarah. Charles first encounters Sarah while walking along the Cobb with his fiancée, Ernestina (Tina). Tina explains that the cloaked figure standing at the end of the Cobb is the 'French Lieutenant's woman', outcast by Lyme society because she is rumoured to have been seduced and abandoned by a French officer, for whom she still pines. Charles subsequently becomes obsessed by Sarah's story. The book features detailed descriptions of Lyme, including the Undercliff, where Charles hunts for fossils. The town received much attention when the award-winning film adaptation of the same name, featuring Meryl Streep and Jeremy Irons, was filmed there.

The French Lieutenant's Woman (1981), screenplay by Harold Pinter

On Chesil Beach (2007)
Ian McEwan

A pebble beach located between the Fleet Lagoon and the Channel, on the southern coast in Dorset, features in Ian McEwan's quietly elegant novella set in 1962. Honeymooners Edward and Florence Mayhew stay in a Georgian hotel overlooking Chesil Beach. They are 'young, educated, and both virgins on this, their wedding night, and they lived in a time when conversation about sexual difficulties was plainly impossible.' The following pages deal with Florence and Edward's disappointments and failed expectations, outlining the decline of their relationship in a time of social and cultural change.

GLOUCESTERSHIRE
Fiction

Coram Boy (2000)
Jamila Gavin

Set in 18th-century Gloucester and London, *Coram Boy* tells of Toby, saved from an African slave ship, and Aaron, the illegitimate son of the heir to a great estate. The story features locations such as Gloucester Cathedral.

Thinks... (2001)
David Lodge

David Lodge's *Thinks...* is set in the (fictional) world of the University of Gloucester. Ralph Messenger is the director of the Holt Belling Centre for Cognitive Science, which is dedicated to exploring the phenomenon of consciousness and brain activity.

Small World

The Rutshire Chronicles

Novelist Jilly Cooper had written several books, including a series of frothy romances, before she published *Riders* (1985). A huge novel filled with steamy sex scenes, light humour, Agas, dogs and horses, it is the first of the so-called 'Rutshire Chronicles', which also includes *Rivals* (1988), *Polo* (1991), *The Man Who Made Husbands Jealous* (1993), *Appassionata* (1996) and *Score!* (1999). Set in the fictional and glamorous English county of Rutshire (Gloucestershire), the books are linked by a series of recurring characters that include Rupert Campbell-Black and his family and arch-villain Roberto Rannaldini. Littered with beautiful, dishevelled women, who make shepherd's pie at the drop of a hat and have affairs with the impossibly handsome, often rich, but dissolute men who happen to live nearby, the books have sold millions. Cooper, who lives in Stroud (about which she says people are very rude), says that Gloucestershire – and Stroud, in particular – has provided the inspiration for 90 percent of her books.

The Tailor of Gloucester (1903)
Beatrix Potter

While visiting her cousin at Harscombe Grange, Potter heard the tale of tailor John Pritchard, commissioned to make a suit of clothes for the mayor of Gloucester. Before he could finish it, someone did so for him, leaving him a note saying 'No more twist'. Potter transformed this story into a book featuring a cat and some helpful mice.

+ http://www.tailor-of-gloucester.org.uk/ (it is possible to visit Pritchard's shop, today a museum, in Gloucester)

Q Lake District – Beatrix Potter Land (feature box)

Non-fiction

Cider with Rosie (1959)
Laurie Lee

Poet Laurie Lee's memoir recalls his childhood in the Gloucestershire countryside. It immortalizes the lovely Slad valley, near Stroud, where Lee grew up.

▢ *Cider with Rosie* (1998), starring Juliet Stevenson

+ www.cotswolds.info/places/stroud/index.shtml (visitors can walk around the landscape that Lee so vividly describes)

Q Spain – *As I Walked Out One Midsummer's Day*

BRISTOL

Fiction

Gone without a Trace (2007)
C. J. Carver

Set in the less salubrious parts of Bristol, Carver's book takes the topical subject of human trafficking and the sex trade as its subject. Former army captain Jay McCauley works for an international aid agency that helps track and unite families separated in war. Her work and her own personal interest in Zamira, a girl from Macedonia who has possibly been trafficked to the UK, leads her to cross paths with Milot Dumani, an Albanian crime boss. A realistic, often grim crime book, *Gone Without a Trace* gives a good insight into the parts of Bristol that are unknown to tourists.

A Respectable Trade (1995)
Philippa Gregory

A Respectable Trade tells the haunting story of the 18th-century slave trade and the fated relationship between Frances and her Yoruban slave, Mehuru. Gregory's meticulous research and eye for historical detail creates a Bristol in which the fine houses of Clifton are juxtaposed with the gritty reality of the docks and the inhumane trade on which much of Bristol's wealth was built.

Shawnie (2006)
Ed Trewavas

Social worker Trawavas sets this hard-hitting book on the Knowle West council estate. Written in the Bristolian dialect, *Shawnie* gives the reader a real insight into many of the problems troubling the city by looking at the lives of the Brewer family.

BATH

Fiction

The Bath Detective (1996)
Christopher Lee

The first in Lee's successful detective series, *The Bath Detective* introduces its hero, the slightly eccentric Inspector James Leonard. Investigating a dead body found outside a Roman bath, Leonard finds himself delving into Bath's society to solve his crime.

Literary Wiltshire

Wiltshire has influenced many writers, both those visiting the area and those born or already living there. Salisbury crops up in the novels of such authors as Charles Dickens (*Martin Chuzzlewit* features the cathedral), Thomas Hardy (*Jude the Obscure*, 1896, in which Melchester is Salisbury), William Golding (*The Spire*, 1964, which is set in the city, where he also taught) and Susan Howatch (*Glittering Images*, 1987, which was written in a flat overlooking the cathedral). The idea for *Barchester Towers* apparently came to Anthony Trollope on a bridge in the city.

Dickens was also influenced by other areas in Wiltshire: Scrooge was inspired by Jeremy Wood of the Gloucester Old Bank and the Beckhampton Inn in Avebury is thought to be the basis for 'The Bagman's Story' in *The Pickwick Papers*. Avebury also appears in Vita Sackville-West's *Grey Weathers* (1923) and Robert Goddard's crime novel set in the city, *Sight Unseen* (2005). Maureen Duffy used Trowbridge as the inspiration for Wortbridge in her autobiographical novel about an evacuee in *That's How It Was* (1962). Other authors who have lived in Wiltshire include Siegfried Sassoon.

The House Sitter (2003)
Peter Lovesey

The eighth book in the series featuring the head of Bath Murder Squad, Peter Diamond, this book finds the burly detective a year on after his wife's murder. Set partly in Bath, where the victim of this book teaches at the university, and partly in Sussex, where her body is found on a beach, *The House Sitter* shows how much Lovesey deserves his British Crime Writers Association Lifetime Achievement Award. Diamond and his team delve into a grim world that exists behind the beautiful Georgian exteriors of the city, such as the celebrated Royal Crescent.

Non-fiction

A City of Palaces: Bath Through the Eyes of Fanny Burney (1999)
Maggie Lane

Focusing on the eventful life and times of novelist, diarist and playwright Fanny Burney (Madame d'Arblay), Lane's slim book provides a great deal of information about Bath in the 18th and 19th centuries. Although Burney's life is explored, from her early visits to the town in 1780 to her retirement there in 1815,

In the footsteps of Jane Austen

Visit Bath and it is almost impossible to ignore the novelist Jane Austen. From the Jane Austen Centre (40 Gay Street), which details the author's life and times, and Number One Royal Crescent, a magnificently restored Regency house, to the Jane Austen festival and parade held every September, Austen is unavoidable. Visitors can also take various walks around the city following in the footsteps of Austen, seeing where she lived and visited and the places in which she set her books.

The Bath that the author knew and lived in (from 1801 to 1806) was a fashionable spa town, a city of great Georgian and Palladian architecture, high fashion, parties and dances, where the upper classes met and mixed for part of the Season. Austen set two of her novels, the Gothic *Northanger Abbey* and *Persuasion* in the city. In the former, the Pump Rooms (http://www.romanbaths.co.uk/), 'where every person in Bath... was to be seen in the room at different periods of the fashionable hours' is where innocent heroine Catherine Morland watches society. In the Lower Rooms of the Assembly Rooms, she is first introduced to Mr Tilney by the real-life Master of Ceremonies, James King. The book features great descriptions of the town, streets, dress and company. For example, the Royal Crescent, today a popular tourist destination, is referred to as the place where people go to 'breathe the fresh air of better company'. In *Persuasion*, heroine Anne Elliot moves to Bath to be with her father, Sir Walter Elliot, who mixes only with the highest echelons of society, although Anne herself has little time for it. Gay Street, today the location of the Jane Austen Centre (http://www.janeausten.co.uk/) and also a street in which the author once lived, is where Admiral and Mrs Croft lodge when they come to town, much to the 'satisfaction' of Sir Walter, who is relieved that they haven't embarrassed him. The book is also partly set in Lyme Regis.

the book also covers the lives of her family and many of her peers. A fascinating read.

BIRMINGHAM
Fiction

The Rotters' Club (2001)
Jonathan Coe

Drawing on his own roots, Coe sets this acclaimed novel in 1970s' Birmingham against a background of the strikes in Longbridge and the city pub bombings. Three grammar-school boys, Ben, Doug and Philip, dealing with growing up, girls, music and political change, inherit the editorship of their school magazine.

📺 *The Rotters' Club* (2005)
🔍 *The Winshaw Legacy: or, What a Carve Up!*

Changing Places: A Tale of Two Campuses (1975)
David Lodge

Changing Places focuses on academic life in Britain and the United States in the late 1960s. A satire, it shows Lodge at his best. Academics Phillip Swallow and Morris Zapp take part in their university exchange programmes: Swallow goes from the University of Rummidge (Birmingham) to Euphoria State University (Berkeley) with hilarious consequences.

🔍 *Small World*

Astonishing Splashes of Colour (2003)
Clare Morrall

This Booker Prize shortlisted book focuses on Kitty, who is dealing with the death of her child and the memories of her own childhood. Set in Birmingham, the novel is deeply moving as the reader follows Kitty's journey as she processes her memories through colour. After being turned down by many publishers, the book was taken by Tindall Street. Established with lottery money, the press was founded to help publish Birmingham authors.

🔍 *The Language of Others*, also set in Birmingham

COVENTRY
Fiction

Middlemarch (1871–72)
George Eliot

Eliot's great classic is set in the wealthy urban town of Middlemarch, believed to be Coventry. Generally considered to be Eliot's best book, it features rich and beautiful Dorothea Brooke who chooses to marry Edward Casaubon. Virginia Woolf described it as 'one of the few novels written for grown-up people'.

📺 *Middlemarch* (1994)
➕ www.nuneatonandbedworth.gov.uk /leisure-culture/tourism-travel/ visiting/george-eliot-country (there are many walking and coach tours that visit sites featured in Eliot's life and books)

NOTTINGHAMSHIRE

Fiction

Lonely Hearts (1989)
John Harvey

The first in John Harvey's acclaimed 'Charlie Resnick' series, *Lonely Hearts* was named by *The Times* as one of the 100 most notable crime books of the 20th century. It introduces Nottingham-based Pole Resnick, a middle-aged, divorced and disillusioned man, who is called in to investigate the murders of two women. The only thing the women have in common is the lonely-hearts column.

The Unfortunates
(1969; reissued 1999)
B. S. Johnson

This beautifully packaged 'book within a box' is actually a series of 27 separately bound chapters, which means they can be read in any order. Based around a journalist (Johnson himself) who goes to Nottingham to cover a football match, it is really about the journalist roaming the city as he looks back to happier times with a friend, Tony, now dead.

Sons and Lovers (1913)
D. H. Lawrence

Lawrence's novels are often informed by his life in Nottinghamshire. *Sons and Lovers*, his largely autobiographical novel written after his mother's death, is no different. In the novel, Eastwood, the mining town near Nottingham in which Lawrence was born, becomes Bestwood. He based several of the characters on people that he knew: Walter Morel is based on his father; Gertrude Morel, the intellectually stifled mother, is based on his mother, Lydia; and Miriam was drawn from his friend Jessie Chambers, with whom he took long walks in the countryside. Jessie's home, The Haggs, became Willey Farm (and Strelley Mill in *The White Peacock*) in the book. Visitors to Eastwood can look in the local library where Lawrence's headstone is on display and see his memorial.

🎬 *Sons and Lovers* (1960), directed by Jack Cardiff and starring Trevor Howard

➕ D. H. Lawrence Birthplace Museum, 8a Victoria Street, Eastwood, Nottinghamshire

Saturday Night and Monday Morning (1958)
Alan Sillitoe

This cult novel is a graphic portrayal and celebration of working-class Nottingham. Protagonist Arthur Seaton is a drinking, womanizing factory worker – the archetypal 'angry young man'. The book immortalizes the area of Nottingham where Sillitoe grew up, among the terraced houses of Radford, and the Raleigh Bicycle Company, where he once worked.

🔍 *Saturday Night and Monday Morning* (1960), starring Albert Finney as Seaton

WOLVERHAMPTON

Fiction

Anita and Me (1996)
Meera Syal

Anita and Me is a poignant account of a Punjabi family living in a West Midlands village (believed to be based on Essington, where Syal spent her early years) near Wolverhampton. Seen through the eyes of Meena, the book details what it is like to be the only non-whites in a small English community in the early 1970s. Meena meets and becomes obsessed with Anita, the rebellious, mouthy girl who is everything her own parents warn her about. The book is about friendship, betrayal and growing up in a turbulent time of change.

Anita and Me (2002), filmed in Nottinghamshire

NEWCASTLE/TYNE AND WEAR

Fiction

Union Street (1982)
Pat Barker

Set in North East England in the 1970s, Pat Barker's grittily realistic portrayal of life in an unnamed industrial city has been described as a northern masterpiece. Focusing on seven women of different ages, from prepubescent Kelly to elderly Alice Bell, the book is bawdy and bitter, evoking the decay and despair of the region at this time.

The Crow Trap (1999)
Ann Cleeves

Introducing Detective Vera Stanhope, *The Crow Trap* is set in an isolated cottage in Northumberland National Park, where three women gather because of an environmental survey. After two murders occur, Stanhope becomes involved. The cottage in the book is based on a settlement called Threestone Burns.

www.northumberlandnationalpark. org.uk/visiting/placestovisit.htm (Northumberland National Park)

Hidden Depths, also set in Northumberland

Tilly Trotter (1999)
Catherine Cookson

For many people, Catherine Cookson put North East England on the world map. *Tilly Trotter* is set in a 19th-century village in County Durham and follows the adventures of Tilly, a strong, independent girl, who is not afraid of anything or anyone. Ignored by the man she loves and branded a witch, Tilly ends up working in a mine. Despite her circumstances, she never loses hope.

Tilly Trotter (1999), a four-part series

Crusaders (2008)
Richard T. Kelly

Set in Newcastle, Richard T. Kelly's plot revolves around John Gore, a clergyman returning to his native North East to establish a church in a deprived area of the city. Along the way, he meets all kinds of characters from all walks of life, finds himself sponsored by the local gangster and embarks on a relationship with a single mother.

The Mercy Seat (2006)
Martyn Waites

London-based but Newcastle-born, Waites decided to set his new series featuring Joe Donovan in Newcastle. He said that he wanted to expose the city's heart, 'full of dark histories and shadows'. Waites also wanted to demonstrate that Newcastle and Gateshead were very different from the *Get Carter* image that many people have of them. The book deals with a predator who preys on runaways in the ward of Byker.

THE LAKE DISTRICT (CUMBRIA)

Fiction

The Maid of Buttermere (1987)
Melvyn Bragg

In the late 18th century, as the Lake District became popular among visitors, books began to mention the local attractions. Increasing references were made to the beautiful daughter of an innkeeper in Buttermere near Keswick. Soon people were calling at the inn to admire Mary Robinson, the 'maid of Buttermere', as she became known. Wordsworth even mentions her in Book VII of *The Prelude*. Mary, however, attracted even more

attention when she fell in love with a fraudster and bigamist. Melvyn Bragg bases his novel on this story.

🏠 www.fish-hotel.co.uk/legend.htm (visitors can stay at the Fish Hotel where Mary lived and worked)

The Cipher Garden (2005)
Martin Edwards

Edwards's 'Lake District Mystery' series, featuring Oxford historian Daniel Kind and Detective Chief Inspector Hannah Scarlett, begins with *The Cipher Garden*. When Daniel and his partner, Miranda, buy a cottage in the valley of Brackdale in the Lake District, Daniel soon finds himself fascinated by a past murder. When the case comes under review, Daniel and Hannah join together to search for the real murderer, who will do anything to conceal his or her identity. Edwards's books evoke the Lake District beautifully. Although Brackdale is fictional, Edwards said he imagined it to be Kentmere and Longsleddale. The book also features Old Sawrey, an imaginary village in Beatrix Potter country.

➕ http://www.nationaltrust.org.uk/ main/w-hilltop (Hill Top, where Beatrix Potter wrote many of her books)

Swallows and Amazons (1930)
Arthur Ransome

Leeds-born writer Arthur Ransome is most famous for the much-loved *Swallows and Amazons* series, which is mostly set in and around the Lake District. Ransome, who learned to sail on Lake Coniston and went to school in Windermere, became a journalist in London. The books, which follow the adventures of the Blackett and Walker children, feature several recognizable Cumbrian locations, including Peel Island (which becomes Wildcat Island, the place to which the Walker children sail) and Bank Ground Farm (which becomes Holly Howe, where the Walkers live).

➕ www.visitcumbria.com/sl/kenmusll.htm (The Arthur Ransome Society is based in the Museum of Lakeland Life)

The Herries Chronicles (1939)
Sir Hugh Walpole

New Zealand-born Walpole wrote the Cumbrian family saga, the *Herries Chronicles*, while living at Brackenburn in the Catbells, overlooking Derwentwater, from 1924 to 1941.

🔍 *The Herries Chronicles – Rogue Herries; Judith Paris; The Fortress; Vanessa*

➕ View Walpole's diaries and the manuscripts of many of his novels at Keswick Museum and Art Gallery

Beatrix Potter land

Although born in South Kensington, London, in 1866, Beatrix Potter considered the Lake District her home. She first visited the area at the age of 16 with her parents, who rented Wray Castle near Ambleside. It was there that she first encountered Hardwicke Rawnsley, the vicar of Wray Church and a future founder of the National Trust. Rawnsley influenced Potter greatly. He impressed on her his love of the area and his belief that the Lake District's natural beauty needed to be preserved. Potter came to share his view. Over the next 20 years or so, Potter continued to visit the area, sketching the landscape and wildlife. She kept in touch with Rawnsley, who encouraged her to write and to publish her first book *The Tale of Peter Rabbit* in 1902. A huge financial success, the book enabled Potter to buy a small farm, Hill Lake, near Sawrey in the Lakes. In the 17th-century cottage, Potter wrote several of her children's stories, including those featuring Samuel Whiskers and Tom Kitten. She later bequeathed the property to the National Trust and it has become a leading tourist destination. In 1909, she bought Castle Farm, a property very near Hill Top, which became her main base. Potter continued to buy property in Cumbria, including Tarn Hows, a beauty spot, in 1929.

When Potter died in 1943, she bequeathed £211,636, 14 farms and 1,620 ha (4,000 acres) of land, together with her flocks of Herdwick sheep to the National Trust (www.nationaltrust.org.uk). The land included Tarn Hows, which is today one of the most visited sites in the region. Her husband's office in Hawkshead is today the site of the Beatrix Potter Gallery (again run by the National Trust). It features an exhibition on the film *Miss Potter*, which starred Renée Zellweger in the title role. In the Tower Bank Arms, near Hill Top, visitors can view one of the sketches for *The Tale of Jemima Puddleduck*.

➕ http://www.hop-skip-jump.com/visit_us.php (The World of Beatrix Potter draws thousands of tourists interested in the author's life, work and characters)

[Q] Beatrix Potter land (box feature)

[home] www.art-travels.co.uk/art-listings/2986.php (visitors can rent Brackenburn Cottage)

[wifi] www.wordsworth.org.uk/ (provides information on the poet, history, Dove Cottage and other places of interest in the area)

[Q] *Guide to the Lakes* (1820; available in new 2004 edition)

'Daffodils' (1807)
William Wordsworth

It might seem strange to include a poem in what is predominantly a collection of books, but it would be impossible, I think, to write on the Lake District without some nod to Wordsworth, one of the 'Lake Poets' so strongly associated with the area. The poem was inspired by some daffodils, which Wordsworth and his sister, Dorothy, spied at Glencoyne Bay, Ullswater, in 1802. Dorothy wrote in her diary, 'I never saw daffodils so beautiful they grew among the mossy stones about and about them, some rested their heads upon these stones as on a pillow for weariness and the rest tossed and reeled and danced and seemed as if they verily laughed with the wind that blew upon them over the lake, they looked so gay ever dancing ever changing.' Today, Wordsworth is strongly associated with Cumbria, where he lived with Dorothy from 1799, at Dove Cottage and Allen Bank, both in Grasmere, where Samuel Taylor Coleridge and Thomas de Quincey also resided, and Rydal House, Ambleside, which has fantastic views over Lake Windermere and 'Dora's field' with its fine display of daffodils. Visitors flock to the Lake District to see these houses, particularly Dove Cottage, which also holds many events.

LIVERPOOL AND MERSEYSIDE
Fiction

An Awfully Big Adventure (1989)
Beryl Bainbridge

An Awfully Big Adventure features aspiring actress Stella, who is rehearsing *Peter Pan* in a Liverpool repertory company in 1950. Written with Bainbridge's usual understated style and bittersweet humour, this book drew on the author's own experiences.

[film] *An Awfully Big Adventure* (1995), starring Hugh Grant and Alan Rickman

[Q] *Master Georgie*, set in Victorian Liverpool and the Crimea

All the Lonely People (1991)
Martin Edwards

The first in Edwards's series featuring Liverpool-based lawyer Harry Devlin, the title (like those of Edwards's other books) is from a song ('Eleanor Rigsby'). Harry returns to the riverside apartment of Liz, the wife from whom he's separated. Before long, Liz is dead and Harry finds himself accused of the murder. All of Edwards's books evoke Liverpool's landscape, people and music.

The Book of Liverpool: A City in Short Fiction (2008)
Margaret Murphy (ed.)

A collection of short stories about the city by its best authors, including Beryl Bainbridge, Roger McGough and Brian Patten, *The Book of Liverpool* looks at what it means to be Liverpudlian and shows how the city has developed over the centuries. The stories feature key historical moments, from the Second World War (1939–45) to 2008 when Liverpool became the Capital of Culture, and are set in a variety of locations, from council estates and the suburbs to the regenerated inner city. An interesting insight into a city undergoing great change.

Non-fiction

Liverpool: A People's History
(1990, third revised edition 2008)
Peter Aughton

A book for anyone wanting to know about the city's history and people, it also features a large fold-out map from the 19th century.

MANCHESTER
Fiction

Turn Home Again (2003)
Carol Birch

A Manchester family saga, Birch's acclaimed novel looks at the lives of three generations of a working-class city family during the 20th century. Birch seamlessly evokes Manchester during different eras – from greyhound racing at the Belle Vue track, Hyde Road, in Gorton, to the factories and foundries of the city.

Manchester Slingback (1998)
Nicholas Blincoe

Blincoe provides a great insight into Manchester's underground culture in this novel, which is set in and around Canal Street. Once a wild child, now a successful man in his 30s, protagonist Jake's past has caught up with him. When his friend is murdered, Jake is taken on a journey back to the past.

Mary Barton (1848)
Elizabeth Gaskell

Gaskell's Manchester books give a real insight into what life was like for the poor in the industrial north. Her sympathetic portrayal of suffering workers in this book drew on her own experiences of helping her husband, minister William Gaskell, work with Manchester's poor in the 1830s. The book was also written out of grief; her husband encouraged Gaskell to pour her energies into writing a novel after the death of their son. Gaskell's book attracted many fans, including Charles Dickens, who is thought to have based the fictional town of Coketown on Manchester and Preston in his novel *Hard Times*. Gaskell's Manchester House is undergoing renovation.

🛜 www.gaskellsociety.co.uk/
(Gaskell Society)

Blue Genes (1996)
Val McDermid

Scottish-born McDermid lived and worked in Manchester for several years and two of the books in her series are set here. *Blue Genes* is the fifth book featuring sassy, ballsy private eye Kate Brannigan dealing with a rash of problems – her partner is moving to Australia, her latest case involves a punk band at odds with a band of skinheads, her best friend is trying to have a baby and her doctor is murdered.

Killing the Beasts (2006)
Chris Simms

Simms's second novel *Killing the Beasts* is set in Manchester in the run up to the 2002 Commonwealth Games, and the author explores the regeneration of Manchester during this time. The book introduces Detective Inspector Jon Spicer, who has to solve a series of seemingly motiveless killings.

24 Hour Party People (2002)
Tony Wilson

This is a novelization of a screenplay about Tony Wilson's time as one of the most influential men in music. A roller-coaster ride, *24 Hour Party People* tells of a time when Manchester was the place to be and its music industry and clubs were among the best in the world. Wilson recounts vividly an important period in the city's history, a time filled with sex and drugs and the rise and fall of Factory Records and the Hacienda.

🎬 *24 Hour Party People* (2002), directed by Michael Winterbottom and starring Steve Coogan as Tony Wilson

YORKSHIRE
Fiction

Behind the Scenes at the Museum (1995)
Kate Atkinson

Set in York (where Atkinson was born), this award-winning book features narrator Ruby Lennox, who unravels the complex story of her family history, setting it against major events in the 20th century. The book features several literary allusions to such novels as Henry James's *The Turn of the Screw* and Emily Brontë's *Wuthering Heights* to help Ruby tell her story, from the moment of her conception onwards.

Wuthering Heights (1847)
Emily Brontë

One of the most famous stories in literary history, *Wuthering Heights* tells of the tortuous love between Heathcliff and Cathy. Set against the sweeping and magnificent landscape of the Yorkshire moors, Emily Brontë's great love story is drawn from the surrounding villages and countryside. The area around Haworth, in West Yorkshire, where the Brontës lived and wrote is now a major tourist destination. Visitors can tour Haworth Parsonage, now a museum owned and maintained by the Brontë Society, where Emily and her sisters lived and wrote. The 400 km (250 mile) Pennine Way, which runs from Derbyshire to Scotland, passes through Brontë country, passing Top Withens, the isolated moorland farmstead, just above Haworth, which is believed to have inspired Wuthering Heights. Ponden Hall, an Elizabethan farmhouse with a Georgian extension, is thought to have inspired Thrushcross Grange. The Hall is also on the Pennine Way, by Stanbury village, and is surrounded by wild hill farmland and heather-covered moors.

🎬 There have been several television and film adaptations of *Wuthering Heights*, but among the most notable are the 1939 film, starring Merle Oberon and Laurence Olivier as Cathy and Heathcliff, and the 1992 version, starring Juliette Binoche and Ralph Fiennes

📶 www.bronte.info/ (Brontë Society and Brontë Parsonage Museum)

🔍 *Jane Eyre*

The Moonstone (1868)
Wilkie Collins

Acclaimed by T. S. Eliot as the first, the longest and the best of modern detective novels, *The Moonstone* is set in a Yorkshire country house in 1842. On her 18th birthday, Rachel Verinder inherits a yellow diamond ('the moonstone'), which has been stolen from a Hindu temple and thus is reputed to bring bad luck to its owner. That night, the stone is stolen and Sergeant Cuff comes to investigate. The book was inspired by Collins's visit to Whitby and is set on the coast between there and Scarborough.

🔍 *The Woman in White*

It Shouldn't Happen to a Vet (1972)
James Herriot

Alf Wight is better known as the author James Herriot, who produced a series of books based on his own experiences as a vet living and working in North Yorkshire. Wight lived in Skeldale House in Thirsk, where he wrote the books, and the town forms the basis for Darrowby. Visitors to Thirsk can relive his experiences at the World of James Herriot, which includes recreated living quarters and sets from the popular television series.

🎬 *All Creatures Great and Small* (1975 film and television series of 90 episodes, transmitted 1978–80 and 1988–90)

📶 www.worldofjamesherriot.org:80/ default.htm (The World of James Herriot)

The Secret Garden (1911)
Frances Hodgson Burnett

This much-loved children's classic tells of Mary, a 10-year-old orphan, who returns from India to live in her uncle's isolated estate on the Yorkshire moors. At Misselthwaite Manor, Mary meets her sickly, spoilt cousin, makes friends with Dickon, a local boy who can charm animals, and discovers an overgrown, walled garden. Gradually, the children begin to clear the garden. By doing so, they transform themselves, the house and Mary's uncle. Visitors to Yorkshire are able to take walking tours around the moors and discover Hodgson Burnett's landscape.

🎬 *The Secret Garden* (1993)
🔍 *A Little Princess*

The Red Riding Quartet (1999–2002)
David Peace

Yorkshire-born writer Peace presents an alternative contemporary history of his native county. *The Red Riding Quartet* focuses on the years between 1974 and 1983, and looks at an area and people traumatized by the Yorkshire Ripper and hit hard by the policies of Margaret Thatcher's government. Peace says, 'Nearly everyone in the north has a story about that time: their fathers being pulled over by the police, walking past murder sites on the way to school.' Influenced by fellow Yorkshire writer Stan Barstow, Peace is today a cult writer, who successfully blends fact with fiction.

🔍 *Nineteen Seventy-Four*; *Nineteen Seventy-Seven*; *Nineteen Eighty*; *Nineteen Eighty-Three*

🔍 Japan, Tokyo – *Tokyo Year Zero*

Dracula (1897)
Bram Stoker

Stoker's stirring Gothic tale of the mysterious Transylvanian Count Dracula has captured many an imagination. Vampires, romance, horror and sexuality are all themes dealt with in the book. Stoker used the beautiful Yorkshire coastal town of Whitby, with its 1,000-year-old port and its abbey, as a source of inspiration and a setting for a large part of the book. While there, Stoker was told of a ship called the *Demetrius*, which founded off the coast and emptied its cargo of coffins into the North Sea. The townspeople told him of the horror of finding decomposing bodies on the beach the next day. Stoker used the tale in his book and Dracula is shipwrecked off the Whitby coast while travelling on the *Demeter*. Dracula first comes ashore at Whitby and it is here that he seduces Lucy, turning her into a vampire.

🎬 Several film and television adaptations have been made of *Dracula*, including Francis Ford Coppola's 1992 version, starring Winona Ryder, Keanu Reeves and Gary Oldman (as Dracula)

➕ www.whitbysights.co.uk/whitby-attractions/draculatrail.html (the Dracula Trail)

Non-fiction

The Road to Wigan Pier (1937)
George Orwell

Based on Orwell's travels around Wigan, Barnsley and Sheffield between 1935 and 1936, *The Road to Wigan Pier* recounts the lives, social conditions and experiences of the working classes in the industrial North. Often shockingly bleak, Orwell's book reveals a world hampered by social injustice, ignorance, exploitation and poverty with devastating honesty and great humanity. A classic.

➕ www.wlct.org/tourism/guidewalks.htm (heritage tour that also highlights other famous people related to Wigan, such as comedian George Formby)

🔍 Burma – *Burmese Days: A Novel*

Brontë country

Each year, tourists flock to the north of England to visit Brontë country (an area covering West Yorkshire and the East Lancashire Pennines). Emily, Anne and Charlotte Brontë were born in Thornton near Bradford, Yorkshire. They moved with their parents, brother and two sisters to the parsonage at Haworth in West Yorkshire, today the site of the Brontë Parsonage Museum, in 1820. After the deaths of their mother and two sisters, Maria and Elizabeth, they began writing to entertain themselves and each other. It was here that the sisters wrote their most successful titles: Charlotte's *Jane Eyre* (1847), Emily's *Wuthering Heights* (1847) and Anne's *The Tenant of Wildfell Hall* (1848). The Brontës were moved and influenced by the dramatic, bleak and beautiful landscape around them, and many of the local houses, villages and monuments of West Yorkshire and nearby Lancashire feature in their books. Examples include: the ruins of Wycoller Hall, near Colne in Lancashire's Pendle Witch country, believed to have inspired Ferndean Manor in *Jane Eyre* and Ponden Hall near Haworth on which Thrushcross Grange is based in *Wuthering Heights*.

🛜 http://www.bronte-country.com/welcome.html
(locations featured in the Brontë novels)

EAST ENGLAND

Fiction

Watch Me Disappear (2006)
Jill Dawson

Set in a small Fenland village, *Watch Me Disappear* features Tina Humber, who returns to the area with her daughter for her brother's wedding in Ely. It is her first visit since her father's suicide. Tina's childhood friend, Mandy, disappeared more than 30 years before and the reader is taken on a journey to discover what happened all those years ago. The Fens, sea horses and beets are recurring images.

The Bookshop (1978)
Penelope Fitzgerald

Fitzgerald's fine novel is a depiction of life in a small parochial seaside town in Suffolk in the 1950s. The plot centres on middle-aged widow Florence, who decides to set up a bookshop in an historic building in Hardborough (thought to be based on Southwold), with unexpected consequences. This is a great study of small-town life in the English countryside.

🔍 *Something Might Happen*
🔍 Germany – *The Blue Flower*

The Sea House (2003)
Esther Freud

Freud explores two adulterous affairs separated by half a century in this evocative novel. Set in the seaside village of Steerborough (based on Walberswick) on the Suffolk coast, the action of *The Sea House* takes place in the present day and 1953.

🛜 www.explorewalberswick.co.uk/
(Walberswick)

The Go-Between (1953)
L. P. Hartley

Set in Edwardian England,
L. P. Hartley's classic novel is
about illicit love and the loss of
innocence set against a Norfolk
landscape. Leo Colston looks back
50 years to 1900 when he spent a
summer with his friend at Brandham
Hall. Leo falls under the spell of
Marcus's older sister and becomes
the go-between, delivering messages
between Marian and the local farmer,
Ted Burgess. Disaster awaits, however.
The 1970 movie was mainly shot
in Melton Constable Hall in North
Norfolk, but other locations include
the village green in Thornage, near
Holt (for the cricket match), and the
Maid's Head Hotel in Norwich, where
Marian takes Leo for lunch (as in the
novel itself).

🎬 *The Go-Between* (1970), directed
by Joseph Loseley and starring
Julie Christie and Alan Bates

🏠 www.foliohotels.com/maidshead/
(Maid's Head Hotel)

🔍 *The Shrimp and the Anemone*

Something Might Happen (2003)
Julie Myerson

Focusing on how the brutal murder of
a woman impacts on the community
of a 'slightly self-satisfied seaside
town', *Something Might Happen*
is based on Southwold in Suffolk,
where the author holidayed as a
child. The book was longlisted for
the Booker Prize in 2003.

The Rings of Saturn (1995)
W. G. Sebald

German-born writer W. G. Sebald,
or 'Max' as he was also known,
wrote this dream-like account of
walking through coastal East Anglia
(Suffolk). A lyrical book, *The Rings
of Saturn* weaves fact, fiction and
memoir as the narrator wends his
way around the region, meeting a
strange array of people. Sebald welds
the past to the present and links
a range of locations and a pastoral
and imperial history to the region.

🔍 *Austerlitz*

Waterland (1983)
Graham Swift

Narrated by history teacher Tom Crick,
Graham Swift's third novel evokes
the eerie flatlands of the Fens. After
Mary, Tom's wife, kidnaps a child,
Tom is forced into early retirement.
Faced with a classroom of bored
teenagers, he abandons the
curriculum to tell them instead about
his childhood in the Fens, where
he grew up during the Second World
War (1939–45). His descriptions of
the marshy, brooding countryside are
hauntingly beautiful. *Waterland* was
shortlisted for 1983's Booker Prize.

🎬 *Waterland* (1992), starring Jeremy
Irons and Sinéad Cusack as Tom
and Mary

🔍 Kent – *Last Orders*

🔍 *The Light of Day*

SCOTLAND

EDINBURGH
Fiction

Greyfriars Bobby
(1912; new edition 2007)
Eleanor Atkinson

Few people visit Edinburgh without hearing the story of Greyfriars Bobby, a tale of love, loyalty and, put simply, a man and his dog. In this classic, Atkinson recounts the true story of Bobby, the devoted Skye terrier who refuses to leave the grave of his beloved master. For 14 years, despite everything the authorities tried to do, at night Bobby returned to sleep by his master's grave. In the end a shelter was created for the dog and, after the law was changed in 1868 to require all dogs to have a licence, the Lord Provost paid for Bobby's and gave him a collar with a brass inscription 'Greyfriars Bobby from the Lord Provost 1867 licensed', which can be seen in the Museum of Edinburgh. Greyfriars is one of Edinburgh's most famous cemeteries and opposite it is now a bronze statue of a small dog, bearing the inscription, 'Greyfriars Bobby – died 14th January 1872 – aged 16 years – Let his loyalty and devotion be a lesson to us all.'

Born Free (1999)
Laura Hird

Set in Edinburgh, Laura Hird's engaging book features a dysfunctional family made up of teenager Jake, his sister Joni and parents Angie and Vic, who live in a city tenement. Hird vividly describes the underbelly of the city. Locations include Shandwick Place and Lothian Road.

🛜 www.laurahird.com/publications.html (author website)

44 Scotland Street (2005)
Alexander McCall Smith

Better known for his Botswana-based series, the *No. 1 Ladies' Detective Agency*, McCall Smith published this novel in serial form in the *Scotsman*. The book, which has been compared by some to Armistead Maupin's *Tales in the City* (perhaps to Maupin's detriment) provides an insight into Edinburgh society through the various room-mates and tenants that central character Pat meets at 44 Scotland Street (a fictional house in a real street) in the New Town. Visitors can stay in Scotland Street and view the setting of McCall's novel for themselves.

🏠 http://www.44scotlandstreet.co.uk /stay.html (book-related B&B)

The Prime of Miss Jean Brodie (1961)
Muriel Spark

Spark's acclaimed novel tells of Miss Jean Brodie, an unconventional, free-spirited and charismatic teacher at Marcia Blaine's School for Girls in Edinburgh. The 1969 film was shot in and around the city in such locations

Rebus's Edinburgh

Ian Rankin's 'Inspector Rebus' novels have sold millions of copies worldwide. Primarily set in and around Edinburgh, the locations are as essential to the plot as the characters. The city that Rankin presents is ever changing, ever evolving, a place where rich and poor are deeply divided. Rankin's first novel, *Knots and Crosses* (1987), introduced the brooding, complex character of John Rebus to audiences and, since then, Rankin's novels have charted the great political, cultural and social changes to the city. Although the books feature locations outside Edinburgh, it is the Scottish capital itself that lies at the heart of all the 'Rebus' novels. Rankin's Edinburgh mixes the familiar city that visitors know and love – the castle, Holyrood, the Royal Mile – with a darker, more sinister and violent, crime-ridden place. Here, tourists rub shoulders with criminals and drug dealers, while gang lords fight to control the city.

Visitors can follow in Rebus's steps, visiting many of the places that appear in the books on one of several tours. Familiar Rebus locations include the city morgue, St Leonard's Police Station, Marchmont and the Meadows (near where Rebus lives), the Scottish Parliament, Leith and, of course, the Oxford Bar (http://www.oxfordbar.com/), where both Rebus and Rankin drink.

📺 *Rebus* (2000–6), starring first John Hannah and then Ken Stott in the title role

📶 http://www.rebustours.com/ (tours)

🔍 *Rebus's Scotland: A Personal Journey* (2005)

as Greyfriars Churchyard, the Grassmarket and Edinburgh Academy.

📺 *The Prime of Miss Jean Brodie* (1969), starring Maggie Smith in the title role

📶 www.scotlandthemovie.com/movies/prime1.html (Scotland film location guide)

Trainspotting (1993)
Irvine Welsh

Edinburgh-born Welsh presents a different view of a city that is usually portrayed as highbrow and genteel. Welsh, who was brought up in Leith's tenements before moving to West Pilton and then Muirhouse, sets *Trainspotting* in the drug-riddled streets of Old Town, New Town and Leith. It follows the lives of a group of working-class Edinburgh junkies, Rents, Sick Boy, Mother Superior, Swanney, Spuds, and Begbie, presenting their lives in the thick local dialect. Darkly funny, the book has been compared to Burgess's *A Clockwork Orange*. Visitors to Edinburgh can take *Trainspotting* tours, which take in some of the places mentioned in the book and film, including Leith Walk, Central Bar and the Dockers' Club.

📺 *Trainspotting* (1996), directed by Danny Boyle and starring Ewan McGregor

📶 www.leithwalks.co.uk/iw/iw1.htm (Trainspotting Tour – Literature Live on Location in Leith)

🔍 *A Clockwork Orange*

GLASGOW

Fiction

Lanark (1981)
Alasdair Gray

Often cited as one of the top 100 Scottish books of all time, *Lanark* is a curious blend of surrealism and realism, hope and despair. A book in four parts, the first (book 3) is set in Unthank (Glasgow), or hell, where Lanark emerges with no memory, and struggles to find love and hope. He is eventually swallowed by a huge mouth and finds himself in an institute recovering. In the second and third parts (books 1 and 2), set in post-war Glasgow, Duncan Thaw struggles to be an artist and suffers a nervous breakdown while painting a mural in a Glasgow church. The final book takes us back to Lanark in the institute and his return to Unthank.

A Very Scotch Affair (1968)
Robin Jenkins

Set in Glasgow, like many of Jenkins's novels, *A Very Scotch Affair* follows the life of Mungo, who escapes a loveless marriage after his wife becomes ill, with devastating consequences for his family. Jenkins's characters are drawn with a fine hand and with devastating humour.

How Late It Was, How Late (1994)
James Kelman

Kelman's controversial Booker Prize-winning novel is written in local dialect and set in Glasgow. It is a stream of consciousness by ex-con Sammy Samuels, who wakes up after a two-day drinking binge and tries to piece together what has happened, only for things to get worse.

Laidlaw (1977)
William McIlvanney

The Laidlaw of the title is Detective Inspector Jack Laidlaw and in this novel William McIlvanney evokes a grittily real Glasgow – as far away from the clichéd image of tartans and drunken louts as is possible. Laidlaw runs his investigation from a hotel in the city and the reader is treated to descriptions of the Victorian architecture. Laidlaw also walks around the city to soak up the atmosphere, allowing the reader an insight into a Glasgow that usually remains hidden from view.

Young Adam (1957)
Alexander Trocchi

This existential cult novel is set on the canals between Glasgow and Edinburgh. Joe, the frustrated young protagonist, works on the barges to make ends meet. Joe and his boss find the body of a young woman in the canal and we gradually discover that the girl and Joe were connected.

🎬 *Young Adam* (2003), starring Ewan McGregor and Tilda Swinton

The Cutting Room (2002)
Louise Welsh

In Welsh's debut novel, the snuff porn industry is explored against the backdrop of Glasgow's streets. Rilke, the gay protagonist, is an auctioneer. In the course of removing belongings from the house of the deceased Roddy McKindless, he comes across some photographs of what look like the torture and murder of a woman. Welsh reveals the seedier side of the city as Rilke traverses it to find out what really happened.

OTHER REGIONS

Fiction

The Crow Road (1992)
Iain Banks

A family saga set in the fictional Gallanach (most probably Oban), the real Lochgair (both in Argyll) and Glasgow. Prentice McHoan negotiates his way through life, while dealing with his eccentric, wealthy family.

📺 *The Crow Road* (1996)
🔍 *The Wasp Factory*

Consider the Lilies (1968)
Iain Crichton Smith

Crichton Smith's novel focuses on the Highland Clearances, the cruel eviction of crofters from their homes between 1792 and the 1850s, as seen through the eyes of an elderly woman. This is an eerily evocative account of this dreadful period in the history of Scotland.

🔍 *The Red Door: The Complete Short Stories, 1949–76*

Under the Skin (2000)
Michel Faber

A strange but curiously addictive novel, *Under the Skin* features beautiful descriptions of the Highlands. The story follows Isserly, a human-looking alien who spends her days driving around the country, picking up hitchhikers on their way to Dundee, Aberdeen, Inverness and other Scottish towns. As the book unfolds, the reader realizes that Isserly is far more than just a female sexual predator.

🔍 *The Crimson Petal and the White*

Sunset Song (1932)
Lewis Grassic Gibbon

Regarded by many as one of the most important Scottish novels, *Sunset Song* is the first part of a trilogy called *A Scots Quair*. The books focus on Chris Guthrie, who grows up in a north-east Scotland farming family on the fictional Estate of Kinraddie in the Mearns. The land that inspired the author is an undulating fertile plain, which lies between Aberdeen and Montrose. Grassic Gibbon was brought up in the area, where his father was a crofter, and the book uses local locations: Arbuthnott is Kinraddie, Bloomfield is Blawearie and the kirk, the school and the mill can all be found in the area. In Arbuthnott, visitors can go to the Grassic Gibbon Centre and follow the Grassic Gibbon trail through the Mearns.

🔍 *Sunset Song* (1932); *Cloud Howe* (1933); *Grey Granite* (1934)

📺 *Sunset Song* (1971)

📶 www.grassicgibbon.com/
(Lewis Grassic Gibbon Centre)

Docherty (1975)
William McIlvanney

His third novel, *Docherty*, won William McIlvanney much critical acclaim. The protagonist, Tam Docherty, is a miner, living in Graithnock in the early years of the 20th century. The book examines working-class Graithnock, a town that is based on Kilmarnock in Ayrshire.

Morvern Callar (1995)
Alan Warner

Warner's debut novel, *Morven Callar*, quickly became a modern classic. Set in a place thought to be based on Oban, the book begins with Morvern waking up to find her boyfriend has committed suicide. The 2002 film was shot in and around Oban.

🎬 *Morvern Callar* (2002),
starring Samantha Morton

WALES

Fiction

The Old Devils (1986)
Kingsley Amis

A modern classic and Booker Prize winner, this book is essentially about growing old disgracefully. Full of booze, dark humour and also poignancy, *The Old Devils* looks at what happens when Alun Weaver and

his wife return to Wales and stir up a lot of trouble among their old friends.

📺 *The Old Devils* (1992), in three parts

The Hiding Place (2000)
Trezza Azzopardi

Azzopardi's debut novel examines the grim lives of a Maltese immigrant family in 1960s' Cardiff. From the father's arrival in Tiger Bay, Azzopardi details the sometimes quite horrific lives of a family dealing with poverty and despair.

On the Black Hill (1982)
Bruce Chatwin

Chatwin is perhaps better known for his travel memoirs. His classic novel *On the Black Hill* is set on the Welsh–English border and chronicles the lives of identical twins, Lewis and Benjamin Jones, who live in a farmhouse there. Chatwin evokes the eerily bleak landscape of the beautiful Black Hills.

🎬 *On the Black Hill* (1987)

🔍 Australia – *Song Lines*

How Green Was My Valley (1939)
Richard Llewellyn

Llewellyn's best-selling novel is set in a South Wales coal-mining village in the late 19th century. It follows the Morgan family and a small mining community, as seen through the eyes of the youngest boy, Huw. The book was made into an Oscar-winning film in 1941.

🎬 *How Green Was My Valley* (1941)
was John Ford's masterpiece

Aberystwyth, Mon Amour (2001)
Malcolm Pryce

The first in a hilarious detective series set in the mean streets of Aberystwyth, Malcolm Pryce's book introduces the oddball character of Louis Knight, the town's private investigator, who finds himself running all over the city to find out why boys are disappearing from its streets.

NORTHERN IRELAND

BELFAST AND ULSTER
Fiction

Divorcing Jack (1995)
Colin Bateman

Journalist Colin Bateman's black comedy focuses on Dan Starkey, a Belfast columnist, who finds himself in trouble both politically and domestically when he's caught in the arms of another woman by his wife. When that woman is murdered, Starkey is a prime suspect. Several of Bateman's books are set in Belfast.

🎬 Divorcing Jack (1998)
🎐 http://www.colinbateman.com
    (author website)

No Bones (2002)
Anna Burns

Burns's depiction of some of the darkest days in Northern Ireland's history is seen through the eyes of protagonist Amelia Lovett. The book

spans the start of the Troubles in 1969 to the ceasefire in 1994, and the Belfast that the author depicts is one haunted and scarred by its past and tortured by unrest.

Reading in the Dark (1996)
Seamus Deane

Set in Derry, from the 1940s to 1970s, *Reading in the Dark* is the personal account of an unnamed Catholic narrator's view of growing up in Northern Ireland. His family is associated with the IRA and through his eyes we learn about the violence, sectarianism and politics of this period.

Cal (1983)
Bernard MacLaverty

Set in Ulster, MacLaverty's novel focuses on Catholic Cal McCluskey, a young working-class boy living on a Protestant housing estate during the Troubles. Pressured into doing a job for the provisional IRA, Cal is consumed with self-loathing and guilt. The book is a great study of Northern Ireland at that time.

🎬 Cal (1984), starring John Lynch in the title role
🔍 Lamb

Eureka Street (1996)
Robert McLiam Wilson

Set in Belfast just months before the ceasefire, McLiam Wilson's descriptive book examines what it is like to live in a city pretty much under siege on a day-to-day basis. The protagonist is Jake Jackson, a Catholic ex-bouncer. Turned into a mini series by BBC NI in 1999, it was shot in and around Belfast, in such places as Garfield Street.

📺 *Eureka Street* (1999), four parts

The Lonely Passion of Judith Hearne (1955)
Brian Moore

Lonely spinster Judith Hearne lives in a Belfast boarding house, desperate for love and dreaming of meeting her perfect man. She falls in love only to have her hopes and dreams dashed.

🎥 *The Lonely Passion of Judith Hearne* (1987), starring Maggie Smith

Swallowing the Sun (2004)
David Park

Park's much-acclaimed fifth novel is set in Belfast. Martin Waring works as a museum guard, lives in the suburbs and seemingly has a happy life. After his daughter's death, he struggles to make sense of his life. This bleak novel gives us an insight into post-ceasefire Belfast, where the paramilitaries have turned to racketeering and the police are demoralized.

Non-fiction

Making Sense of the Troubles (2000)
David McKittrick and David McVea

Northern Ireland has a complicated and layered history, one that is difficult to understand. This book gives a concise, analytical overview into the Troubles. It is seen by some as one of the definitive works on the subject.

MIDDLE EAST

Afghanistan | Iran | Iraq | Israel | Jordan

Lebanon | Palestine | Saudi Arabia | Syria | Yemen

MIDDLE EAST

GENERAL

Fiction

***Tales from the Bazaars
of Arabia: Folk Stories from
the Middle East*** (2002)
Amina Shah

This dazzling collection of classic
folk stories from Arabia, Turkey,
Afghanistan and Persia is alive
with princes, kings, djinns, witches,
apes and snakes dealing with fate
and karma and fighting for good
against evil. Compiled by Amina
Shah, *Tales from the Bazaars of Arabia*
brings together some of the best
stories from this region of the world.

Non-fiction

***The Great War for Civilisation:
The Conquest of the Middle East*** (2005)
Robert Fisk

Fisk's brilliantly passionate book
presents 50 years of the history of
the Middle East. It draws on more
than three decades of the author's
experiences of living and working in
this turbulent region. Journalist Fisk's
encounters with such people as
Osama bin Laden inform the text,
bringing it and the region to life.
Whether you hate or love Robert
Fisk, this book is an excellent
introduction to, and examination of,
the people and politics of this highly
complicated place.

AFGHANISTAN

Fiction

Flashman (1969)
George MacDonald Fraser

Fraser's hugely popular series featuring
anti-hero Sir Harry Paget Flashman
begins with this book. Inspired by
Tom Brown's Schooldays in which the
character features as a cowardly bully,
Flashman embarks on a military
career after being expelled from
Rugby. His adventures lead him to
Afghanistan, where his exploits
culminate in his participation in the
disastrous retreat from Kabul (1842).
Through his own cowardly behaviour,
Flashman not only survives but is
lionized as the 'Hector of Afghanistan'.
Fraser gives a great insight into
19th-century British colonial history
as witnessed first-hand by this
entertaining character. Visitors to
Kabul can stay at the Gandamack
Lodge, named after Flashman's
fictitious home in Leicestershire.

🎬 *Flashman* (1967)

🔍 *Tom Brown's Schooldays* by
  Thomas Hughes

🏠 http://www.gandamacklodge.co.uk
  (Gandamack Lodge)

The Mulberry Empire (2002)
Philip Hensher

This ambitious and sprawling novel
draws on the writings of earlier
authors such as H. Rider Haggard
and Sir Arthur Conan Doyle. The
story focuses on the British dealings
with Afghanistan in the late 1830s,

when they decided to replace the independent-minded Dost Muhammad Khan with a puppet ruler. The Army of the Indus was created to help bring about the change, but the British failed to take into account the Afghan tribes who objected to their scheme and who consequently united to drive the British out of their country with tragic consequences. A book that blends fact with fiction, in which real-life characters walk arm in arm with made up ones, *The Mulberry Empire* is a Great Game novel and gives the reader a very interesting overview of this fascinating period of imperial history.

The Kite Runner (2003)
Khaled Hosseini

This best-selling book is a story of loss and redemption in modern Afghanistan. Following a phone call from an old family friend, Amir, a novelist living in California, returns to his homeland, Afghanistan. The journey back to Afghanistan causes Amir to recall his childhood in the 1970s with his friend, Hassan, the son of Amir's father's servant and a member of the minority Hazara. The day of the local kite-flying competition, which Amir is desperate to win, with Hassan's help, is the day that everything changes and neither boy can foresee how much their lives will change. Tracing the final days of King Zahir Shan's reign to the battlefield that the country became, first under the Soviets and then under the Taliban, *The Kite Runner* is also a deeply moving examination of friendship.

🎬 *The Kite Runner* (2008)
🔍 *A Thousand Splendid Suns* (2007)

The Swallows of Kabul (2002)
Yasmina Khadra

This powerful novel follows four Afghan people living under the Taliban regime. Mohsen lives with his wife Zunaira in Kabul. Both had dreams that ended with the outbreak of the war with Russia and it is only at home that they can be themselves. Following a series of dreadful events, Zunaira finds herself in prison, where she awaits execution. There, Atiq, a part-time jailer, watching over those condemned to die, is drawn to her. Atiq's own wife is dying of cancer. In the words of author J. M. Coetzee 'Khadra's Kabul is hell on earth: a place of hunger, tedium and stifling fear.'

The Patience Stone (2010)
Atiq Rahimi

One rarely hears or reads much about the lives of the ordinary people of Afghanistan, especially women; Rahimi's book, translated from its original French, now fills this gap. *The Patience Stone* is written in the form of a monologue of a wife to her husband, a jihadist soldier, who lies in a coma after being shot. As soldiers storm the streets, shells explode and the mullah calls people to prayer, the wife begins to speak to her husband, telling him her secrets, fears, resentments, dreams and sexual desires. The man becomes her 'patience stone', an object of Persian myth that absorbs the words of the penitent until the day it explodes.

Non-fiction

The Sleeping Buddha:
The Story of Afghanistan through the Eyes of One Family (2004)
Hamida Ghafour

A moving and personal book, *The Sleeping Buddha* is journalist Ghafour's account of her journey in 2003 back to Afghanistan, the country that she and her family left in 1981 when Soviet tanks arrived. While reporting on the country's reconstruction post 9/11, Ghafour delves deeper and deeper into her family's past. She introduces us to the many colourful characters who haunt it, including her poetess grandmother, the great-uncle who wrote the first constitution and her parents, who searched for the perfect pomegranate.

A Bed of Red Flowers:
In Search of My Afghanistan (2005)
Nelofer Pazira

A Canadian-based film-maker, Pazira spent her childhood growing up in Kabul, the daughter of two liberal-minded professionals. At the age of 5, her life changed when her father was imprisoned for refusing to support the Communists. In 1979, the Soviets began their 10-year occupation of the country and

Pazira and her friend Dyana planned acts of rebellion and Pazira became involved in the resistance movement. After Pazira's family finally fled to Canada, via Pakistan, Pazira and Dyana corresponded, the latter revealing the reality of life in an oppressive regime in which women are subjugated. Pazira returned to post-Taliban Afghanistan to find her friend and the subsequent search formed the basis for her highly acclaimed film *Kandahar*.

🎬 *Kandahar* (2001)

IRAN

Fiction

My Father's Notebook (2000)
Kader Abdolah

Abdolah's book presents Iranian history as seen through the eyes of the deaf mute father of Iranian dissident Ishmael. Left his father's notebooks, which are written in cuneiform, Ishmael struggles to decode the past, while dealing with his own new life in a Dutch city built on reclaimed land.

The Blood of Flowers (2007)
Anita Amirrezvani

Set in 17th-century Iran, Amirrezvani's beautifully detailed novel follows an unnamed heroine living in a rural village with her mother and beloved father, who is a rug-maker. After her father dies, the family falls on hard times and is forced to go to the historic city of Isfahan (between Fars and Tehran in central Iran), where they work for the girl's uncle, a carpet-maker of international repute. Encouraged by her uncle, the girl discovers her talent as a carpet-maker and she begins to feel that life is finally changing for the better for her and her mother.

➕ http://www.art-arena.com/ esfahan.htm (Isfahan)

The Prince (1969)
Hushang Golshiri

Golshiri's highly acclaimed novel is set in the Iran of the 1920s. Through the memories of the dying Prince Khosrow Ehtejab, it presents the Qujar dynasty that ruled Isfahan, the town in which the author grew up. The prince is haunted by memories and taunted by the ghosts of his ancestors, who become more real to him than the world he actually inhabits as they reveal to him the brutality and also the beauty of the past. Golshiri was persecuted for his stand against censorship under both the shah's and the ayatollah's regimes and many of his books were banned in Iran.

📶 http://www.golshirifoundation.org/ english/index.asp (Hooshang Golshiri Foundation)

The Blind Owl (1937)
Sadeq Hedayat

Acclaimed for his brilliant short stories, Hedayat originally published his novella *The Blind Owl* in India.

Regarded as his masterpiece, it has been translated into many languages from its original Persian. Hedayat's narrator is an invalid who takes opium and much of the story has a dreamlike feel. The three women who have impacted on his life recur throughout the book: the ethereal beauty, who reminds him of everything he lacks and will never be; the little girl with whom he played in his childhood; and the woman who became his wife. *The Blind Owl* is a study of the narrator's descent into madness and was much admired by other writers, including Henry Miller.

Drunkard Morning (1998)
Fataneh Haj Seyed Javadi

This best-selling novel is set in 1940s' Iran and tells of a woman who defies her upper-class family to marry beneath her. When her new carpenter husband turns out to be abusive, she breaks with tradition and, in a radical move, leaves him to marry someone else.

Caspian Rain (2007)
Gina B. Nahai

Yaas, the Jewish–Iranian narrator of Nahai's fourth book, is an unwelcome child – a girl – and her mother cries tears of despair at her birth. However, she wants Yaas to succeed, where she has herself failed. She wants her daughter to have some relevance in a society that deems her irrelevant because of her gender. Set 10 years before the Iranian Revolution (1978–9), *Caspian Rain*

The Thousand and One Nights

One of the greatest and best-known tales, *The Thousand and One Nights* (known more commonly in the West as *The Arabian Nights*) is part of most people's psyche today, in one form or another. The stories, originally believed to have been compiled by Abu abd-Allah Muhammed el-Gahshigar in the ninth century, began to filter through to the West during the Middle Ages, but weren't translated until the French scholar Galland did so in the 18th century. The tales spring from a multitude of sources, storytellers and places, originating for the most part in Persia, Arabia and India.

In other versions discovered since Galland's translation, some of the stories vary but they essentially deal with a king who is in the habit of taking a wife and executing her after their first night together. His plans are thwarted by the ingenuity of Scheherazade, the vizier's daughter, who weaves a story for the king, only to have her execution delayed because she failed to finish it in one night. The next night she begins a new story as soon as she ends the first one, and again the king puts off his new wife's execution, and so this goes on for 1,001 nights. The stories that Scheherazade tells are in a mixture of styles, probably to maintain her husband's interest, and include love stories, tragedies, comedies and historical tales. Although the reasons for the ending may vary in the different collections, the king always gives his wife a pardon and a stay of execution. Many of the stories have been adapted for film, television or radio, including those featuring Sinbad and Ali Baba and the Forty Thieves.

gives the reader some insight into Persian life prior to 1979. It is a fascinating read.

🛜 http://ginabnahai.com/
(author's website)

🔍 *Sunday's Silence*

My Uncle Napoleon (1973)
Iraj Pezeshkzad

A social farce set in a garden in 1940s' Tehran, *My Uncle Napoleon* was hailed as a classic in Iran and was turned into a highly successful television series. It follows a large extended family dominated by a paranoid patriarch and shows what happens when the narrator, Uncle Napoleon's least favourite nephew, falls in love with his cousin, Layli.

📺 *My Uncle Napoleon* (1976)

The Septembers of Shiraz (2007)
Dalia Sofer

This lyrical novel is set in Iran, the country of Sofer's birth, after the Iranian Revolution. At its centre lies the Amin family, Isaac, Farnaz and their two children, Parviz and Shireen. An Iranian Jew, Isaac, who has never been particularly religious, finds himself in trouble under the new regime. Sofer seamlessly conjures up the terror and insecurity of living in post-shah Iran, showing how the Amin family's lives fall apart.

Non-fiction

Reading Lolita in Tehran (2003)
Azar Nafisi

For two years prior to leaving Iran for the United States in 1997, Azar Nafisi arranged for a group of seven of her best female students to meet at her house each Thursday to discuss forbidden pieces of Western literature. A former lecturer, Nafisi had either been sacked or resigned from her various posts under the totalitarian theocracy. Her former students came from different religious and social backgrounds and gradually opened up as they discussed *Lolita*, *Pride and Prejudice* and other books, finally opening up about their own thoughts and dreams.

📶 http://azarnafisi.com/
(author's website)

Persepolis (2001)
Marjane Satrapi

Set during the Islamic Revolution, Satrapi's brilliant graphic novel, *Persepolis* (the Greek name for Persia) is autobiographical. Originally published in French, in the grand tradition of Spiegelman's *Maus*, Satrapi presents the politics of the time as seen by a child through illustration. The young Satrapi witnesses the overthrow of the shah, experiences the terror of the Khomeini years and watches her liberal parents try to cope with a new regime that becomes increasingly more fundamentalist. Iran's history also unfolds through Satrapi's family's past (her grandfather was Naser al-Din Shah, Persian emperor from 1848 to 1896). Darkly funny and moving, *Persepolis* was dismissed by Iranian authorities as 'Islamaphobic'; something that the author denies.

🎬 *Persepolis* (2007)

IRAQ

Fiction

They Came to Baghdad (1951)
Agatha Christie

Christie at her best ... a mixture of romance and espionage in an exotic locale, *They Came to Baghdad* is located in a city that Christie knew very well. Protagonist Victoria Jones yearns for adventure and certainly finds it when a spy whispers his final words to her before dying in her hotel room – now she must just make sense of them. In the background a secret superpower summit and a Middle Eastern underground organization planning sabotage complicate matters.

The Nightingale (2009)
Morgana Gallaway

Essentially a romance, *The Nightingale* is perhaps all the more interesting because it is set in contemporary Iraq, where Gallaway's protagonist is a young Iraqi girl from a prominent family in Mosul. Leila yearns to be a doctor but after Hussein's regime crumbles so do her dreams. Her previously modern family becomes more conservative and the city that Leila knows becomes more violent. After being harassed at the hospital where she works, Leila becomes a translator at a US base outside Mosul but hides her job from her family. There, she meets and begins a relationship with a Special Forces captain, but her eyes are opened to what is happening in her country when she starts to witness first-hand the violence and horrors of war.

Saddam City (2004)
Mahmoud Saeed

Saeed's beautiful but disturbing book describes life in Iraq during Saddam Hussein's rule. Focusing on the arrest and long incarceration of Mustafa Ali Noman, a teacher in Baghdad, the book examines the brutality and inhumanity that many civilian Iraqis suffered at the hands of the secret police.

When the Grey Beetles Took Over Baghdad (2000)
Mona Yahia

This award-winning novel is set in Baghdad in the aftermath of the Six-Day War (1967). Here, 14-year-old Lina lives as part of a middle-class Jewish family. As the Jewish community becomes increasingly more vulnerable, Lina's father loses his job and her brother is arrested. Lina struggles to live a normal life in an increasingly perilous city and when her family

decides to leave the country, she must keep their plans secret. Yahia evocatively brings to mind the smells, colours and atmosphere of the city during the 1960s. The author was herself born in Baghdad.

Non-fiction

The 8.55 to Baghdad (2004)
Andrew Eames

British journalist Andrew Eames follows in the footsteps of crime writer Agatha Christie from London to Baghdad. In 1928, with her first marriage at an end, Christie decided to take a break, anxious to escape the suffocating life in Sunningdale, Berkshire. She had intended to visit the Caribbean, but a chance meeting at a dinner party with a couple who had been in Iraq led Christie to travel there instead. At the time, Iraq was an outpost of the British Empire and a train, the Nairn Line, ran across the desert from Beirut via Damascus to Baghdad. Eames traces the famous crime writer's route with much greater difficulty, as he journeys across a region that is on the brink of war. He does stay at many Christie sites, however, including the Baron Hotel, where Christie and many other literati stayed and also the dig-house at Ur, the capital of the ancient civilization of Sumeria, where Christie was introduced to Max Mallowan, the man she would later marry.

http://www.atlastours.net/iraq/ur.html (Ur)

Ibn Fadlan's Journey to Russia: A Tenth-Century Traveller from Baghdad to the Volga River (2005)
Richard Frye (translator and editor)

In AD921, Ibn Fadlan was part of a diplomatic mission that travelled from Baghdad to the court of the king of the Bulghars in the Volga Valley. Ibn Fadlan wrote a *risala*, an account of his journey (and an invaluable historical document), which described the customs and cultures of the various tribes that he met on his way. Frye's translation is the first in English. Michael Crichton based his novel *Eaters of the Dead* on Ibn Fadlan. The 1999 film adaptation, *The 13th Warrior*, was mainly filmed in Canada.

🎬 *The 13th Warrior* (1999), starring Antonio Banderas as Ibn Fadlan

War of Necessity, War of Choice: A Memoir of Two Iraq Wars (2009)
Richard N. Haass

There has been a huge amount of literature – fiction and non-fiction – prompted by the two Iraq wars and it would be remiss not to include at least one of them. Richard Haass is president of the Council on Foreign Relations and was a member of the National Security Council under George H. W. Bush during the Persian Gulf War (1990–1). He also advised Colin Powell on the Iraq War (2003–). This memoir is an honest account of why the United States went to war and also of Haass's opinion that the first war was one of necessity; the second, one of choice. This book is an insightful history, as well as a

personal and professional memoir. It perhaps gained wider attention through Angelina Jolie carrying it around on a film set, rather than for its own particular merits.

ISRAEL

Fiction

The Little Drummer Girl (1983)
John le Carré

With his usual flair, John le Carré creates an intriguing world of espionage and terrorism with Israel this time as the focus of attention. In *The Little Drummer Girl*, Charlie, a beautiful English actor with a penchant for lying, is recruited by an Israeli intelligence officer to take part in a dangerous plot to capture a Palestinian terrorist.

🎬 *The Little Drummer Girl* (1984), starring Diane Keaton as Charlie

When I Lived in Modern Times (2000)
Linda Grant

Grant's award-winning novel begins with protagonist Evelyn Sert on a boat to Palestine in 1946. It follows her life in this strange, new country during a period of great historic change and the formation of the new state of Israel.

To the End of the Land (2010)
David Grossman

Internationally renowned author David Grossman has written many books about Israel but *To the End of the Land* has particular resonance and possibly is among his best. Started in 2003, Grossman finished the book after the death of his son, Uri, on 12 August 2006, towards the end of the Second Lebanon War. The book focuses on middle-aged mother Ora, who leaves home after her soldier son, Ofer, goes off to fight again, to avoid anyone notifying her of his death. She goes walking in Galilee with her former lover Avram, telling him about Ofer and keeping him very much alive through the power of her words.

🔍 *See Under: Love* (1980)

My Michael (1968)
Amos Oz

A profoundly moving book, *My Michael* focuses on the disintegration of a young couple's marriage. Set in the neighbourhoods of 1950s' Jerusalem, Hannah Gonen's fantasy life begins to overtake her real life with husband, Michael as the years pass.

Operation Shylock: A Confession (1993)
Philip Roth

In this bizarre but quite brilliant book, the protagonist, Philip Roth, a Jewish–American novelist, travels around Israel telling Jews to return to their homelands. Meanwhile the real Philip Roth (or is he?) tries to stop him, even if it means impersonating his own impersonator.

The Lover (1977)
A. B. Yehoshua

This haunting novel, set just after the Yom Kippur War, is focused on a husband searching for his wife's lover. Using multi-character perspectives, Yehoshua builds up a layered story and allows us to see different viewpoints of the same event.

Exodus (1958)
Leon Uris

Uris's best-seller tells the story of the birth of a nation – Israel. To research the story, Uris travelled the country 'by train, plane, Vauxhall and Austin, jeep and by foot', interviewing more than 1,000 people to create the background for his plot. The protagonists Ari Ben Canaan and American nurse Kitty Fremont are at the heart of the story, but the epic events that led to the creation of Israel are the greater story. Otto Preminger turned the book into a film, but Uris is alleged to have thought that the director destroyed his work. Most of the film was shot on location and is faithful to the book.

🎬 *Exodus* (1960)

Non-fiction

Israel: A History (1998)
Martin Gilbert

Eminent historian Martin Gilbert offers this extraordinary account of the making of Israel, evoking the events and personalities who made the formation of this state possible in 1948 and the events that have led it to become such an important country in world politics, since.

In the Land of Israel (1983)
Amos Oz

This collection of essays by novelist Amos Oz is based on his travels in and around Israel and the West Bank and his conversations with the real people – labourers, soldiers, zealots, fanatics and idealists – whom he met.

JORDAN

Fiction

Appointment with Death (1936)
Agatha Christie

An Hercule Poirot novel situated outside of England, *Appointment with Death* draws on Christie's own experiences of travelling with her archaeologist husband in the Middle East. Opening in Jerusalem, but moving to Jordan, our Belgian sleuth finds himself once more embroiled in murder and mayhem after the detestable and sadistic Mrs Boynton is found dead in the magnificent rose city of Petra. Memorable for its location and Christie's atmospheric evocation of place, this is perhaps not one of the strongest novels featuring Hercule Poirot, but it is entertaining none the less.

Appointment with Death (2008), starring David Suchet as Hercule Poirot

Pillars of Salt (1996)
Fadia Faqir

Set in Jordan during and after the British Mandate of 1921, Fadia Faqir's novel focuses on two women, Maha and Um Saad, forced to share a room in an Amman mental hospital. Maha, a Bedouin woman, recounts her story directly to the reader, Um Saad's story is revealed through conversations with Maha and a separate narrator also tells Maha's story but from a different viewpoint, allowing the story and plot to become more layered. The different strands reveal how the women ended up in the asylum and the reader gains an understanding of the brutal regime in which Maha's beloved husband, a member of the resistance, was killed by the British and Um Saad suffers the humiliation of her husband bringing home a new young wife.

LEBANON

Fiction

Somewhere Home (2004)
Nada Awar Jarrar

Jarrar tells the story of three Lebanese women each trying to reach or seek a house that represents her home. Maysa leaves Beirut to return to her grandparents' house, the place where she went as a child, situated on the slopes of Mount Lebanon; Aida, returns from exile, to recapture her past and the spirit of the Palestinian refugee who was a second father to her during her childhood; and Salwa,

T. E. Lawrence's Arabia

One of the most fascinating characters of the 20th century, T. E. Lawrence is possibly best known to a popular audience as 'Lawrence of Arabia'. Revered by many, Lawrence's *Seven Pillars of Wisdom* (1926) is one of the last romantic discussions of war, with the author's often poetic use of language harking back to the time of classical war literature. Based on Lawrence's own experiences, the book deals with the Arab Revolt against the Turkish Empire and Lawrence's role in it as a liaison between British and Arab forces. It provides a good overview of this period of Middle Eastern and British history. Lawrence is an iconic figure and fans can visit many places associated with him through tours such as the T. E. Lawrence trek, which traces his steps from Wadi Rum in Jordan – where he was based during the Great Arab Revolt (1917–18) and also the setting for the film *Lawrence of Arabia* – to Mudawarra, on the Jordan–Saudi Arabian border, where visitors can see the wrecked trains and bridges that Lawrence blew up in 1917. Tourists can also go on an 11-km (7 mile) walk in Dorset, England, that takes in the author's own house, Clouds Hill, in Wareham and Moreton Cemetery, his last resting place.

📶 http://telsociety.org.uk/telsociety/index.htm (T. E. Lawrence society)

✈ http://www.rumguides.com/archives/23-The-T.-E.-Lawrence-trek-optional-return-5-days.html (T. E. Lawrence trek)
http://www.visitswanageandpurbeck.co.uk/things_to_see__do_in_purbeck/activities/walking/the_lawrence_of_arabia_trail.aspx (The Lawrence of Arabia Trail, Dorset)

🎬 *Lawrence of Arabia* (1962; David Lean's iconic film starring Peter O'Toole as Lawrence)

---

the eldest of the women, recalls the land of her youth, from a hospital bed far from Lebanon.

Gate of the Sun (1999)
Elias Khoury

Written by Lebanese Khoury, *Gate of the Sun* is an epic work about Palestinian exile 'based on the stories of every village and starting with tales from the "great expulsion of 1948"'. The author collected them from refugee camps. Khalil nurses Yunes, an old Palestinian freedom fighter, who may never regain consciousness from a coma in a refugee camp on the outskirts of Beirut. Khalil recounts

Yunes's extraordinary life and his 'love affair' with his wife, whom he can meet only secretly at Bab al-Shams (the Gate of the Sun).

🎬 *Bab el Sham* (2004) by director Yousry Nasrallah

Ports of Call (1999)
Amin Maalouf

First published in French in 1996, *Ports of Call* is a love story. Protagonist Ossyane, the descendant of a leading Ottoman family, leaves Beirut and his father's revolutionary aspirations for him, to study in France, but war breaks out and he is drawn into the

Resistance there. Returning to Beirut and hailed as a hero, Ossyane falls in love with Clara whom he marries. The Jewish–Muslim couple settle in Haifa, but as war breaks out in Israel, Ossyane is forced to return to Beirut only to have the border shut behind him and to find himself separated from the woman he loves.

Beirut Blues (1992)
Hanan Al-Shaykh

Through the letters that her protagonist Asmahan writes Al-Shaykh evokes a Beirut that few people are privileged enough to view. Asmahan struggles to make sense of the chaos caused by civil war, writing letters to her loved ones that may never reach their destination. A lyrical book, *Beirut Blues* is a beautiful evocation of a country's past and present.

Non-fiction

The Prophet (1923)
Kahlil Gibran

It perhaps seems odd that a book of less than 20,000 words and philosophical in nature should have become a modern classic, but Kahlil Gibran's *The Prophet* has done just that. The book is essentially the guidance given by a wise man, before he departs for his birthplace of Almustafa, to the people of Orphalese on everything from love and children to marriage. Gibran himself was born in Bsharri, about 120 km (75 miles) from Beirut, but was brought up in the United States. Although Gibran

spent his most productive time in America, visitors to Bsharri can see more than 400 drawings and paintings, pieces of manuscript and bits of furniture from his studio in New York all located in the Gibran Museum.

🛜 http://www.friendsofgibran.org/html/gibran_national_committee.html (Gibran Museum)

Beirut (2010)
Samir Kassir

Kassir's last book before being assassinated by a car bomb in 2005, *Beirut* has been widely lauded as the definitive history of Beirut. Spanning more than 4,000 years of history, the book examines the city from ancient to modern times, showing its growth through the 19th and 20th centuries and evoking a vibrant and changing Middle Eastern city.

The Hills of Adonis: A Quest in Lebanon (1967)
Colin Thubron

Travel writer Thubron walked 800 km (500 miles) in the 1960s through Lebanon in search of Astarte and Adonis, the deities of the region. Through his interactions with local peoples, Thubron does what he does best, detailing the minutiae of everyday life, culture and society. This is the Lebanon of historic coastal towns, of the ruins that tell of the Phoenicians, Greeks and Romans; this is the Lebanon that people often overlook. Thubron has written many other travel books, including *In Siberia* (1999).

PALESTINE

Fiction

The Secret Life of Saeed: the Pessoptimist (1974)
Emile Habiby

Habiby's greatest novel combines fantasy and fact: the protagonist Saeed is a Palestinian living in Israel, who is an informant for the state. Written as a series of letters after tragicomic figure Saeed has escaped to outer space, the book challenges the reader's sense of what is real and what is artificial, while presenting the complexity of the situation in this region. Habiby, himself a Palestinian living in Israel, won the highest awards for literature from both the PLO and the Israeli government. He sat in the Knesset and was an award-winning journalist.

Wild Thorns (1998)
Sahar Khalifeh

Wild Thorns addresses one essential question: how do Palestinians survive under occupation? Khalifeh deals with this problem through two cousins, both widely opposed in their outlook. One of the cousins is Usama, newly returned from the Gulf, whose stance is that political independence and survival are essentially the same thing and who is politically active, and the other cousin is Adil, who fights for his own and his family's survival. Essentially a chronicle of real life in the West Bank under occupation and examining the conflicts that exist within Palestinian society as

well as between Palestinians and Israelis, this novel is a fascinating and thought-provoking read.

A Lake Beyond the Wind (1998)
Yahya Yakhlif

Set in one of the most devastating years in Palestinian history, 1948, Yakhlif's book is a fictional account of the devastation of Samakh, a small town north of Jerusalem, by the Arab Liberation Army, causing most of its inhabitants to flee into exile. Yakhlif was born in Samakh and has spent much of his life as a refugee.

Non-fiction

Sharon and My Mother-in-Law: Ramallah Diaries (2003)
Suad Amiry

An insightful account of architect Suad Amiry's experiences of living in the West Bank in the 1980s, which was enlivened by her 92-year-old mother-in-law forced to stay during the 42-day curfew imposed by the Israeli army on Ramallah residents in 2002. Arising out of email exchanges to keep her sane, Amiry's account is full of the humour, frustration and anger of living in Ramallah. This is an extraordinary account of the Palestinian–Israeli conflict as seen by someone dealing with it on a daily basis. The book, which has been widely translated, won Amiry the prestigious Italian Viareggio Literary Prize in 2004.

SAUDI ARABIA

Fiction

Adama (2003)
Turki Al-Hamad

Al-Hamad's extremely popular book is a coming-of-age novel that follows an 18-year-old boy in 1960s' Saudi Arabia. Hisham spends his days reading banned novels and questioning the society in which he lives, one torn between the traditional ways of the old and modern world. Gradually, he finds himself increasingly involved in the struggle for change.

Girls of Riyadh (2007)
Rajaa Alsanea

A best-seller when it was published in Arabic in 2005, the book caused an uproar in Saudi Arabia and was subsequently banned. *Girls of Riyadh* is a Saudi *Sex and the City*. It follows four girls, members of the wealthy elite 'velvet class', their lives, dreams, trials and tribulations. Told by an anonymous narrator who posts their stories on the Net, Alsanea's book also depicts a society in which the characters are banned from driving and do not have a free choice over their education, career or marriage.

Eight Months on Ghazzah Street (1988)
Hilary Mantel

Based on Mantel's experiences of living in Saudi Arabia, this novel is a powerful portrayal of how women live and survive in this male-dominated region. Focusing on a cartographer, who moves to Jeddah with her husband, Mantel creates a vivid depiction of a woman forced to adapt to a culture she doesn't understand who slowly loses all sense of herself.

The Saddlebag (2000)
Bahiyyih Nakhjavani

Nakhjavani's lyrical novel, set in the 19th century, follows nine characters on the road from Mecca to Medina and relates what happens when they come across a strange saddlebag, which seems to have the power to change their lives.

Non-fiction

A History of the Arab Peoples (2005)
Albert Hourani

A highly readable, comprehensive and informed history of the Arab peoples, Hourani's book covers a vast swathe of history, from pre-Islamic to modern times. The book is probably one of the best introductions to Arab peoples, culture and society, and is an updated edition of his earlier book.

Jarhead: A Soldier's Story of Modern War (2003)
Anthony Swofford

Swofford's best-selling combat memoir of life as a marine during the Persian Gulf War (1990–1) demystifies the reality of war and is a classic. The author presents the tedium, loneliness and humour of life in a pre-war desert deployment and then writes honestly and powerfully about the war itself.

🎬 *Jarhead* (2005), directed by Sam Mendes

Arabian Sands (1959)
Wilfred Thesiger

This classic focuses on Thesiger's time in the 'Empty Quarter' of Arabia, where he travelled for five years from 1945, just before the discovery of oil in the region changed it forever. Thesiger, often at great risk as a Christian infidel, travelled among the Bedu people, taking part in their daily lives, dealing with the threat of starvation and the extreme weather conditions.

SYRIA

Fiction

Grandfather's Tale (1998)
Ulfat Idilbi

Written by one of Syria's best-loved novelists, *Grandfather's Tale* is set in 19th-century Damascus. Told in the manner of *One Thousand and One Nights*, the narrator describes how her grandfather came to live in Syria, travelling from Chechnya to Damascus.

Just Like A River (1984)
Muhammad Kamil al-Khatib

Khatib's first novel is set in early 1980s' Syria and is perhaps as much an insight into the country's politics

and society today as of that time. Damascus, in particular, is brought to life through Khatib's vivid portrayal of the conflict existing between an old, traditional way of life and a new, more radical society. The tensions are shown through the voices of a multitude of characters, including Chief Sergeant Yunis, a veteran of the Syrian Army and Yusuf, a radical university lecturer.

Non-fiction

Come, Tell Me How You Live: An Archaeological Memoir (1946)
Agatha Christie

Christie accompanied her husband, the archaeologist Max Mallowan, on his digs to Syria and Iraq in the 1930s, a journey that was later to inform some of her own writing. This entertaining memoir is an account of Christie's daily life and paints a charming and humorous picture of the author herself, her husband, their friends and also the local people with whom they interacted. When Christie was in Palmyra she stayed at the Zenobia hotel.

🔍 Jordan – *Appointment with Death*
🏠 www.zenobia-hotel.com (hotel)

YEMEN

Fiction

Salmon Fishing in the Yemen (2007)
Paul Torday

This charming book was a runaway

The Baron Hotel

Situated in Aleppo, northern Syria, the Baron Hotel has been a favourite among the literati. Built in 1909, it was intended to be a luxury hotel for travellers on their way to Jerusalem and has since housed kings, politicians and celebrities, from T. E. Lawrence ('Lawrence of Arabia') and Agatha Christie to Theodore Roosevelt and Julie Christie. Many of the guests before the Second World War were predominantly British or German and some were spies masquerading as archaeologists. Many key political decisions were negotiated within the confines of the hotel. Today, visitors can stay in the room where Lawrence of Arabia rested his weary head (202) and see his bill on display in the lounge, soak up the atmosphere of room 203 where Christie wrote part of *Murder on the Orient Express* and stand on the balcony of room 215 from where King Faisal declared Syria's independence.

success when it was published in 2007. Dr Alfred Jones, a low-level bureaucrat and fisheries expert, is set the unlikely task of introducing salmon into Yemen. Through his interaction with a sheikh, who dreams of a more peaceful world, Alfred finds his vision of his own life changing radically and as it does he becomes increasingly more obsessed with the idea of bringing salmon to Yemen.

🎬 *Salmon Fishing in the Yemen* (2012), directed by Lasse Hallstrom and starring Ewan McGregor.

Like Nowhere Else (2005)
Denyse Woods

Woods, the daughter of an Irish diplomat, knows the Middle East well. In this novel she beautifully evokes the atmosphere, landscape, sights and smells of the Yemen. Essentially a love story, *Like Nowhere Else* centres on Vivien Quish, who, dreaming of being a great traveller, arrives

in the city of Sana'a only to meet anthropologist Christian Linklater. As Vivien falls in love with the beauty of Yemen, she also becomes enthralled with Christian.

📶 http://www.yemennic.info/English%20site/SITE%20CONTAINTS/Tourism/Touristic%20sites/Al-mahweet/Al-mahweet.htm (information about the city of Sana'a)

INDEX